WALKING THE KING CHARLES III ENGLAND COAST PATH: NORTH WEST

NATIONAL TRAIL - Cumbria, Lancashire and Merseyside Coast

by Ange Harker

JUNIPER HOUSE, MURLEY MOSS,
OXENHOLME ROAD, KENDAL, CUMBRIA LA9 7RL
www.cicerone.co.uk

© Ange Harker 2025
First edition 2025
ISBN: 978 1 78631 027 9
eISBN: 978 1 78362 678 6

Printed in Singapore by KHL Printing on responsibly sourced paper.

A catalogue record for this book is available from the British Library.
All photographs are by the author unless otherwise stated.

 Route mapping by Lovell Johns www.lovelljohns.com

© Crown copyright 2025 OS AC0000810376. NASA relief data courtesy of ESRI
Cicerone's EU representative for GPSR compliance is Easy Access System Europe, Mustamäe tee 50, 10621 Tallinn, Estonia. Email gpsr.requests@easproject.com.

Updates to this guide

While every effort is made by our authors to ensure the accuracy of guidebooks as they go to print, changes can occur during the lifetime of an edition. Any updates that we know of for this guide will be on the Cicerone website (www.cicerone.co.uk/1027/updates), so please check before planning your trip. We also advise that you check information about such things as transport, accommodation and shops locally. Even rights of way can be altered over time. We are always grateful for information about any discrepancies between a guidebook and the facts on the ground, sent by email to updates@cicerone.co.uk.

Register your book: To sign up to receive free updates, special offers and GPX files where available, create a Cicerone account and register your purchase via the 'My Account' tab at www.cicerone.co.uk.

Front cover: Some of the best mountain and estuary views can be seen from Askam pier (Stage 11)

CONTENTS

Map key 5
Route summary table 6
Overview profile/staging options 8
Stage facilities planner 12

INTRODUCTION 23
What is the England Coast Path? 25
Origins 25
Planning and wayfinding 26
What is Coastal Access? 26
Adaptability 27

The north-west coastal landscape 28
Geography 28
Geology 28
Natural history 29
Human and cultural histories 34

Practicalities 37
Fitness and variations to the itinerary 37
Transport 37
Accommodation 38
Communications 39
Money 39
When to go 39
North or south? 40
Coastal safety 40
Emergencies 40
What to pack 41
Maps 42
Using this guide 43
Accessibility 44

PART 1 – CUMBERLAND 45
Stage 1   Gretna to Knockupworth 47
Stage 2   Knockupworth to Bowness-on-Solway 51
Stage 3   Bowness-on-Solway to Abbeytown 56
Stage 4   Abbeytown to Silloth 61

Stage 5	Silloth to Maryport	66
Stage 6	Maryport to Whitehaven	72
Stage 7	Whitehaven to Seascale	78
Stage 8	Seascale to Ravenglass	85
Stage 9	Bootle to Silecroft Beach	89
Stage 10	Silecroft Beach to Green Road	93

PART 2 – MORECAMBE BAY 99

Stage 11	Foxfield to North Scale	101
Stage 12	North Scale to Vickerstown	107
Stage 13	Vickerstown to Bardsea	112
Stage 14	Bardsea to Cark	118
Stage 15	Cark to Grange-over-Sands	124
Stage 16	Arnside to Hest Bank	129
Stage 17	Hest Bank to Overton	135
Stage 18	Overton to Conder Green	140
Stage 19	Conder Green to Fleetwood	144

PART 3 – WYRE TO WALES 149

Stage 20	Fleetwood to Lytham	151
Stage 21	Lytham to Preston	157
Stage 22	Preston to Tarleton	161
Stage 23	Tarleton to Crossens	165
Stage 24	Crossens to Formby	170
Stage 25	Formby to Seaforth	175
Stage 26	Seaforth to New Brighton	180
Stage 27	New Brighton to Parkgate	184
Stage 28	Parkgate to Welsh border/Chester	190

Appendix A	Accommodation table	198
Appendix B	Useful contacts	220
Appendix C	Day walk options	222
Appendix D	Further reading	224

Acknowledgements

Whilst this guide was written on a freelance basis I'm one of hundreds of people nationwide whose day jobs involve developing the KCIIIECP, and one of tens in the north west alone. This book is dedicated to all those colleagues past and present in the North West Coastal Access Delivery Team – Mags Bradley, Neil Coles, Jen Green, Liz Hayes, James Lawrence, John Manning, Jane Moore, Danny Moores, Dai Parry, Kathy Poulton-Cope, Danielle Radley, Kerry Rennie, Gerry Rusbridge (KCIIIECP north west delivery leader), Kath Sallabank, Bethany Thomas and Sarah Wiseman – and the many, many more in the national KCIIIECP team – not least mapmakers extraordinaire Susannah, Nick and Huw, the Open Access and National Trails team (Kevin, Sara, Deb et al), and the national leadership of Neil, Paul, Chris, Lone, Martin and Hills. There are too many colleagues to list from the Cumbria and Cheshire to Lancashire area teams including Protected Sites and NNR staff whose shared expertise and support were so vital. Thanks also to the many external partners and landowners who worked with us, including the Solway and Arnside & Silverdale National Landscapes, Lake District National Park, the Wales Coast Path teams, RSPB, National Trust and the Cumbria, Lancashire and Cheshire Wildlife Trusts. The final dedications must go to the access authorities who carried out the physical establishment of the trail and continue to manage the open stretches – thanks to John, David G, Bob, Geoff, the late Dave C, Hazel, Helen, Julie, Brian, Mike, Robin, Dan, Sian and Andy from, in turn, Cumberland, Cumbria, Westmorland & Furness, Lancashire, Sefton, Liverpool, Wirral and Cheshire West & Chester councils.

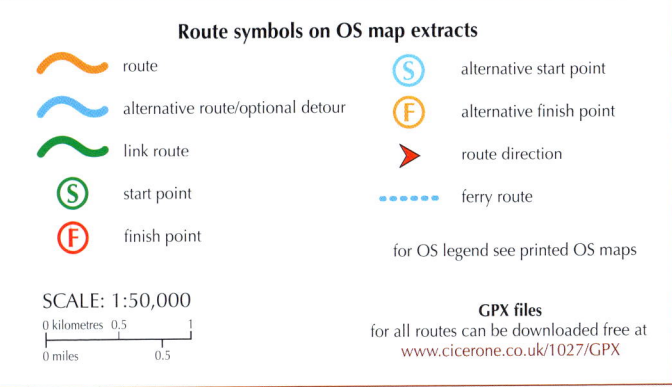

ROUTE SUMMARY TABLE

Stage	Start	Finish	Time	Distance (km)	Ascent (m)	Page
1	Gretna	Knockupworth	5hr 35min	21.1	100	47
2	Knockupworth	Bowness-on-Solway	6hr 30min	25.4	80	51
3	Bowness-on-Solway	Abbeytown	6hr 30min	25.4	30	56
4	Abbeytown	Silloth	4hr 30min	16	20	61
5	Silloth	Maryport	5hr 30min	20.8	70	66
6	Maryport	Whitehaven	6hr 50min	25.7	290	72
7	Whitehaven	Seascale	7hr 40min	26	610	78
8	Seascale	Ravenglass	3hr 35min	13	80	85
9	Bootle	Silecroft Beach	3hr 55min	14.4	160	89
10	Silecroft Beach	Green Road	4hr 50min	18.6	25	93
11	Foxfield	North Scale	6hr 15min	23	150	101
12	North Scale	Vickerstown	6hr 25min	24.6	50	107
13	Vickerstown	Bardsea	5hr 55min	22.3	115	112
14	Bardsea	Cark	6hr 20min	24.2	90	118
15	Cark	Grange-over-Sands	4hr 55min	18.1	160	124
16	Arnside	Hest Bank	6hr 45min	23.6	270	129
17	Hest Bank	Overton	5hr 35min	21.2	80	135
18	Overton	Conder Green	4hr 55min	19	40	140
19	Conder Green	Knott End	5hr 40min	22.6	30	144
20	Fleetwood	Lytham	7hr 15min	28.6	65	151
21	Lytham	Preston	5hr 45min	22.1	40	157
22	Preston	Tarleton	4hr 40min	18.4	20	161
23	Tarleton	Crossens	3hr 55min	15.3	15	165
24	Crossens	Formby	5hr 10min	18.6	20	170
25	Formby	Seaforth	4hr 35min	16.5	40	175
26	Seaforth	New Brighton	2hr 55min	11.7	35	180
27	New Brighton	Parkgate	7hr 20min	28.4	100	184
28	Parkgate	Chester	6hr 15min	23.9	55	190

Red sandstone outcrops provide geological interest below Maryport prom (Stage 5)

WALKING THE KING CHARLES III ENGLAND COAST PATH: NORTH WEST

OVERVIEW PROFILE/STAGING OPTIONS

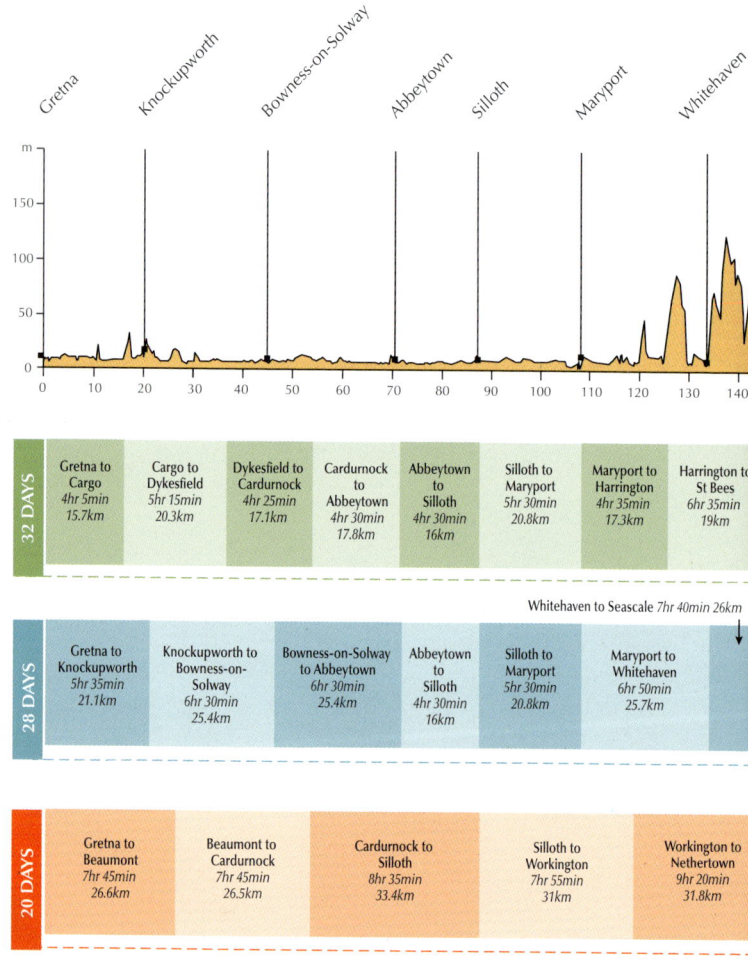

Overview profile/staging options

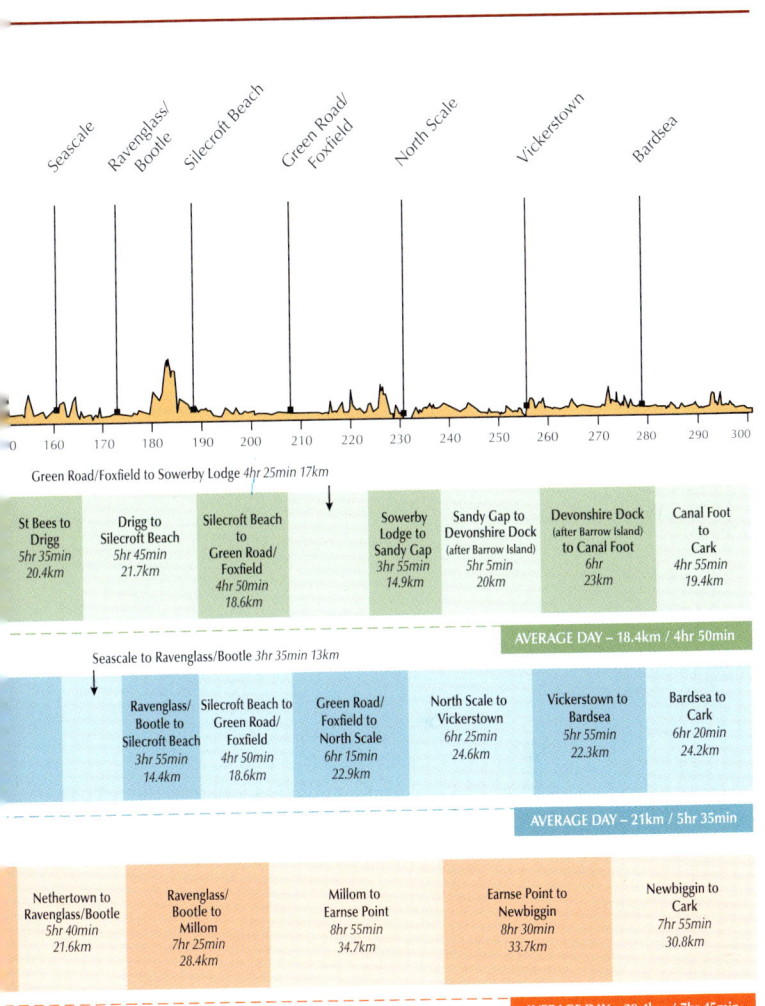

WALKING THE KING CHARLES III ENGLAND COAST PATH: NORTH WEST

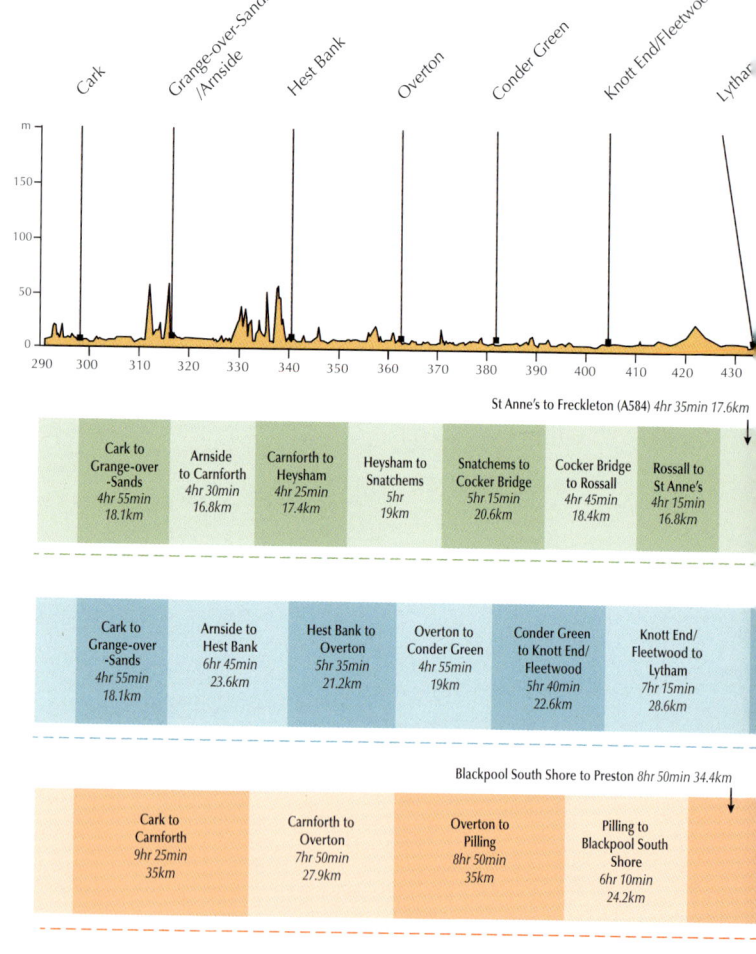

Overview profile/staging options

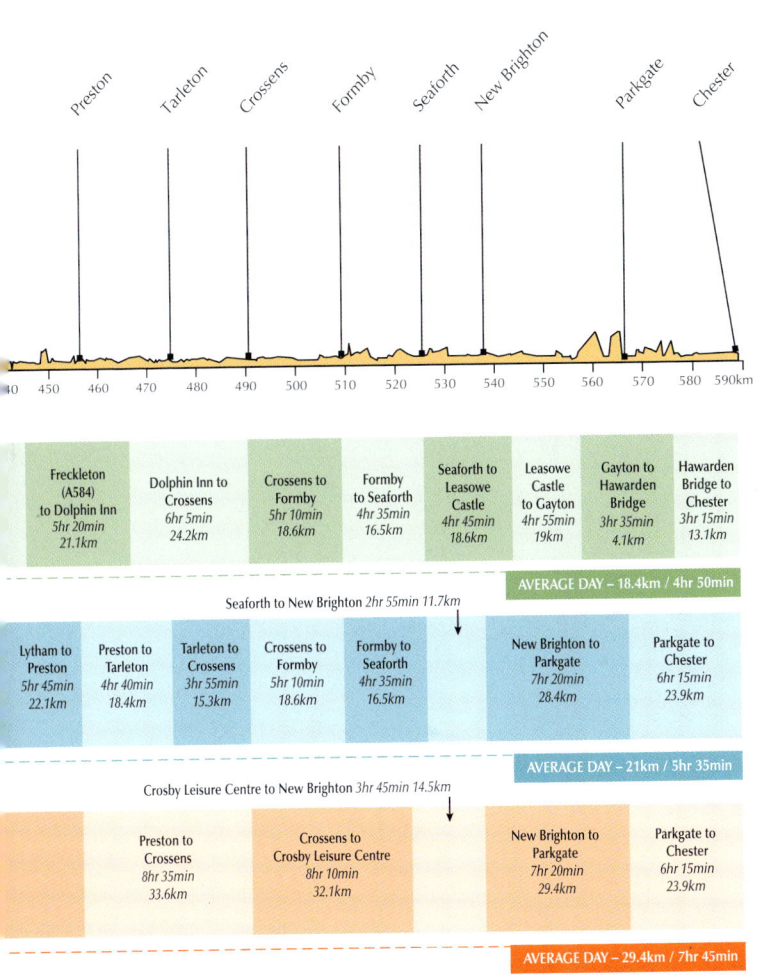

WALKING THE KING CHARLES III ENGLAND COAST PATH: NORTH WEST

STAGE FACILITIES PLANNER

Walking times and distances given do not include off-trail sections. Where included against off-trail facilities, this is the walking time and distance to the relevant exit point on either the main trail or the alternative route, where the exit point is not already listed.

🔺 general accommodation   🟢 camping
🟠 refreshments   🟤 shop   🅰️ ATM
🔵 train/tram   🔵 bus

Stage	Place	Walking time	Distance (km)		Facilities				
1	**Gretna**	-	-			🟠	🟤	🅰️	🔵
1	Metal Bridge	1hr 10min	4.5	🔺		🟠			🔵
1	Rockcliffe	1hr 50min	7.1	🔺		🟠			🔵
1	Cargo (accommodation on trail before village, buses 1km off-trail)	1hr 20min	4.5	🔺					🔵
1	**Knockupworth**	**1hr 15min**	**5.1**	🔺					🔵
2	Carlisle area (3–4km off-trail, buses available)	1hr 15min	4.9	🔺	🟢	🟠	🟤	🅰️	🔵 🔴
2	Beaumont	15min	0.7	🔺					🔵
2	Monkhill (1km off-trail)					🟠			🔵
2	*Burgh-by-Sands (on high tide route, 1.5km off main trail)*	*40min*	*2.5*			🟠			🔵
2	Dykesfield	1hr 50min	9.6						🔵
2	Boustead Hill	10min	1.2	🔺	🟢				🔵
2	*Easton (0.7km off-trail)*	*30min*	*2*	🔺					
2	Drumburgh	10min	0.7						🔵

STAGE FACILITIES PLANNER

Stage	Place	Walking time	Distance (km)	Facilities
2	Glasson	30min	1.8	🔴 · · · · 🔵
2	Port Carlisle	40min	2.7	🔴 · 🍴 · · 🔵
2	**Bowness-on-Solway**	**40min**	**1.9**	🔴 🟢 🍴 · · 🔵
3	Cardurnock	1hr 45min	7	🔴 · · · · 🔵
3	Anthorn	1hr 5min	4.4	🔴 🟢 🍴 · · 🔵
3	*Angerton (on high tide route, 0.5km off main trail)*	*55min*	*3.7*	🔴 · · · · 🔵
3	*Kirkbride (1km off high tide route; accommodation 2.5km)*			🔴 · · · ATM 🔵
3	*Newton Arlosh (on high tide route, 1km from main trail)*	*50min*	*3.5*	🔴 · 🍴 · ·
3	**Abbeytown** *(facilities 1.3km off-trail)*	**1hr 55min**	**6.7**	· 🟢 🍴 🔵 ATM 🔵
4	*Wheyrigg (4.5km off-trail, buses available)*			🔴 · · · · 🔵
4	Skinburness	3hr 35min	12.6	🔴 · · · · 🔵
4	**Silloth**	**55min**	**3.4**	🔴 🟢 🍴 🔵 ATM 🔵
5	*Blitterlees (1km off-trail)*	*30min*	*2*	🔴 🟢 🍴 · · 🔵
5	Beckfoot	55min	3.5	🔴 🟢 · · · 🔵
5	Mawbray	45min	2.5	🔴 🟢 · · · 🔵
5	Old Kiln Farm	45min	2.4	🔴 🟢 · · · 🔵
5	Allonby	30min	1.9	· · 🍴 🔵 · 🔵
5	Blue Dial	35min	2.4	🔴 · 🍴 · · 🔵
5	**Maryport**	**1hr 30min**	**6.1**	🔴 · 🍴 🔵 ATM 🔴

WALKING THE KING CHARLES III ENGLAND COAST PATH: NORTH WEST

Stage	Place	Walking time	Distance (km)	Direction	Access	Food	Bank	ATM	Parking	Station
6	Flimby	55min	3.6							●
6	Workington	1hr 50min	7.1	←		🍴	🏦	ATM	●	●
6	Harrington	1hr 40min	6.7	←		🍴	🏦	ATM	●	●
6	Lowca (0.5km off-trail)	55min	3.7							
6	Parton	30min	2	←					●	●
6	**Whitehaven**	**1hr**	**2.6**	←		🍴	🏦	ATM	●	●
7	St Bees	3hr 30min	11.2	←	✓	🍴	🏦			●
7	Nethertown	1hr 40min	5.	←	✓					
7	Braystones	45min	2.7	←	✓					
7	Beckermet (2.5km off-trail)					🍴				
7	Sellafield	55min	3.7	←						●
7	**Seascale**	**50min**	**3**	←	✓	🍴	🏦	ATM	●	●
8	Drigg (accommodation 1.3km off-trail)	1hr 30min	5.5	←		🍴	🏦			●
8	Holmrook (1km off-trail)	20min	0.9			🍴		ATM		
8	Saltcotes (accommodation 1km off-trail)	1hr 10min	4.3	←	✓					
8	**Ravenglass**	**35min**	**2.3**	←	✓	🍴				●
9	Newbiggin (1km off-trail at Eskmeals; 6km from Bootle station)				✓					
9	**Hycemoor (Bootle station)**	**Train**	**Train**							●
9	Tarn Bay	30min	2	←						

STAGE FACILITIES PLANNER

Stage	Place	Walking time	Distance (km)						Facilities	
9	Selker	35min	2.3	◀						
9	Gutterby Lane Ends *(for Whitbeck accommodation, 2km off-trail)*	1hr 20min	4.9	◀						
9	**Silecroft beach**	**1hr 5min**	**5.2**		🍴					
10	*Silecroft village (1.3km off-trail)*			◀	🍴			⬤		
10	Haverigg	2hr	7.3	◀	🍴	🏧			⬤	
10	Millom	1hr 40min	6.5	◀	🍴	🏧	⊕	⬤		
10	*The Hill (1.2km off-trail)*	40min	2.8	◀						
10	**Green Road**	**30min**	**2**					⬤		
10	*The Green (1.5km off-trail)*				🍴					
10	*Duddon Bridge (3.5km off-trail)*						⊕			
10	*Broughton-in-Furness (2km off-trail)*			◀	🍴					
10	**Foxfield**	**Train**	**Train**	◀	🍴			⬤	⬤	
11	Kirkby-in-Furness	1hr 5min	4.2	◀	🍴			⬤	⬤	
11	Askam-in-Furness	1hr 25min	5.4		🍴	🏧	⊕	⬤	⬤	
11	Barrow-in-Furness (north)	3hr 15min	11.3		🍴	🏧	⊕	⬤	⬤	
11	Vickerstown (north)	15min	1		🍴				⬤	
11	**North Scale**	**15min**	**1.1**						⬤	
12	North Walney	1hr 50min	7.1			🏧			⬤	
12	Biggar Bank	40min	2.6		🍴				⬤	

WALKING THE KING CHARLES III ENGLAND COAST PATH: NORTH WEST

Stage	Place	Walking time	Distance (km)		Facilities
12	South Walney	1hr 35min	5.9	←	🚉
12	Biggar village	1hr 25min	5.5		🍴
12	**Vickerstown**	**55min**	**3.5**	←	🍴 🍽 🚉
13	Barrow-in-Furness (central)	1hr	3.8	←	🍴 🍽 ATM 🚉
13	Concle	1hr 30min	6.4		🍴 🍽 ATM 🚉 ⬛
13	Roa Island (1km off-trail)				🍴
13	Piel Island (1km + ferry off-trail)			◄(green)	🍴
13	Rampside	10min	0.5		🍴 🚉
13	Newbiggin	1hr 15min	4.8	←	🍴
13	Moat Farm	20min	1.1	←	
13	Aldingham	25min	1.3		
13	Baycliff (facilities 0.5km off-trail)	20min	1.3	←	🍴
13	**Bardsea** (accommodation 0.5km off-trail)	**55min**	**3**	←	🍴 🚉
14	Ulverston (2km off-trail)			←	🍴 🍽 ATM 🚉 ⬛
14	Canal Foot	1hr 10min	4.6	←	🍴
14	Greenodd rest stop (facilities 0.3km off trail)	1hr 40min	6.2	◄(green)	🍴 🍽 🚉
14	**Cark** (train station 0.6km off-trail)	**3hr 30min**	**13.4**	←	🍴 🍽 ATM 🚉 ⬛
15	Flookburgh (on high tide route, 1km from main trail)			←	🍴 🚉
15	Lakeland Leisure Park	1hr 25min	5.5	◄(green)	🚉

STAGE FACILITIES PLANNER

Stage	Place	Walking time	Distance (km)	Arrow	Viewpoint	Food	Toilet	ATM	Parking	Accommodation
15	Allithwaite (on pre-ECP route, 1.2km off main trail once open)	2hr 5min	7.8							●
15	Kents Bank	40min	1.6						●	●
15	**Grange-over-Sands**	**45min**	**3.2**	←		🍴	⊕	ATM	●	●
15	Meathop (3.5km off-trail)			←		🍴	⊕			
15	Sandside & Storth (2km off-trail)			←		🍴				
16	**Arnside**	**Train**	**Train**	←		🍴	⊕	ATM	●	●
16	New Barns	45min	2.5	←		🍴				
16	Far Arnside	55min	3.1	←	◆					
16	Silverdale	45min	2.3	←	◆	🍴	⊕		●	●
16	Warton (facilities 1km off high tide route, 1.5km off main trail)			←						
16	Cote Stones	2hr 25min	8.3	←		🍴			●	●
16	Carnforth (1km off-trail)	0.9	0.9	←	◆	🍴	⊕	ATM	●	●
16	Bolton-le-Sands (trail)	1hr 10min	4.2	←		🍴	⊕	ATM	●	●
16	Bolton-le-Sands (facilities 1km off-trail)					🍴	⊕	ATM		●
16	**Hest Bank**	**45min**	**2.3**	←		🍴	⊕	ATM	●	●
17	Bare (1km to station)	40min	2.2	←		🍴	⊕	ATM	●	●
17	Morecambe (north)	20min	1.1			🍴	⊕	ATM	●	●
17	Morecambe (central) (campsite 1.5km off-trail)	20min	1.1	←	◆	🍴	⊕	ATM	●	●

WALKING THE KING CHARLES III ENGLAND COAST PATH: NORTH WEST

Stage	Place	Walking time	Distance (km)		Facilities				
17	Morecambe (south)	25min	1.6	←	food				■
17	Heysham	1hr 20min	5.1	←	food	water	ATM	●	■
17	Middleton Sands	1hr 5min	4.3	←					■
17	**Overton**	**1hr 25min**	**5.8**		food				■
18	Snatchems	2hr 15min	8.4	←	food				
18	Lancaster (north bank)	30min	2		food	water	ATM		■
18	Lancaster (south bank)	5min	0.3		food				■
18	*Lancaster central (facilities 0.5–1.5km off-trail)*			←	food	water	ATM	●	
18	*Ashton with Stodday (1km off-trail)*	1hr 45min	7.1	←	food				■
18	**Conder Green**	**20min**	**1.2**	← ✓	food				■
19	Glasson Dock	20min	1.2						■
19	Cockerham Sands	1hr 30min	6	←					
19	*Cocker Bridge (Cockerham facilities 1.5km off-trail)*	40min	2.8		food				■
19	*Pilling (on winter route 1.5km from summer route)*	1hr 40min	6.5	←					■
19	Preesall	2hr 45min	11	← ✓	food	water			■
19	**Knott End**	**25min**	**1.6**	←	food	water	ATM		■
20	**Fleetwood**	**Ferry**	**Ferry**	←	food	water	ATM	●	■
20	Rossall	1hr 30min	5.8		food	water	ATM	●	■
20	Cleveleys	35min	2.4	←	food	water	ATM	●	■

STAGE FACILITIES PLANNER

Stage	Place	Walking time	Distance (km)		Facilities
20	Bispham	50min	3.3	◀	● ● ATM 🏦 🍴
20	Blackpool (north)	25min	1.3	◀	● ● ATM 🏦 🍴
20	Blackpool (central)	30min	2.5	◀	● ● ATM 🏦 🍴
20	Blackpool (south)	30min	1.9	◀	● ● ATM 🏦 🍴
20	Starr Gate	35min	2.2	◀	● ● 🏦 🍴
20	St Anne's	1hr	3.6		● ● ATM 🏦 🍴
20	Ansdell/Fairhaven	30min	2.3	◀	● ● ATM 🏦 🍴
20	**Lytham**	**55min**	**3.3**	◀	● ● ATM 🏦 🍴
21	Warton (2km off-trail)	1hr 15min	4.6	◀	● 🏦 🍴
21	Freckleton	1hr 50min	6.6	◀	● ● ATM 🏦 🍴
21	Savick Bridge (A583)	1hr	4		● ATM 🏦 🍴
21	Preston docks/north bank	1hr	4		● ATM 🏦 🍴
21	**Preston (Penwortham Bridge area)**	**40min**	**2.9**	◀	● ● ATM 🏦 🍴
22	*Preston (central; 0.5–1.5km off-trail)*	2hr 25min	9.8		● ATM 🏦 🍴
22	Longton (trail)			◀	🏦
22	*Longton (2km off-trail)*	25min	1.6		● ATM 🏦 🍴
22	*Walmer Bridge (2km off-trail)*	20min	1.4		● ATM 🏦 🍴
22	*Much Hoole (2km off-trail)*	45min	2.8	◀	● ATM 🏦 🍴
22	A59 east				●

Walking the King Charles III England Coast Path: North West

Stage	Place	Walking time	Distance (km)	Direction	Facilities
22	Bretherton (2km off-trail)			←	🚌 ☕
22	**Tarleton**	**45min**	**2.8**	←	🚌 ATM 🏧 ☕
23	Becconsall & Hesketh Bank (0.5–1km off-trail)	30min	2	←	🚌 ATM 🏧 ☕
23	Banks (1.5km off-trail)	3hr 20min	13.2	▶	🚌 ATM 🏧 ☕
23	**Crossens** (Buses near trail, other facilities up to 1km off-trail)	**5min**	**0.1**		🚌 ATM 🏧 ☕
24	Southport (facilities up to 1.2km off-trail)	1hr 35min	6	←	🚌 🚆 ATM 🏧 ☕
24	Birkdale (0.5–1.5km off-trail)	35min	2		🚌 🚆 ATM 🏧 ☕
24	Ainsdale (facilities 1–2km off-trail)	1hr 20min	4.5	←	🚌 🚆 ATM 🏧 ☕
24	**Freshfield (trail)**	**1hr 40min**	**6.1**	▶	🚌 🚆 ☕
25	Freshfield/north Formby (1.5km off-trail)				🚌 🚆 ATM 🏧 ☕
25	South Formby (1.2km off-trail)	1hr 40min	5.9	←	🚌 🚆 ATM 🏧 ☕
25	Hightown	40min	2	←	🚌 🚆
25	Blundellsands (trains 0.6km off-trail)	1hr	3.8	←	🚌 🚆 🏧 ☕
25	Crosby (trains 0.7km off-trail)	30min	1.9	←	🚌 🚆 ATM 🏧 ☕
25	**Seaforth** (trains 1km off-trail)	**45min**	**2.9**	←	🚌 🚆 ATM 🏧 ☕
26	Bootle (A565) (trains & other facilities 0.5km off-trail)	25min	1.5	←	🚌 🚆 ATM 🏧 ☕
26	Liverpool dockside (Regent Road)	1hr	4	←	🚌 🚆
26	Pier Head/Albert Dock (trains, buses & Albert Dock accommodation 0.5km off-trail)	35min	2.5		🚌 🚆 ATM 🏧
26	Liverpool centre (0.5–2.5km off-trail)			←	🚌 🚆 ATM 🏧 ☕

STAGE FACILITIES PLANNER

Stage	Place	Walking time	Distance (km)	Facilities				
26	Seacombe	Ferry	Ferry					●
26	Egremont	15min	1					●
26	**New Brighton**	**40min**	**2.7**	🍴		ATM		●
27	Wallasey	40min	2.8	🍴	🍺	ATM	●	●
27	Leasowe	35min	2.6	🍴				●
27	Meols	1hr	3.9	🍴				●
27	Hoylake *(facilities up to 0.6km off-trail)*	35min	2.5	🍴		ATM	●	●
27	West Kirby	45min	3.1	🍴	🍺	ATM	●	●
27	Thurstaston (Country Park)	1hr 20min	5	🍴				
27	Heswall *(facilities 1.5–3.5km off-trail)*	55min	3.3	🍴	🍺	ATM	●	●
27	**Parkgate**	**1hr 25min**	**5.2**	🍴	🍺	ATM	●	●
28	*Neston (1km off-trail)*			🍴	🍺		●	●
28	Little Neston	30min	2	🍴				
28	*Burton (1.5km off-trail)*	30min	2					●
28	Wales Coast Path link route – industrial estate	1hr	4					●
28	Hawarden Bridge station	40min	2.7				●	
28	*Shotton (0.5km off-trail)*	10min	0.4	🍴	🍺	ATM	●	●
28	*Queensferry & Garden City (facilities up to 1km off-trail)*	25min	1.7	🍴	🍺	ATM	●	●
28	*Higher Ferry (facilities 1km off-trail)*	1hr 30min	5.8					
28	**Chester**	**1hr 25min**	**5.7**	🍴	🍺	ATM	●	●

New Brighton's sunsets can make for a spectacular end to your day (Stage 26)

INTRODUCTION

The highest cliffs in the north west await just south of Whitehaven (Stage 7)

The King Charles III England Coast Path (KCIIIECP) will be the longest managed coastal footpath in the world. This groundbreaking development in UK outdoor access creates almost globally unparalleled opportunities for long-distance walking; but most importantly, its ease of use makes our glorious coastlines available to so many more of us, locals and visitors alike.

The north-west of England is a beautiful place to start, and entails a whopping 590km (367 miles) of the KCIIIECP. Gretna, on the Scottish border, is your gateway to the wild Solway Firth and the open Cumbrian coast, with astounding views of the Lake District fells. Next comes the vast expanse of Morecambe Bay's famous sands and a string of iconic seaside towns heading towards the Ribble Estuary. Sefton's dunes lead to Liverpool, which might be considered the modern cultural centre of the route, and a circuit of the heritage-rich Wirral peninsula leads nicely to Chester, the Welsh border and of course the Wales Coast Path.

There are few truly strenuous days in comparison with areas such as the south-west coast. The terrain is often reasonably friendly, and high cliffs and rocky sections are seldom. Public transport allows easy access and variability in day length in many areas. This doesn't mean the north-west should be overlooked by experienced long-distance or hill walkers. The very fit can rack up some significant daily mileage, or simply enjoy having time to absorb all the spectacular landscapes, cultures and heritage this part of the world has to offer.

Natural and human histories abound across the north-west coast. Much is protected for its rare habitats and species, with Morecambe Bay's muds, marshes and sands being one of the largest wading bird habitats in the country. Human stories range from Mesolithic burial sites to nuclear submarines via docks, abbeys, castles, Roman remains, World Heritage Sites, and agricultural heritage along the way.

This guide suggests daily itineraries and logistics for long-distance walkers, including alternative routes where sections may not be open before publication; but with such variability and flexibility en route you'll hopefully also find everything you need to adapt your journey – whether in bite-size chunks or epic expeditions – to be everything you need it to be.

Passing through Haverigg's extensive dune system, approaching the mouth of the Duddon Estuary (Stage 10)

WHAT IS THE ENGLAND COAST PATH?

There are great views of Piel Island and Castle from the ECP on south east Walney (Stage 12)

ORIGINS

The King Charles III England Coast Path and its associated Coastal Access rights grew from years of campaigning from various access groups and the resultant Marine and Coastal Access Act 2009, which enshrined in law the duty for Natural England, the government's advisor on the natural environment, to make it happen.

Rather than just connecting existing rights of way, this new National Trail would create brand new access, against a set of legal criteria. Tens of thousands of landowners, conservationists and partners were consulted to achieve the required 'fair balance' between those who visit and those who manage the land; whilst maintaining protection of extremely sensitive natural environments.

The Coastal Margin was also mapped: the strip of land between the trail and the sea, allowing the public to legally access many new parts of the coast using new Coastal Access rights.

Stretch by stretch, final proposals went to public consultation and approval by Government, via the Planning Inspectorate who determined the minimal objections received (from only 2% of landowners).

Regional councils installed the necessary infrastructure and waymarking – in the north-west, these were Cumberland, Westmorland & Furness, Lancashire, Sefton, Liverpool, Wirral and Cheshire West & Chester councils.

The 2023 Coronation prompted a surprise rebrand as the King Charles III England Coast Path, although for convenience this guide will still refer descriptively to the 'England Coast Path' or 'ECP'.

The result is a fully waymarked, easy-to-use National Trail with all-new infrastructure enabling as many people as possible to access coast and country. Indeed, some of the biggest benefits of the trail and margin are simply in connecting local communities to each other, off-road, for the first time.

PLANNING AND WAYFINDING

As with all National Trails, look for the trade mark acorn logo. The England Coast Path (on later waymarks, the King Charles III England Coast Path or KCIIIECP) should be well waymarked throughout, including seasonal, high-tide or other diverted routes. Information panels will often provide more context and clarity.

Ordnance Survey 1:25,000 Explorer® and 1:50,000 Landranger maps will mark the ECP using their standard diamond lozenges, and the Coastal Margin with a pink wash (on Explorer maps only).

The new access rights will also be shown on DEFRA's Magic Map, and the National Trails website. The latter's interactive map is helpful for planning your trip, checking diversions, and downloading GPX files. Be aware, some stretches may download as a number of separate files.

WHAT IS COASTAL ACCESS?

Coastal Access and Open Access are close siblings, with only a few subtle differences. In places, existing Open Access has been replaced by Coastal Access as the legal access type, or you may find both in close proximity. The main difference is actually that you will find more restrictions within Coastal Access, due to the far more complex nature of the land. These are:

- **Directions** Access exclusions (e.g. 'no public access') or restrictions (e.g. 'dogs on leads') which may be year-round or seasonal. Check these on openaccess.naturalengland.org.uk.
- **Excepted land types** Land automatically excluded from Coastal Access rights, including golf courses, caravan sites, burial grounds, arable land, railways, schools, parks and gardens, and buildings and their curtilage. The trail may pass through some of these, but rights do not extend across the margin.

Due to the changeable nature of the coast's land use, exclusions, restrictions and excepted land won't be shown on maps of the Coastal Margin as they'll often soon be out of date.

Some blanket 'national restrictions' also apply, most notably that dogs must always be on a lead around farm animals on Coastal Access land – whether the trail or the margin – as opposed to 'effective control' on a public footpath.

ADAPTABILITY

Unless by coincidence, the trail is not a Public Right of Way (PROW) in itself, but a strip of Coastal Access land. As well as the Coastal Margin, adaptability has been built into the legislation to ensure long-term continuity.

- **Rollback** If the trail is damaged by natural processes, a new route can be installed without a formal consultation process.
- **Variations** The trail can adapt more easily than a PROW to development or changes in conservation or land management needs, via a Variation Report.

Art works and information boards celebrate the natural heritage of the Fleetwood coast (Stage 20)

THE NORTH-WEST COASTAL LANDSCAPE

Left to right: Six-spot burnet moth, golden-ringed dragonfly and common blue butterfly

GEOGRAPHY

Modern trends for realigning administrative boundaries mean this guide will refer to a number of overlapping regions. From north to south, the 1974 county of Cumbria has again reverted to separate unitary authorities for Cumberland (north and west Cumbria), and Westmorland and Furness (some of which was north Lancashire pre-1974). The Arnside and Silverdale National Landscape straddles the border of Cumbria (Westmorland) and Lancashire. Beyond Lancashire, the Merseyside county encompasses the Sefton, Liverpool and Wirral boroughs – before you reach a small corner of Cheshire near the border.

GEOLOGY

The landforms of the north-west coast, as everywhere, are entirely underpinned by their geology. The ever-present Lake District volcanic and slate mountains and the Lancashire gritstone moors give way to much lower coastal plains, formed of glacial and estuarine deposits, leading to the Irish Sea. This makes for refreshingly less taxing walking than some coastlines, but there are plenty of exceptions where the underlying bedrock memorably rears its head.

Cumberland's coastal bedrock consists mainly of sandstones, as the dramatic Triassic red cliffs of St Bees Head demonstrate. Crumblier cliffs between Ravenglass and Silecroft are formed from recent glacial deposits before giving way to estuary once more as the River Duddon runs out to sea.

East of the Duddon, glacial deposits also formed the 11-mile 'barrier island' of Walney, separated from mainland Barrow-in-Furness by the tidal Walney Channel, and Morecambe Bay's Carboniferous limestones begin appearing in outcrops at Dunnerholme Rock, Plumpton, Cartmel, Humphrey Head, Arnside, Silverdale and Warton. The Arnside and Silverdale National Landscape is a highlight for fossil-hunters.

Sandstone returns in mainly Permian outcrops near Lancaster, Morecambe and Glasson Dock. Otherwise, from Morecambe to Liverpool, classic sandy beaches and expanses of dune formed since the ice age cover the underlying bedrocks; intersected by the Lune, Wyre and Ribble estuaries.

Around the Wirral peninsula, lying above a deeper layer of coal, Triassic sand- and mudstones are mainly exposed as red sandstone outcrops at Hilbre Island, Red Rocks and Burton Marsh. Superficial boulder clays otherwise overlie the whole area, forming very crumbly cliffs in places, finally superseded by estuarial silts as you reach the River Dee.

NATURAL HISTORY

Beach and dune

The open coast is a place of wonder, and on any visit to the beaches of the north-west, you may glimpse exciting species such as dolphins, harbour porpoise and the grey seals of Walney Island and the Wirral. But the close-ups are just as fascinating.

Seabirds like Sandwich or little tern, and visiting gannets from southern Scotland, might be spotted diving for fish. Terns, oystercatcher and ringed plover nest on sand and shingle. 'Vegetated shingle' is itself protected for its delicate plant species such as sea kale, sea pea, sea beet and the striking sea holly. The intertidal sands of Allonby Bay are known for the Solway's 'honeycomb reef', created by the honeycomb worm.

Half the UK's population of rare natterjack toads live in Cumbria, with more again on the Sefton and Wirral coasts. In winter, these yellow-striped toads hibernate in sandy dune soils; in summer they're mainly nocturnal, but their rattling croak can be heard for some distance.

Removal of over-stabilising spiky marram grass and invasive Japanese Rose is often key to dune restoration projects. Loose sand is favoured by species such as sand lizard and the extra-rare northern dune tiger beetle, found mainly around Ainsdale. Dune slacks (dips) often host ponds or wetlands rich in insects, amphibians and dune plants – from sea buckthorn to orchids to Grass of Parnassus, the county flower of Cumbria.

Cliff

RSPB hides atop St Bees Head, the highest sea cliffs in the north-west, create excellent summer viewing spots for nesting herring gulls, kittiwake, fulmar, cormorant, razorbill and guillemot, with handy

Coastal plants to look out for include (clockwise from top left) Walney geranium, Carline thistle, sea holly, sea spurge and sea lavender

species-identification boards nearby. Elsewhere, Arnside and Silverdale's cliffs host specialist limestone plants and flowers in very shallow, alkaline soils. Many of the coast's cliffs are protected for both their biological and geological features, including the crumbly red cliffs of south-west Cumbria and the Wirral.

Estuary and wetland

Where river meets sea, estuary is created, and where multiple rivers converge, you'll find the epic intertidal swathes of the Solway Firth or Morecambe Bay. With great ranges of saltmarsh, muds and sands exposed at low tide, hundreds of thousands of waterfowl, geese and wading birds feed and roost there – in winter, look for thousands-strong clouds of pink-footed and barnacle geese migrating from marsh to marsh on the Solway Firth.

Waders such as redshank and curlew feed from the muds and sands, while little egret – white herons which have experienced something of a population boom in recent years – enjoy fishing in shallow waters. Avocet populations are spreading across the Ribble, Morecambe Bay and Solway estuaries. Look out also for ducks and wildfowl both common and scarce, such as the ever-present shelduck; and from Morecambe Bay northwards, the eider, or 'Cuddy duck'.

Inland extensions of coastal wetlands include the RSPB's Leighton Moss and Burton Mere reserves, where bitterns may be heard

Stonechats can often be seen on coastal perches and rocks near the path

'booming' from the reedbeds at dawn and dusk in spring. Lowland peatlands like Duddon Mosses and Roudsea Woods & Mosses in Cumbria store carbon and water, whilst proving valuable heath and bog habitat. Look for raptors such as marsh harrier, kestrel and short-eared owl soaring above free-roaming deer and the far more elusive adder – alongside spring floral extravaganzas along the estuaries' tributary rivers.

Woodland and scrub

Gorse-lined coastal slopes such as those south of St Bees are loved by small nesting birds and raptors; and around areas of rugged limestone cliffs like Silverdale's, remnants of ancient woodland abound. Lancaster whitebeam is a notable local rarity. Roudsea Woods and Mosses National Nature Reserve (NNR) features a mixture of ancient woodland and wetter coastal forest. The Sefton coast in turn offers lengths of scrubby and wooded dunes, culminating in the famous Sefton pines, growing in the dunes themselves and home to red squirrels.

Farmland

Most of the north west's farmland is livestock-focused, often similar to nearby upland hill farms, alongside more fertile arable land on the Lancastrian plains around the Ribble Estuary. Hedges, scrub, dry stone walls, trees, ponds and streams are home to birds, small mammals, fish and invertebrates, from the common to the less so. Many farms are under environmental stewardship, and conservation grazing has also been introduced in places to mimic the natural patterns of prehistoric herbivores. You'll notice this on many dunes, such as Mawbray Banks (to loosen sands and open up slacks) and marshes such as Rockcliffe (to create space for ground-nesting birds).

Urban

Even on the most urban of seafronts, plenty of birds enjoy tidal feasts and beach roosts. Look out for turnstone flipping pebbles for tasty treats beneath, listen for oystercatcher peeping, and don't forget to guard your chips from the gulls! Dock and harbour walls host seaweeds, algaes, and huge clumps of mussels and barnacles which are exposed at low tide. Birds like Barrow-in-Furness's dockside eiders sometimes nest under bridges, and in Liverpool, towering landmark buildings may even host peregrine falcons alongside (or because of) the pigeons.

Protections

Environmental protections are rightly frequent, but often multi-layered, throughout the north west coast. These complex protections played one of the strongest roles in where the ECP could be aligned, and where Coastal Access rights may or may not apply within the Coastal Margin, so you're likely to see reference to them on signage and reading material. The main UK and European (still enshrined in UK law despite Brexit) sites on the ECP are Sites of Special Scientific Interest (SSSI), Special Protection Area (SPA, for birds), Special Areas of Conservation (SAC, for habitats), Ramsar (for wetlands), and National Nature Reserves (NNR).

How can I help?

The first port of call for responsible outdoor access guidance is always the Countryside Code, but there are some extra considerations which coastal walkers should be aware of.

NATURAL HISTORY

Good boys and girls are very welcome on the coast path, but may need to stay on their lead at times like here on North Walney (Stage 12)

Beach, dune, shingle, marsh, estuary Migrating and wintering birds need to conserve every calorie they can when feeding and roosting in these areas. Even being on alert for intruders uses energy.
- Keep away from wildlife like seals and birds, keep dogs on leads, and avoid the shore two hours either side of high tide
- Assume birds and nests are there on the ground even if you can't see them
- Pick up dog poo, as it damages soil quality

Cliff Use hides to view seabirds and watch your footing around delicate clifftop plants.

Floodbanks and sea walls The silhouetting of humans and dogs – potential predators – against the sky is known as 'skylining', and causes stress to birds, and dogs running onto beaches and marshes can disturb them. Please follow requests to remain behind a floodbank or keep dogs on paths or leads.

Natterjack toads In dune slacks or coastal marshes, avoid shallow pools and puddles (including ruts in the path): flea treatments can harm them, and spawn can suffocate in stirred-up silt.
- Keep dogs on leads and out of water
- Watch your footing – tiny toadlets may be on the move

Farm animals Safety for walkers is an extra factor here, alongside the wellbeing of livestock.
- Avoid getting between adults and their young
- Pick up dog poo – disease can lay dormant for a long time
- Keep dogs on leads around livestock unless threatened by cattle (your dog can probably outrun them)
- Remember dogs aren't 'just playing' if you're an animal – stress alone can cause miscarriage and illness

Looking back to gentle cliffs near Bolton-le-Sands (Stage 17)

HUMAN AND CULTURAL HISTORIES

Pre-Industrial Revolution

The north west's human history is as varied as anywhere else in the country. The oldest post-glacial human remains in the north have been found around Morecambe Bay, near Great Urswick and Kents Bank, at 11,000 and 10,000 years old respectively. Stone circles and other Mesolithic, Neolithic and Bronze Age remains can be found throughout the north west coast, including Birkrigg Stone Circle near Bardsea – a worthwhile detour from the ECP. Two primary Celtic tribes then ran the Iron Age north west: the Brigantes up to Lancashire and the Carvetii in Cumbria.

Next came the Romans. Evidenced by place names such as Lancaster, and other physical traces, their main north-western legacies – Hadrian's Wall and Chester – neatly sandwich this journey. Hadrian's Wall in particular is ever-present as far as Ravenglass in west Cumbria, through a series of fortlets guarding the coast as well as the land border. Almost 2,000 years old, the Wall is a central part of the international 'Hadrian's Wall and Frontiers of the Roman Empire' World Heritage Site.

Anglo-Saxon rule eventually took most of England over, despite the Celts holding on to Cumbria for some time. As Christianity began to take over from paganism, notable saints included Patrick, said to have been born at Ravenglass and whom the 8th-century ruined chapel at Heysham is named for, and St Bega, who fled Ireland to her now namesake St Bees.

The Vikings' arrival was split between Danish invasions from the east into Lancashire, Merseyside and Cheshire; and Norse immigrants, via Ireland and the Isle of Man, integrating with existing Cumbrian communities and upland areas, which their home terrain would have well prepared them for.

HUMAN AND CULTURAL HISTORIES

Place names throughout the north west are a lasting legacy of many of these communities: Old English (Black Combe, Broughton, '-ton', '-ingham'), Viking (Drigg, Haverigg, Formby, Meols, 'fell', 'dale') and Celtic (the rivers Calder, Derwent, Ehen, Esk, Leven) are all abundant.

Although the Norman conquest arrived in 1066, northern Cumbria's control continued to fluctuate until 1092, when William the Conqueror's son Rufus won Carlisle and built the castle. You won't find Cumberland in the Domesday Book – it was part of Scotland at the time.

Notable monarchs of Medieval England include Edward I, who succumbed to dysentery on Burgh-by-Sands marsh en route to take on Robert the Bruce, the location marked by a sizeable monument; Henry VI, who fled the battle of Towton and was found and sheltered at Muncaster Castle; and Mary, Queen of Scots, who fled Scotland to Workington Hall before being held at Carlisle Castle. In Tudor England, Henry VIII's dissolution of the monasteries which had owned and controlled much of the land in Medieval times, had a sweeping impact across the north. Coastal abbeys and priories dissolved in the 16th century include St Bees, Furness, Cartmel, Cockersand, Lytham and Chester.

Modern industry and culture

Meanwhile, various industries sprang up around the coast, first for local subsistence, then on a bigger scale as technologies and transports developed. From the first forest-clearing Neolithic farmers, the development of agriculture, stone and metal tools, clothing, art and their associated

Flimby beach (Stage 6)

trade routes led to enterprises such as mining, quarrying, fishing, salt production and shipping, until the 18th century and the Industrial Revolution transformed them into large-scale industries.

New towns, canals and later railways sprang up around major centres, such as Millom's iron mines, Whitehaven's coal, Workington and Liverpool's docks, Lancashire and Cheshire's textile mills and Barrow's shipbuilding. Agriculture also developed as coastal marshes were drained, and labour became mechanised.

While some of these histories may once have been a source of pride for the British Empire, many ports and industries were complicit in the transatlantic slave trade, which saw goods and enslaved people traded between England, Ireland, Africa and the Americas in horrific conditions, with ships and plantations built, bought and established by wealthy British families and companies – meaning much of the architectural and maritime interest on the north west coast was built in part from the proceeds of slavery. Thankfully, this is much more widely recognised nowadays.

Since the Revolution, nuclear power, the modern military, and tourism have established a strong coastal presence. Sellafield Nuclear Decommissioning Site is a household name and huge employer, joined by Barrow-in-Furness where BAE Systems blend nuclear power and the town's shipbuilding history in its military submarines. Lancashire's BAE Warton Airfield builds and tests fighter jets; elsewhere, World War 2 airfields are now in commercial aviation, agricultural or wind energy use, and others remain in military possession like RAF Woodvale at Ainsdale. Military defence and training histories pepper the coast: Walney Island was a World War 1 and 2 training ground; and pillboxes and lookout posts are frequent.

Tourism's influence goes without saying. Romantic artists and writers like Turner and the Wordsworths inspired others to travel to their featured coastal destinations, with Wainwright's illustrated guidebooks promoting walking in the region from the 20th century. Architecture and landscape art like Anthony Gormley's 'Another Place' statues at Crosby draw modern crowds.

Railways enabled a boom in Victorian seaside towns such as Blackpool, Southport and Morecambe, and in turn their music-hall culture and TV stars such as Eric Morecambe; but for musical legacies few trump The Beatles, whose statues stand at Pier Head between the Liver Building and Gerry Marsden Ferry terminal – itself named for the author of that inevitable earworm as you approach your 'Ferry Cross the Mersey' in the final stages of the trail.

PRACTICALITIES

Native Herdwick sheep graze Drigg dunes under the watchful gaze of England's highest mountains in Wasdale (Stage 8)

FITNESS AND VARIATIONS TO THE ITINERARY

Fitness-wise, many lengths are fairly steady, with the most strenuous sections being the hilly west Cumbrian cliffs, and the loose sand of the Haverigg and Sefton dunes. Joints can often be protected from tarmac promenades using adjacent beaches, greens and gardens.

The majority of the trail is very adaptable thanks to coastal public transport services – many stages could be split into two, or two days stretched across three. Tables of alternative itineraries are included. For a selection of day trips or short sections see Appendix D.

TRANSPORT

Getting to the trail

If you're travelling by air from outside the UK, Glasgow, Edinburgh, Newcastle, Manchester and Liverpool should all have decent transport connections to key locations on the route. Carlisle and Gretna train stations are closest to the start of the route, with rail and bus connections between the two. At the end of the ECP, Neston and Hawarden Bridge are the closest stations to the ECP itself. National Express coaches serve Carlisle, Lancaster, Blackpool, Preston, Liverpool, Birkenhead and Chester; the Megabus goes to Carlisle,

Deep tidal channels are just one of the hidden saltmarsh hazards that can catch out an unsuspecting walker, as here in Millom (Stage 10)

Lancaster University, Preston and Liverpool.

On the trail

Public transport is very good where railways and urban centres exist. A few weak spots rely on the survival of vulnerable local bus services (which will therefore be grateful for trade), or taxis. The Maryport to Heysham, Fleetwood to Lytham and Southport to Neston lengths are all well served by train (although some stops are 1 or 2km inland), barring the odd estuary. Buses intermittently connect most of the days, but take a little more planning, especially as some rural services are seasonal or limited; the best resources are council websites for Cumberland, Westmorland & Furness, Lancashire and Cheshire West & Chester; merseytravel.gov.uk between Southport and the Wirral; and the national traveline.info website.

Longer days may be necessary on the Gretna to Maryport, Ravenglass to Silecroft, Bardsea to Cark and Heysham to Lancaster sections – but there are always enough road crossings to split a day using local taxis, though this can be expensive. In time, baggage transfer services may hopefully expand to cover the ECP (especially on the Solway alongside Hadrian's Wall), including customised or passenger services.

ACCOMMODATION

B&B accommodation is plentiful in many places and easy to find by searching on websites such as airbnb.co.uk, booking.com and regional Tourist Information Centres.

Websites like ukcampsite.co.uk and pitchup.co.uk are great for camping, but for now expect a lack of cheap backpackers' campsites and hostels, although recent additions suggest this will improve as the ECP develops and awareness of backpackers' needs increases over time.

Campervanners will find things far simpler, as there are plenty of offerings via the Camping and Caravanning Club, Camping and Motorhome Club, and other membership websites and social media groups such as BritStops, Pub Stopovers, and SearchForSites. There are also plenty of holiday parks and lay-bys – allowing you to choose a base near a station and use public transport to link to each day's linear walk.

The same principle can be applied to budget Travelodge-type hotels in a handful of larger towns and cities such as Carlisle, Maryport, Workington, Whitehaven, Barrow, Blackpool, Southport, Liverpool and New Brighton.

Otherwise, this guide lists some of the main pubs, hotels, campsites and occasional hostels on the route, but do conduct your own searches to see what's changed since the time of writing.

COMMUNICATIONS

As well as poor signal in some remote places, your phone may also jump to the Isle of Man's network in West Cumbria. Plan ahead, check the weather forecast, write down train and bus times, taxi numbers, tide times and heights, and don't forget your map (or this book) in case of phone data or battery failure, and some change for any surviving phone boxes.

MONEY

Contactless payments are fairly universal nowadays, but once more, the odd rural or takeaway business, taxi or car park may require cash, so keep some on you as ATMs (cash machines) may be few and far between. Even in urban areas, ATMs can be some distance inland, and often inside shops with limited opening hours. Searching 'ATM' within your mobile phone's map app may help.

WHEN TO GO

Spring and summer are the obvious choices due to extended daylight hours, (hopefully) gentler weather and fewer stormy high tides. That said, gazing across yellow sands to snow-capped mountains or crunching across frost-encrusted winter beaches is an experience in itself. Autumn brings its own beauties, and there's joy to be had in having the trail to yourself in quiet season. Rural public transport links may often be reduced or non-existent between October and Easter though, so off-season walks will require careful planning.

NORTH OR SOUTH?

This guide has been written from north to south to correlate with Cicerone's Wales Coast Path and South West Coast Path guides for walkers wishing to carry on around the coast, but the information here and good waymarking on open stretches should easily enable a reverse route – something to consider in winter when the prevailing south-westerlies are at their most enthusiastic.

COASTAL SAFETY

Staying safe is usually a matter of common sense – avoid cliff edges, especially if crumbly, cracked or overhung, and check the tide times – bearing in mind that forecast times can vary by an hour or so in some locations. Tide heights are relevant – treat 8+ metre tides with caution, and avoid 9–10 metre tides. Some dangers aren't so obvious though, which is why some access exclusions are in place due to 'unsuitability for public access'. Morecambe Bay's deadly sinking sands are well known, and the invisible danger spots can move daily and occur very close to the shore. North-west England also has one of the highest tidal ranges in the world at 10 metres, and the gradual gradient means this height difference can cover miles of sand on each tide – creating tides said to be faster than a galloping horse in places.

Saltmarshes can catch walkers out as deep, muddy channels are not easily visible, but can fill hours before the tide covers the marsh. These channels often lie along the back of a marsh and can completely block an escape on what appears to be a clear route. Even solid saltmarsh ground can be lower towards the back, and flood early – so stick to the path. If you think you've been caught out, call for help as soon as possible to ensure it arrives before high tide. Similarly, lowland peat bogs ('mosses') may be up to 10m deep, even when they appear solidly vegetated.

In all of these situations, please keep dogs on a lead (for their own safety as well as protecting wildlife) or close to you on the trail, to avoid these invisible hazards.

Otherwise, potential hazards are more commonplace – cattle, as mentioned above (including on marshes – there can be hundreds grazing) and traffic being key examples. Urban areas may also be daunting at times, but are generally safe on the ECP route, although it's worth avoiding walking later in the evening, especially on the approaches to Workington and Liverpool.

EMERGENCIES

In a coastal emergency (anything on the water, shore, saltmarsh, or anywhere that might be easier to access via them), call 999 and ask for the Coastguard. The Coastguard, RNLI, Bay Search and Rescue and various local Inshore Rescue teams will between them have the means to cross coastal terrain as appropriate. Where land access would be easier but you're away from a road (such as on a clifftop), ask for the Police, who may decide to deploy Search and Rescue or Mountain Rescue instead. The nearest A&E hospitals to the route are Carlisle, Workington, Barrow, Lancaster, Blackpool, Preston, Liverpool and Chester.

WHAT TO PACK

Much of this depends on your itinerary and how long you need to sustain yourself between facilities. However, even if you were aiming to to camp as much of the route as possible, you'll rarely be more than two days without resupply options. In terms of everyday essentials, assume changeable weather, and remember the north-west is subject to the UK's predominantly south-westerly winds – so warm layers and waterproofs should be carried at any time of year, along with a survival blanket or bag, first aid kit, sunglasses, suncream and sunhat for the better days. Take plenty of water in any case – the chances of finding pure spring water are very low, and enroute refreshments not guaranteed. A power bank for mobile devices is a worthwhile investment.

The secluded Fleswick Bay from above (Stage 7)

MAPS

As yet, the most concise but detailed map resources for the whole of the north-west ECP are this guide's companion map booklets, but in time others may crop up, such as Harvey Maps' long distance trail maps. GPX files for use with mobile mapping software and GPS devices can be downloaded from the Cicerone or National Trails websites (see 'Interactive Map'), although these work better with some apps than others due to the multiple 'shapefiles' within each stretch download.

Which paper (or digital equivalent) map you use depends on your priorities – if you're keen to see the extent of the Coastal Margin, then Ordnance Survey 1:25,000 Explorer maps will have both the trail and the margin added as stretches open, via its pink wash (but see notes above regarding excepted and restricted land). The following OS maps apply:

Map number & name	Section of ECP	Route stages
1:25k Explorer maps		
315 Carlisle	Gretna to Boustead Hill	1–2
314 Solway Firth	Boustead Hill to Beckfoot	2–5
OL4 English Lakes North West	Beckfoot to Flimby	5–6
303 Whitehaven & Workington	Flimby to Sellafield	6–7
OL6 English Lakes South West	Sellafield to Baycliff	7–13
OL7 English Lakes South East	Baycliff to Carnforth	13–16
296 Lancaster, Morecambe & Fleetwood	Carnforth to Bispham	16–20
286 Blackpool & Preston	Bispham to Banks	20–23
285 Southport & Chorley	Banks to Little Crosby	23–25
275 Liverpool	Little Crosby to Pier Head	25–26
266 Wirral & Chester	Seacombe to Chester & Shotton	26–28
1:50k Landranger maps		
85 Carlisle & Solway Firth	Gretna to Milefortlet 21	1–5
89 West Cumbria	Milefortlet 21 to Seascale beach	5–8
96 Barrow-in-Furness & South Lakeland	Seascale beach to Grange-over-Sands	8–15
97 Kendal & Morecambe	Roosebeck to Heysham Port	13–17
102 Preston & Blackpool	Heysham Port to Marshside	17–24
108 Liverpool	Marshside to Gayton	24–27
117 Chester & Wrexham/Caer a Wrecsam	Gayton to Shotton & Chester	27–28

USING THIS GUIDE

Plover Scar lighthouse rising above the waters at high tide (Stage 19)

and a little extra for slow terrain, but don't include rest stops. If you're happy map-reading, the companion map booklets and GPX downloads (www.cicerone.co.uk/1027/GPX) should keep things simple on the go; either way this guide hopes to aid in forward planning to ensure a smooth day-to-day journey.

As the ECP will be continually evolving around the ever-changing coastline, even once fully open the routes described here will change frequently. Check www.nationaltrail.co.uk for updates on open stretches – any problems you find can be reported via that website to the relevant trail officer.

A little egret fishing in the shallows. Egret numbers have boomed in the UK in recent decades

USING THIS GUIDE

As emphasised above, this trail is what you want to make of it. If the mileage suits you, this 28-day plan should enable all days to be connected by bus or train with a little forward planning, but alternative itineraries have been suggested and a table in Appendix A lists accommodation available at each potential stopover. Notes are included on each stage's introduction as to the terrain, accessibility, transport, interest points en route, ECP status, and interim alternatives if you're heading out before it's fully finished. Timings are given for walking time based on 4km per hour, 10 minutes per 100 metres of ascent,

Walking the King Charles III England Coast Path: North West

ACCESSIBILITY

The ethos of the England Coast Path is to enable as many people as possible to get into walking and explore the natural coastal environment – whether country- or city-based; for long-distance walkers this might include enabling family and friends to join you for sections. Stiles are replaced with pedestrian and field gates, or large stockproof kissing gates, sometimes with RADAR locks to enable wheelchair access, and these should further improve over time.

For wheelchair access, built environments are generally okay assuming dropped kerbs are present. On rural sections, some mobility or a companion may help with tricky gates, terrain and vegetation growth; over time, footfall (animal and human) can also muddy or erode ground around bridges, gates and flagstones. As such, this book does not make judgements on whether the basic terrain is wheelchair friendly.

Sensory impairments, fatigue, balance, chronic pain, dexterity, neurodivergence (dyslexia, autism, dyspraxia etc.) and low income create different challenges: there's no such thing as 'fully accessible'. Be aware toilets can shut without warning. Notes on terrain, transport, potential wheelchair accessibility and extreme sensory inputs (e.g. loud noises) are made for each stage, but for guidance only, due to changeability. Light-sensitive walkers may benefit from a north to south approach to avoid sea-glare.

Finally, bear in mind that the statistics in this book are based on 4km per hour, so you may wish to adjust accordingly.

Eventually, Trail Partnerships and third parties will hopefully test and promote more accessible lengths. Visit www.nationaltrail.co.uk/access-for-all for more information including a promoted wheelchair section from Allonby to Maryport.

PART 1 – CUMBERLAND

Boats in Maryport harbour (Stage 6)

Walking the King Charles III England Coast Path: North West

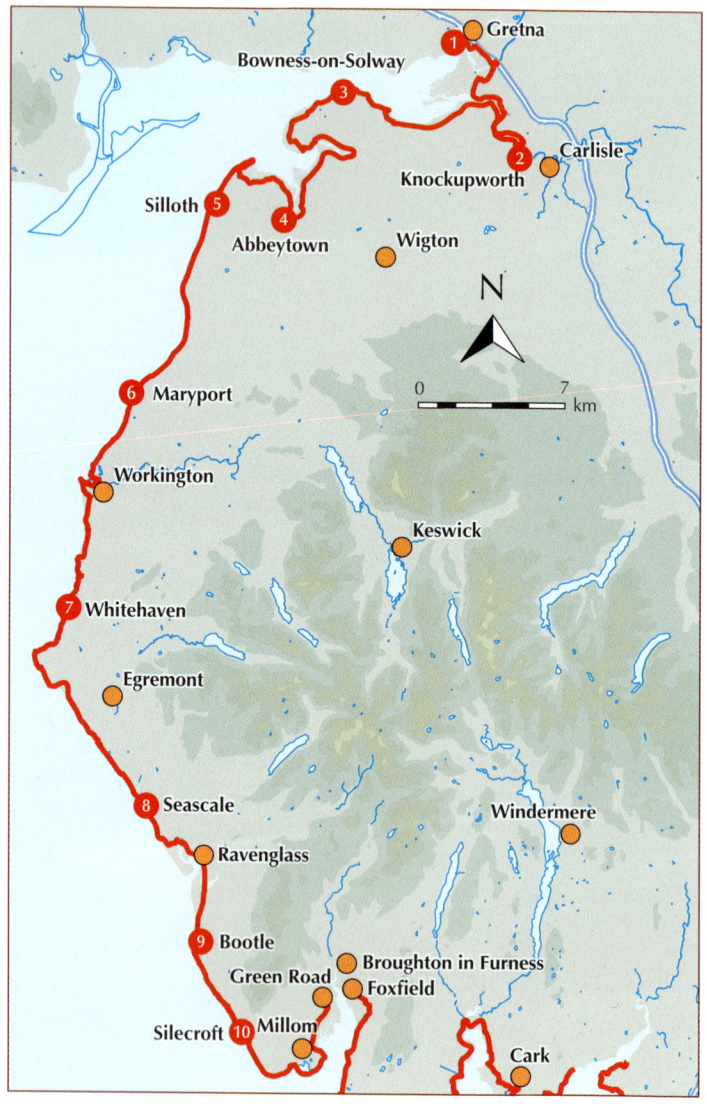

STAGE 1
Gretna to Knockupworth

Start	Sark Bridge, Gretna, NY 327 669
Finish	Knockupworth Bridge, Carlisle, NY 372 569
Time	5hr 35min
Distance	21.1km (13 miles)
Ascent	100m
Terrain	Grass or gravel riverside, floodbank and country lanes
Refreshments	Various in Gretna; Metal Bridge Inn; Crown & Thistle, Rockcliffe (400m off-trail)
Toilets	Caledonia Park retail centre, near start
Transport	Trains and buses between Gretna and Carlisle. Buses 63 to Rockcliffe & Cargo, 382 via Metal Bridge, 93 between Carlisle, Knockupworth Farm and Bowness-on-Solway; pre-booked taxis
Accessibility	Tricky terrain and steps, especially over railway at Metal Bridge. Rockcliffe and Demesnes Marsh circuit step-free with RADAR kissing gates
Parking	Caledonia Park (South) free car park, Gretna, NY 325 671
Accommodation	Various in Gretna and Carlisle; Metal Bridge Inn, huts and motorhomes; occasional B&Bs and holiday cottages
KCIIIECP status in 2025	Open

At the southern end of Gretna, the King Charles III England Coast Path officially starts (or indeed finishes) halfway across the Sark Bridge, where the Scotland–England border runs up the middle of the River Sark below. It's a matter of metres until you're off the road and gazing across the Solway Firth. Beyond Gretna, unless splitting your day early, the next bus is at Knockupworth, on the road into Carlisle. While logistics for the first two days may require some research – the easiest overnight option may well be Carlisle or Bowness – this is as difficult as it gets, and taxis are an option close to the city. Early marshside sections are but a teaser for the days ahead, as the Eden riverside draws you inland, ready for a return to the Solway on Stage 2.

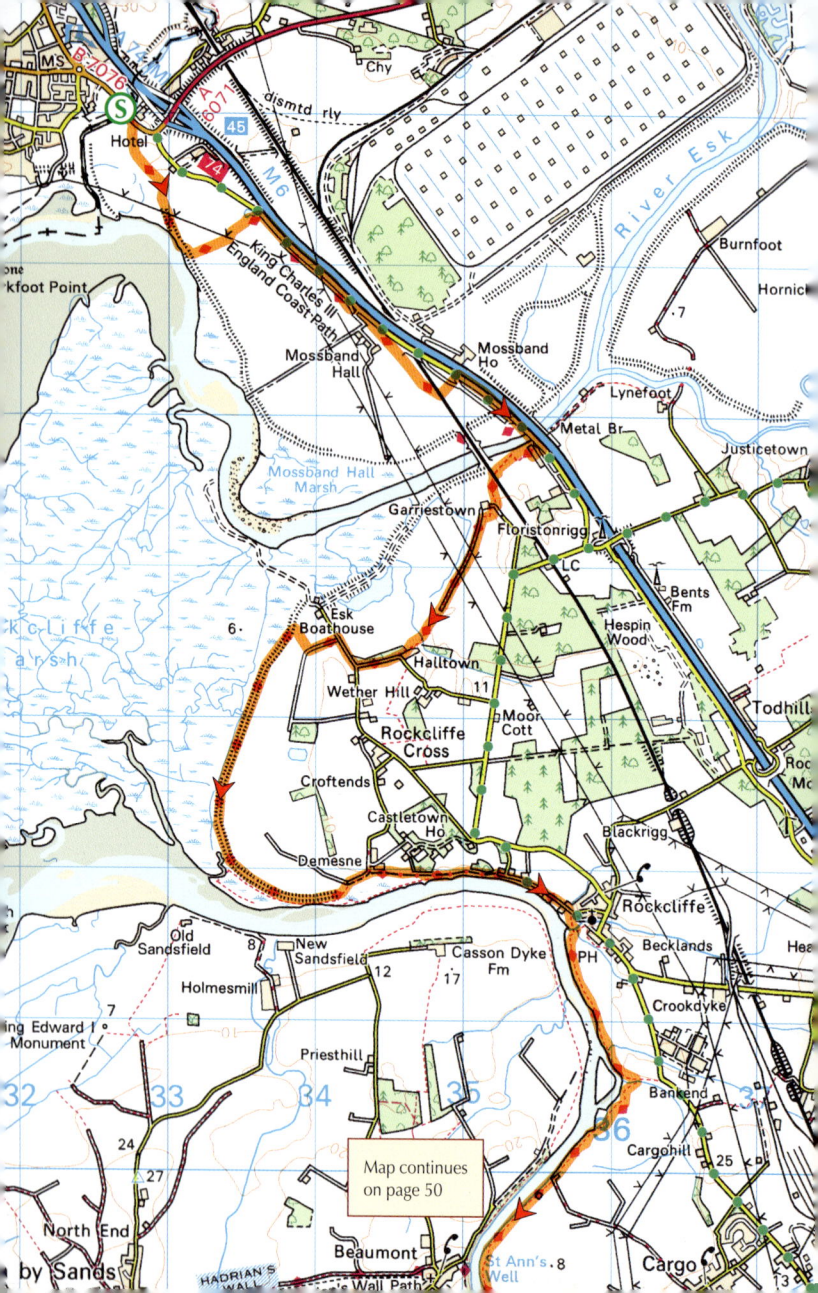

STAGE 1 – GRETNA TO KNOCKUPWORTH

GRETNA

From 1612, Gretna was a border customs post, and prehistoric megaliths prove much older origins; but now, the name is synonymous with one thing. England's 1753 Marriage Act introduced a requirement for parental consent for under-21s – and for many runaway couples heading north to elope, Gretna was the first cross-border stop. The most famous site is the Old Blacksmith's Shop in the northern Gretna Green end of town; but even at the border, venues advertise thousands of marriages conducted over the years. The ECP would make a fantastically long engagement or honeymoon!

Gretna to Metal Bridge (4.5km, 1hr 10min)

Cross Sark Bridge, and shortly after the path drops to a kissing gate into fields below right. Follow a fence to the left, to a floodbank; stay on it. About 1km from the road, turn inland along a hedge, then right over a bridge before a road. The bank and marsh beyond are the first of many wildlife refuges which are excluded from Coastal Access. Follow a path along the back of fields then on tarmac past a small wetland, then down a hedged lane, to the railway/M6 intersection.

Drop into another field for 300m, then pass under the railway and straight ahead along a field edge to more tarmac. Turn right to meet the river by the road bridge. Zigzag left through a gate and along roadside, doubling back through road barriers onto pavement. Cross the bridge, then turn right through a large wooden fence to the hamlet of **Metal Bridge**.

Estuary views soon open up across the Solway

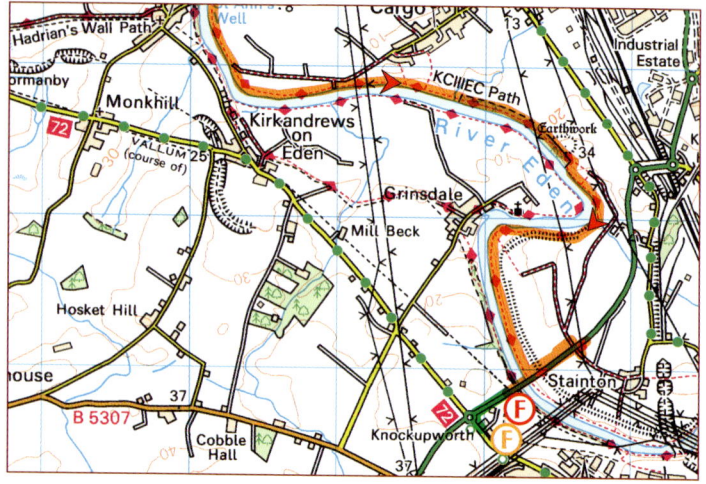

Metal Bridge to Rockcliffe (7.1km, 1hr 50min)

Turn briefly right, then left before the pub to circuit its campsite. Rejoin the riverside then cross the railway bridge soon after. Brace yourself for lots of steps! Keep half-left on another hedged lane for 200m, then right on tarmac towards **Garriestown Farm**. Turn left just before buildings to follow the right-hand edges of two enclosures to another enclosed lane, field edge, small wooded section and finally field to Halltown Farm. Keep right then right again on the Esk Boathouse road.

Halfway down, turn left to circuit a cattle field and rejoin the floodbank. With great views across the marshes to Scotland, head left on this bank for around 2.5km. Continue along the back of the marsh past Demesne Farm, which eventually narrows to an enclosed track, becoming road, straight ahead to **Rockcliffe**, on the River Eden.

Rockcliffe to Knockupworth (9.5km, 2hr 35min)

Cross the green half-right. Cross a bridge and take a gate just to the left. Pass right of a cricket pitch to continue inside fields along the river, veering inland to cross bridges over creeks (very muddy after rain). Stay more or less with the riverside for another 7km, climbing above a large bank, the historical site of a Jacobite camp, just beyond Cargo. Turn left just before the A689 road bridge, past a small wetland then zigzag under the road and up onto pavement over the bridge.

Continue on the road to a roundabout and turn left to Knockupworth Farm (NY370565) for the (unmarked) bus stop and safe taxi pull-in.

STAGE 2
Knockupworth to Bowness-on-Solway

Start	Knockupworth Bridge, Carlisle, NY 372 569
Finish	King's Arms, Bowness-on-Solway, NY 223 627
Time	6hr 30min
Distance	25.4km (16 miles)
Ascent	80m
Terrain	Riverside, floodbank, road, saltmarsh
Refreshments	Pubs in Burgh-by-Sands, Port Carlisle and Bowness; café in Bowness
Toilets	Portaloo, Kirkandrews village hall
Transport	93 bus between Carlisle, Knockupworth Farm and Bowness, or taxis
Accessibility	Kissing gates and uneven terrain on riversides; some steps
Parking	Free roadsides in various locations, residential roadsides in western Carlisle
Accommodation	Various in Carlisle and en route; pub in Port Carlisle; pub, B&Bs and campsites in Bowness; bunkhouse at Boustead Hill
KCIIIECP status in 2025	To Kirkandrews: open; to Dykesfield: check National Trails website; to Bowness: walkable

Some planning is needed around tides and storms, and the status of the ECP, on this stage – but alternatives are present. Between Beaumont (pronounced 'bee-mont') and Holmesmill, a closed public footpath needs reinstating, which the ECP will follow once open. That route is described below, but in the meantime, you'll need to use the minor road from Beaumont to Holmesmill instead. From there, it's all walkable, but very high tides may affect Burgh Marsh (pronounced 'bruff'). Bus stops en route enable shorter days.

Knockupworth (A689 bridge) to Kirkandrews-on-Eden (4.9km, 1hr 15min)
Double back under the bridge on a track leading to a wooded riverside path. Follow this, alternately in trees and field, and down steps to a bridge. Cross and continue on this path to another footbridge which takes you leftwards. Cross it, keeping straight ahead in this field to a road. Turn right through the village of **Grinsdale**.

HADRIAN'S WALL AND EDWARD I

The Edward I monument at the scene of his death on Burgh Marsh

The Hadrian's Wall Path (HWP) starts (or finishes) at Bowness-on-Solway, passing various forts and 'Milecastle' fortlets en route. Now a World Heritage Site, the wall was built 1900 years ago by the Emperor Hadrian to keep the 'barbarian' Scottish Picts out. Burgh-by-Sands was home to the first recorded African community in Britain, as featured on the BBC's 'Black and British' series – the Roman fort of Aballava housed a unit of Moors from north African provinces under Emperor Marcus Aurelius.

You'll also meet Edward I, 'Hammer of the Scots', who perished from dysentry en route to facing Robert the Bruce. A monument on Burgh Marsh marks the spot, and the HWP and ECP high tide routes pass his statue in the village.

Continue to the end of the tarmac, keeping right on a grassy lane to the former chapel of St Kentigern. At its entrance, take a stone step stile and steps to the riverbank before passing back into a field. Follow the river for 3km, mainly inside field edges (and a short section of lane), meandering east then west. Approaching Kirkandrews-on-Eden, take a flight of steps towards the village above you..

Kirkandrews to Old Sandsfield (6.6km, 1hr 40min)

Turn right through the woods halfway up the steps, and follow this path until you meet road again. Until the ECP opens beyond Kirkandrews, turn left at the top of the steps past the village hall (where there is sometimes a public portaloo), then right on road. At Beaumont go right, then left after the church, to Holmesmill.

Keep right, and right again at a fork. A gravel track passes through trees, then drops to the back of a marsh. Follow the waymarked route through grazing marsh

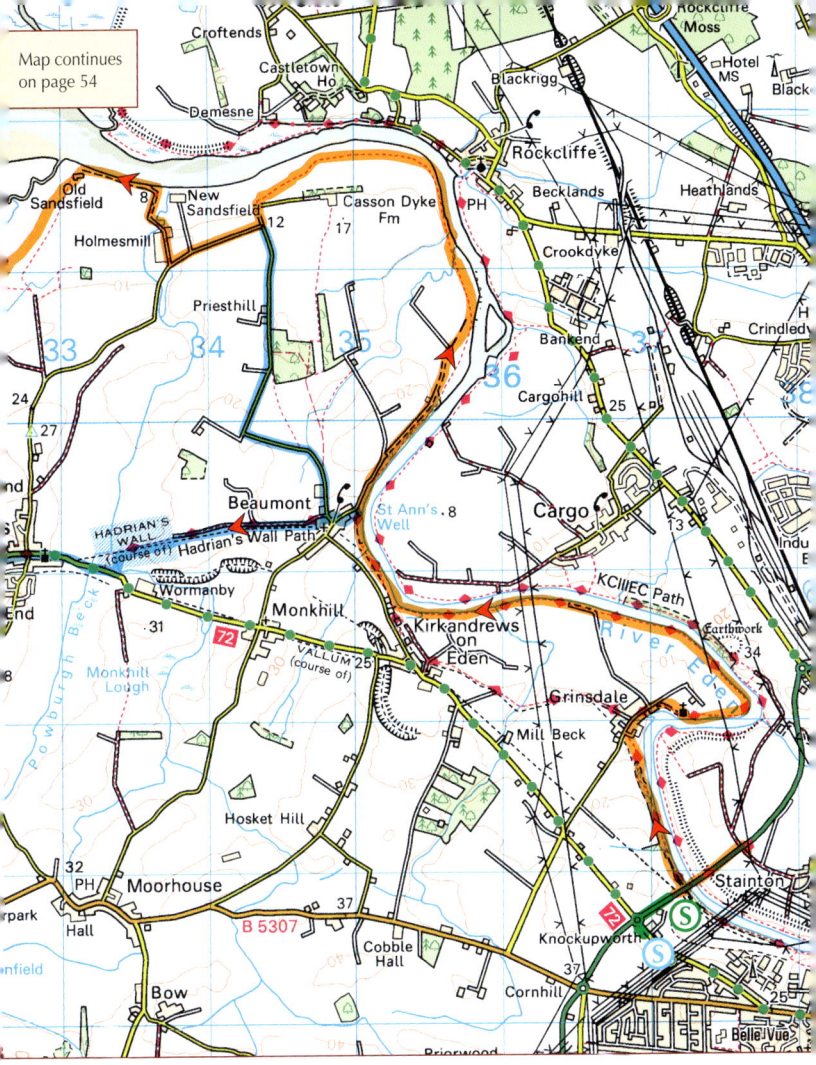

then riverside for about 2.5km. When the fence moves away to your left, take a diagonal line inland. At a lane, turn right, soon right again, and right once more at the next road junction to pass **Holmesmill** and rejoin the riverbank. Turn left towards **Old Sandsfield**.

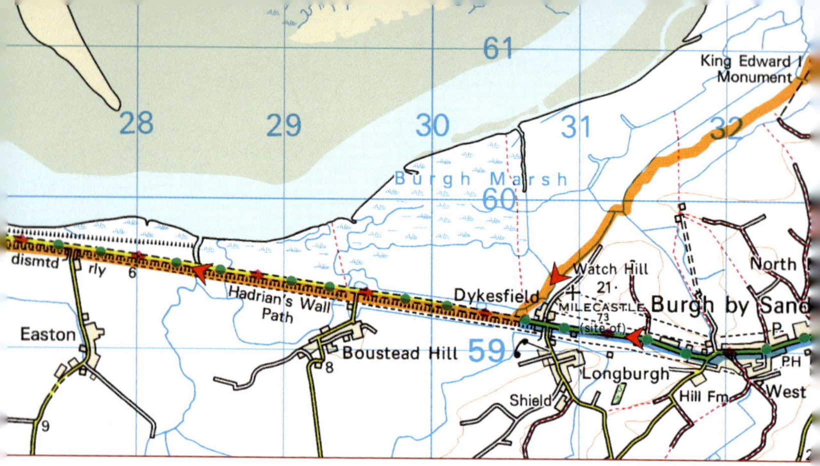

Old Sandsfield to Dykesfield (3.8km, 1hr)

Just past the house, go through a gate and veer left onto Burgh Marsh. The highest, driest and most direct line heads to the Edward I Monument, about 200m out on the marsh. Alternatively, the treeline offers walkers some camouflage if curious cattle are present.

From the monument, the driest line crosses ridge and furrow remnants towards the seaward end of the treeline ahead. Go around the corner there, following the marsh boundary now for about 1km. On the final section, follow a small ditch to the road at **Dykesfield**. For the bus stop, turn left on the road to a junction.

The ECP passes through the Hadrian's Wall Path start/finish shelter at Bowness-on-Solway

Stage 2 – Knockupworth to Bowness-on-Solway

Alternative routes, Beaumont to Dykesfield (removes up to 2.2km)

During very high tides (check in advance), take the Hadrian's Wall Path from Beaumont village to **Burgh by Sands** and on to Dykesfield. Alternatively, to avoid cattle on Burgh marsh, minor roads and footpaths are available from Holmesmill to Burgh by Sands.

Dykesfield to Bowness-on-Solway (10.2km, 2hr 35min)

Turn right onto floodbank (also HWP) for 3.5km. Approaching **Drumburgh**, from April to August, cross the road and pass the village on floodbank and field edges until the road and path re-converge. From September to April, and until open, use the road to Drumburgh, Hadrian's Wall Path to Glasson, then keep straight ahead on road then footpath, rejoining the coast beyond a trig point. Follow a roadside path on marsh then through trees. Pass the stone remains of the 18th-century **Port Carlisle**, marking the end of the former Carlisle Canal, then rejoin the road for 2km to Bowness-on-Solway. Follow HWP waymarks on a short detour behind buildings for estuary views and the HWP start/finish shelter.

The HWP/ECP returns to the road near the bus stop, King's Arms pub and other facilities.

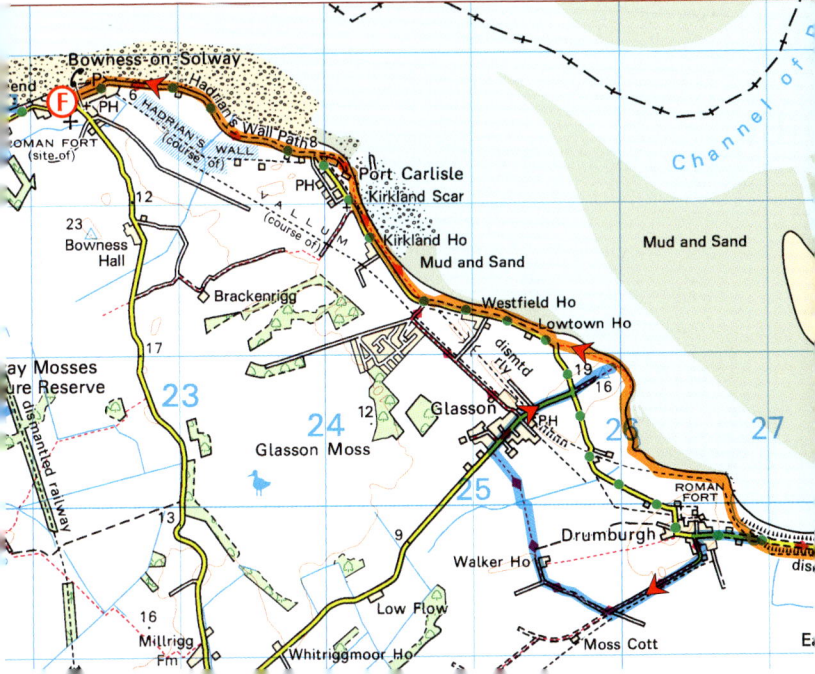

STAGE 3
Bowness-on-Solway to Abbeytown

Start	King's Arms, Bowness-on-Solway, NY 223 627
Finish	Abbeytown riverside (for Abbeytown village), NY 172 517
Time	6hr 30min
Distance	25.4km (15¾ miles); plus 1.3km to Abbeytown
Ascent	30m
Terrain	Road, marsh, field edges
Refreshments	Pubs at Angerton, Newton Arlosh, and Abbeytown on second half; Midtown Stores, Kirkbride
Toilets	Holme Cultram Abbey, Abbeytown
Transport	Buses 93 around Anthorn peninsula to Carlisle and 400 from Abbeytown to Silloth
Accessibility	All tarmac if using high tide routes; beware traffic
Parking	Free roadsides in most locations
Accommodation	B&Bs and pubs in Angerton, Kirkbride and Newton Arlosh
KCIIIECP status in 2025	Not yet open but all walkable using high tide routes

This stage introduces a new character to the estuarine landscapes as the Eden channel widens out with extensive views to southern Dumfries and Galloway, and a circuit of Anthorn Radio Station. The second half follows the Solway's final two tributaries, the Wampool and Waver, to Abbeytown. The interest en route makes up for a tarmac-heavy day – it's unavoidable in the first half, but check afternoon tide times as the marshes beyond Anthorn can flood – and the high routes are primarily more road. Abbeytown itself requires a small detour inland, but the day can be split elsewhere using the 93 bus, or the hotel in Newton Arlosh.

Bowness to Anthorn Bridge (10.2km, 2hr 30min)

Continue westwards on the coast road. After Bowness, the next 10km sits on or alongside the road overlooking the coastal part of the RSPB's Campfield Marsh, and the main channel of the Solway Firth towards Annan in Scotland and its

Stage 3 – Bowness-on-Solway to Abbeytown

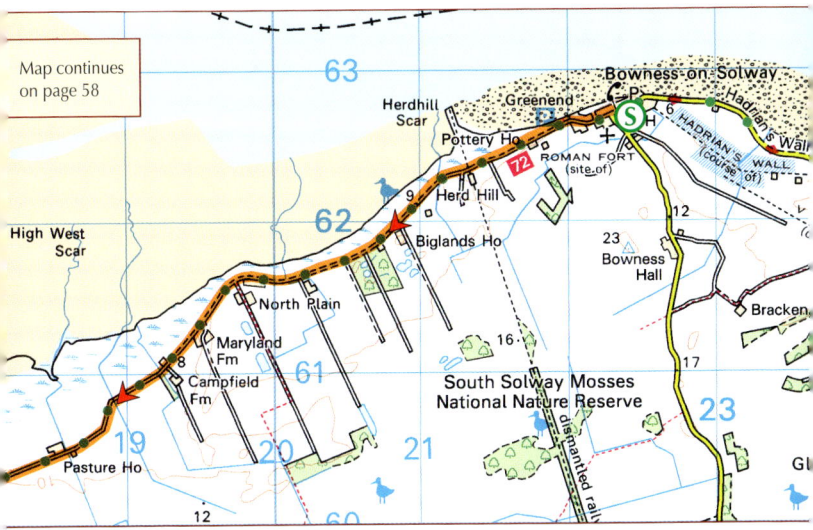

industrial sites and hills beyond, before heading south through **Cardurnock**, then east, passing the radio station.

> **Anthorn Radio Station**, which can be seen from far and wide but looms large over this stage, is a naval and government radio transmitting station which was originally a World War 2 military airfield.

Anthorn Bridge to Newton Marsh (8.4km, 2hr 15min)

Pass the first few houses at Anthorn Bridge, heading north-east now, and the first half of **Anthorn's** housing estate. When the road moves inland, take a path on your right leading to the marsh. Use the road at high tide and until ECP opens.

Follow marsh and field edges for about 2km. When the road returns, follow it through **Whitrigg** for about 750m, then turn right at the road junction to cross Whitrigg Bridge.

Turn right straight after the bridge to follow the banks of the River Wampool downstream. Until open, use high tide route from Whitrigg Bridge to Salt Coates as described below, then follow the road to Abbeytown. Stay with the back of the marsh when the channel opens out. After 3.5km there's a footpath inland if you need to escape tides or access facilities in **Newton Arlosh**.

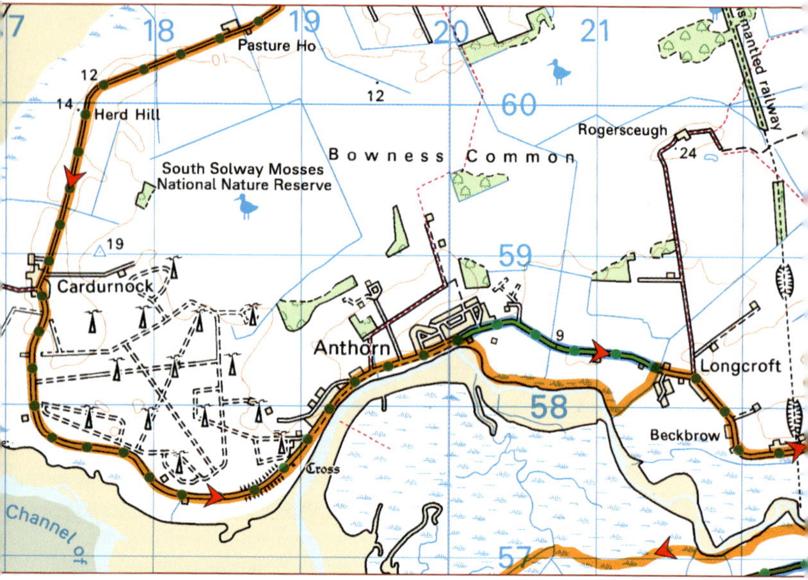

Walking the King Charles III England Coast Path: North West

The ECP connects the Hadrian's Wall Path with the Roman frontier's coastal outposts at Maryport and Ravenglass

Newton Marsh to Abbeytown
(6.8km, 1hr 45min)

After another 3.75km of waymarked marsh path generally south-west then south, turn right onto a minor road just west of **Salt Coates**.

After 1km turn right onto a path primarily following a disused railway, dropping temporarily into fields partway.

Opened in 1869 to connect Cumbria's iron ore mines and Lanarkshire's furnaces, the **Solway Junction Railway** once ran from Kirtlebridge in Scotland to Aspatria in Cumbria. It crossed the Solway on a 1.8km-long viaduct between

STAGE 3 – BOWNESS-ON-SOLWAY TO ABBEYTOWN

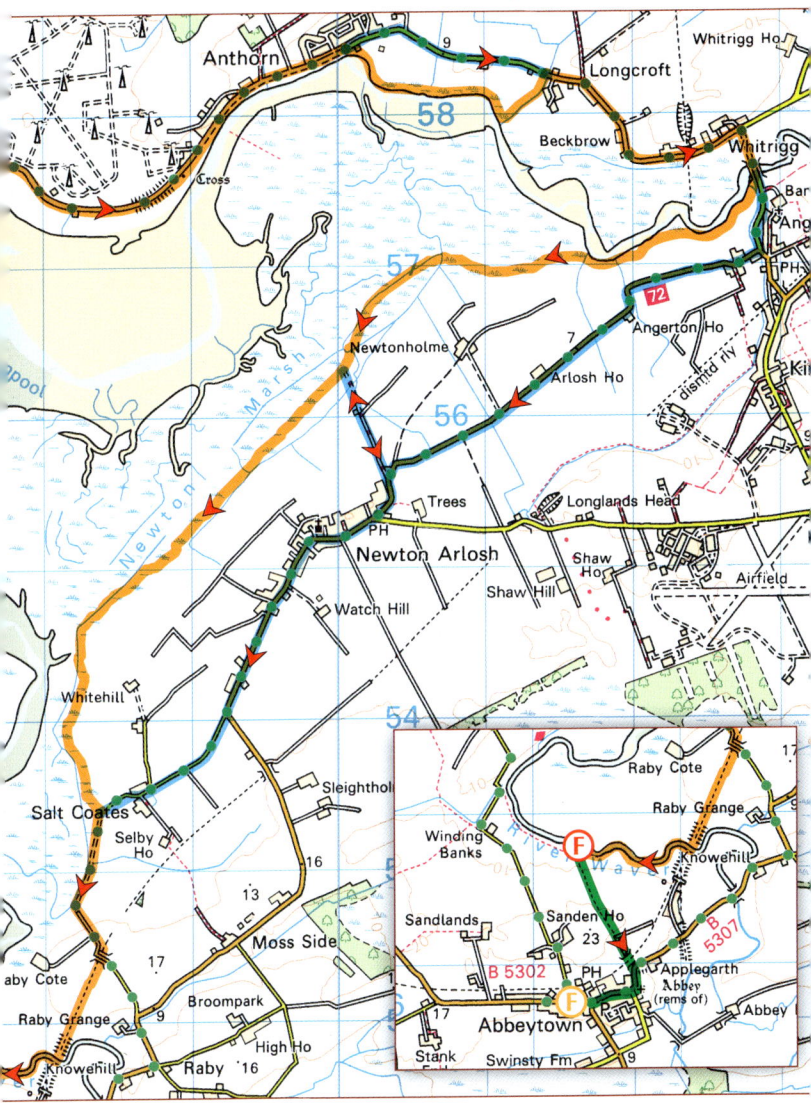

WALKING THE KING CHARLES III ENGLAND COAST PATH: NORTH WEST

Holme Cultram Abbey is your welcome to Abbeytown and well worth a look inside

Bowness-on-Solway and Annan in Dumfriesshire, but repeated storm, ice and tide damage led to closures and an eventual dismantlement in 1934.

Cross the River Waver, and turn right on the riverside for 1km to a path junction by a small footbridge by the riverside.

Alternative route, Whitrigg Bridge to Salt Coates

(removes 1.2km)
Continue on road from Whitrigg Bridge to **Angerton** and take the first right to **Newton Arlosh** and **Salt Coates**. There's a midway link via a public right of way from Newton Arlosh to Newton Marsh.

Abbeytown link route   (1.3km, 20min)

If you're finishing at Abbeytown, turn left on a public footpath through field edges, becoming a lane, and through an underpass, which can be very wet underfoot! Now turn right on the road, passing Holme Cultram Abbey, and keep right on this road through Abbeytown. A toilet, occasional café and museum displays are available in the Cistercian Holme Cultram abbey, which is worth a visit. The bus stop is just past a road junction, near a Spar.

Looking across part of the RSPB Campfield Marsh reserve to Scotland

STAGE 4
Abbeytown to Silloth

Start	Abbeytown riverside, NY 172 517
Finish	Criffel Street/Station Road crossroads, Silloth, NY 109 535
Time	4hr 30min
Distance	16km (10 miles); plus 1.3km from Abbeytown
Ascent	20m
Terrain	Riverside, grassland, promenade and 6km of sometimes muddy marsh
Refreshments	Pubs and cafés in Abbeytown and Silloth; fish & chips in Silloth
Toilets	Holme Cultram Abbey, Abbeytown; seasonal in Skinburness (seasonal); in Silloth RNLI station and Criffel Street
Transport	Buses 400 from Abbeytown to Silloth and 60 from Skinburness to Silloth, Maryport & Workington
Accessibility	Tricky terrain on marsh; RADAR kissing gates near Brownrigg and round Grune Point. High stile and narrow roads on high tide route. Open grass and prom to Silloth
Parking	Roadsides at Holme Cultram Abbey, Abbeytown and Silloth; car park at Skinburness NY 127 559 (all free)
Accommodation	Pubs, B&Bs and holiday parks in Silloth; scatterings elsewhere on booking sites
KCIIIECP status in 2025	Open

In the right conditions, this is a fantastic day's walking, but does require some planning. Skinburness and Calvo Marsh, the last of the Solway saltmarshes, may be affected by high tides, and is grazed by large herds of cattle from May to November – also contributing to very muddy conditions when wet. GPS may be useful on this section. A waymarked high tide route is available (same length as main trail), but expect a very steep stile at Highwath Bridge. High tide means above 9.5m, or 8.5m in storms – and including the two hours either side. However, time it right and the marsh offers a spectacular sense of openness and isolation, with views to Scotland and Anthorn, and in winter, thousands of migratory geese regularly sweeping the skies. Grune Point is a delight, intersecting the eastern marshes and your first views of the wider Solway seascape to the west, before you join the promenade towards Silloth.

WALKING THE KING CHARLES III ENGLAND COAST PATH: NORTH WEST

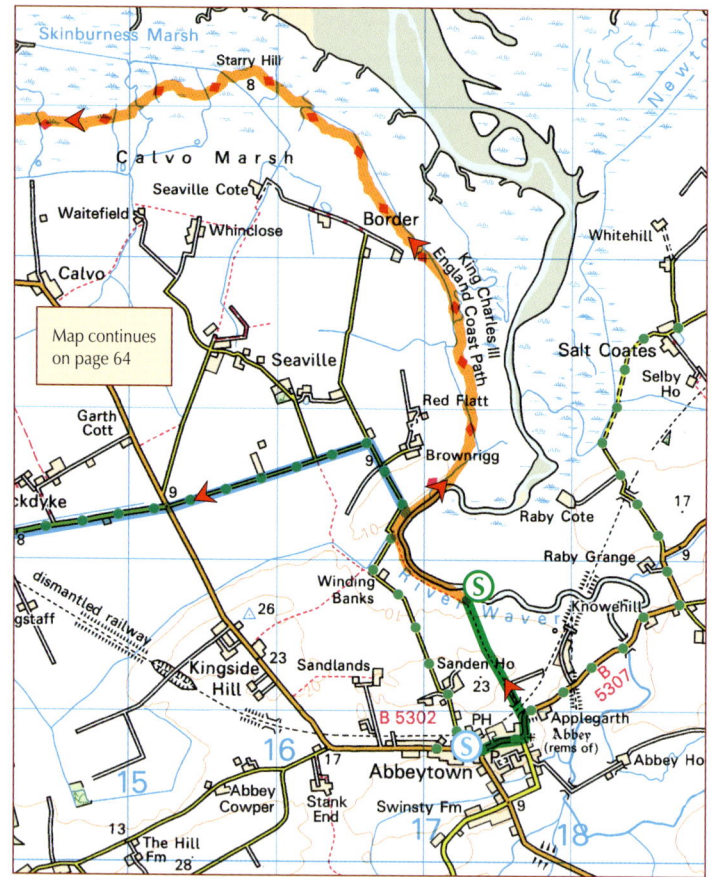

Abbeytown riverside to East Border (3.5km, 1hr)
Back at the riverside, turn left and cross two footbridges. Follow the river until you're forced briefly onto the road and over the small Rumbling Bridge. Shortly after it, drop back to a riverside – becoming saltmarsh – path. Look for waymarks and flat, subtle sleeper bridges over channels and boggy patches to a path junction at **East Border** (marked as Border on 1:50,000 OS map), about 2.5km in. The only real escape opportunity – head south on road to join the high tide route near Brownrigg.

STAGE 4 – ABBEYTOWN TO SILLOTH

Skeins of geese are a spectacular sight over the Solway marshes in winter

East Border to Sea Dyke End (4km, 1hr 15min)
Stay ahead on the waymarked and bridged route, loosely following the seaward edge of a more rushy, sometimes scrubby area of ground, which leads you further out on open ground. After some gorse, the path swings left and into a different enclosure, still on saltmarsh. Handrails now make bridges easier to see, but the ground can still be very wet – take care. Follow the bridges, eventually turning back inland towards a farmhouse and crossing a few more bridges to meet the road just right of the house at **Sea Dyke End**; also the end of the high tide route. At least one culvert across the final channels is difficult to see, especially if cows are present. At the road, dogleg briefly left to a ramp accessing the flood bank.

Alternative route, Rumbling Bridge to Sea Dyke End (same distance)
For the high tide route, or to avoid cattle on the open marsh, stay on the road. Turn left after Brownrigg, then the third right. Take a track just behind a farm on your right, then left along field edges, and half-right in the final field to a farm. Cross the road to a very high stile down to a channel. Turn left on the next road to **Sea Dyke End**.

Sea Dyke End to Skinburness, via Grune Point (5.1km, 1hr 20min)
Now keep right on the bank, crossing the road partway, to Skinburness. At its end, turn right down the lane, passing a few houses. Note the high tide waymark just in

WALKING THE KING CHARLES III ENGLAND COAST PATH: NORTH WEST

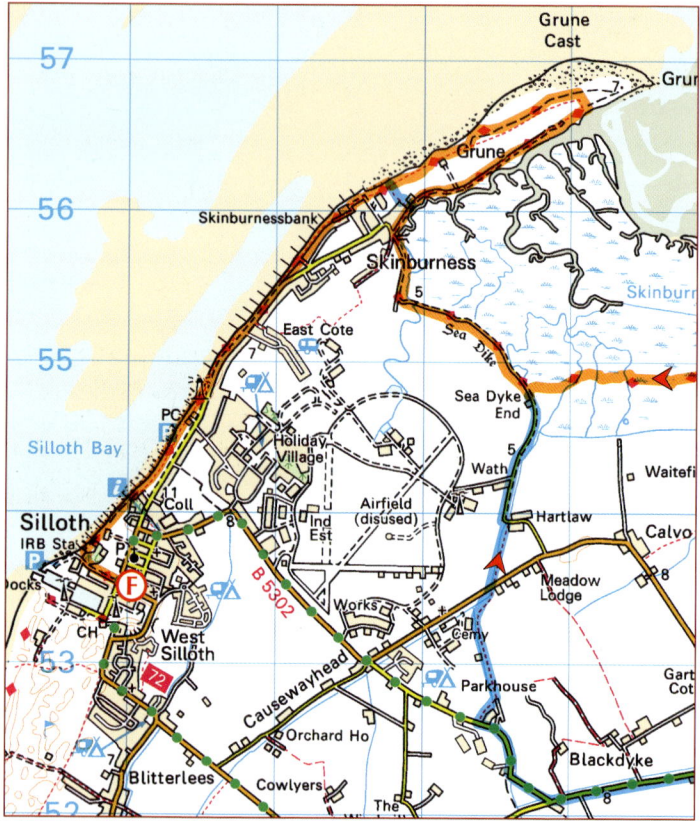

case. Continue ahead alongside the river and saltmarsh, through a few gates, then turn left when waymarked, before a quirky World War 2 pillbox. Worth a visit – but beyond it is a favourite refuge for birds, so do return to the path.

More waymarks lead you back down the western side of the peninsula on grass then through scrub, to the seaward end of Dick Trod Lane in **Skinburness**.

Skinburness to Silloth (3.4km, 55min)

Keep ahead on tarmac, diverting briefly landward of the final house, after which gravel soon opens out onto grass. After 1km, the sea defence takes a dogleg:

continue either on grass or a lower concrete promenade. After another 1.7km, past the amusement arcade, go inland around the RNLI station and along the edge of Silloth Green, to its south-eastern corner by the Criffel Street/Station Road crossroads. Turn left for the bus stop.

> The small town of **Silloth** retains many aspects of its Victorian heyday, including pretty cobbled streets, a large public green and garden, the striking East Cote lighthouse and restored pagoda above the prom. Information panels reveal a much longer history via Hadrian's Wall Milefortlets 10 and 11. More recent additions include Ray Lonsdale's 'Big Fella' sculpture – a giant peering out to sea from his huge prom-side bench – and Stage 5's dockside industries. On the shore, spot waders like redshank and turnstone.

Ray Lonsdale's 'Big Fella' sculpture on Silloth prom

STAGE 5
Silloth to Maryport

Start	Criffel Street/Station Road crossroads, Silloth, NY 109 535
Finish	Maryport old harbour bridge, NY 034 365
Time	5hr 30min
Distance	20.8km (13 miles)
Ascent	70m
Terrain	Dunes, cycle path and promenade
Refreshments	Cafés and pubs in Silloth, Allonby and Maryport; Moody Cow at Blue Dial
Toilets	Silloth Criffel Street, Maryport High Street and Irish Street; Allonby's northern playground
Transport	Trains to Maryport. Buses 400 & 60 at Silloth, 30 & 60 at Maryport and Workington, and 60 at Allonby
Accessibility	Tricky terrain in dunes; wheelchair accessible from Allonby to Maryport
Parking	Free roadsides in Silloth centre, Maryport King Street (along prom north of town) and numerous dune car parks; paid at Maryport aquarium (South Quay)
Accommodation	Various around Silloth, Allonby and Maryport, plus holiday parks and motorhome/camping sites throughout
KCIIIECP status in 2025	Open

As soon as you're past Silloth Docks, Stage 5 is all about the dunes. Initially it's natural vegetated dune and low sandy cliffs, so expect some slower walking on soft terrain to Allonby. The Mawbray dunes were part of a restoration project called Dynamic Dunescapes in the early 2020s – see Stage 11 for more information on dune conservation. The ECP then joins National Cycle Route 72 from Allonby to Maryport. Even the roadside section is very pleasant walking, well-separated by a corridor of greenery, and passing the Roman Milefortlet 21 ruins and historic Crosscanonby Saltpans, close to the sea; before joining the promenade with fantastic views across the Solway as you approach Maryport.

STAGE 5 – SILLOTH TO MARYPORT

Descending the dune bank between Dubmill Point and Allonby

Silloth to Mawbray (8km, 2hr 10min)

At the crossroads in Silloth, turn right and keep going past the dock entrance signs, then right in front of the golf club. At the end of this dockside track, cross a car park then turn left on a footpath, soon following a fence for a short while. Stay on the waymarked dune path for 3.75km, merging briefly with a cycle path approaching Beckfoot, then rising to the roadside. When the road swings inland, follow the seaward dune edge for around 750m to the start of a fenced enclosure.

Avoid cattle by keeping right of the fence; otherwise pass through the fence and enclosure when directed.

Mawbray to Allonby (4.3km, 1hr 10min)

At the far end, near the Mawbray Banks car park, the waymarked high tide route heads left; for the main trail take a short dogleg right to stay seaward of the next enclosure, then follow the path back to the road at **Dubmill Point**. Erosion is progressing rapidly at this point, so be prepared for temporary diversions. Now follow the road, crossing when directed, to the second road junction at **Oldkiln Farm**, where the high tide route also rejoins the coast. Both the erosion and tidal pinch points lie at this southern end; if in doubt, use the waymarked high tide route from Mawbray via Edderside to avoid retracing all those steps.

After another 500m of roadside path, cross back to the coast edge. You'll meet another cycle path near **Allonby**; take this over a small bridge and through the town.

Toilets are by a playground at the northern end; there's also a pub, fish and chip shop, ice cream and a small shop.

Allonby to Maryport (8.5km, 2hr 10min)

Beyond the village, the path crosses the road at **Blue Dial Farm**. In 800m **Milefortlet 21** perches on the cliff above you and the saltpans are over the road. For the Milefortlet access, continue 375m down the road then double back up the field to your left. 1.7km later, keep right on the golf course road to a concrete promenade all the way to **Maryport**, with views to Criffel and southern Scotland. Above you is the Senhouse Roman Museum, accessible via the town if you wish.

MILEFORTLET 21 AND CROSSCANONBY SALTPANS

Milefortlet 21 is one of the most prominent of the Roman coastal defences reaching to south west of Cumbria. Sitting atop a small rise, the 15x18m fortlet would have commanded excellent views of sea and land.

Behind agriculture and fishing, salt was Cumbria's third-biggest industry in Anglo-Saxon times, with place names such as Saltcotes extending south as far as Millom. The Crosscanonby pans date from the 17th and 18th centuries. While many Cumbrian remains have been tide- and time-damaged, these are protected – for now – and publicly accessible between road and sea defence, directly below the Milefortlet. The main structure is the circular 'kinch pit' where salt was dried out.

A harbourside Maryport sculpture references its history, including its Roman name, 'Alauna'

STAGE 5 – SILLOTH TO MARYPORT

Approaching the harbour, either go through a gap in the concrete wall on your left and keep ahead along Strand Street, or keep right to use a new boardwalk along the short beach, avoiding the road. Now turn left to follow this old harbour wall to a bridge.

Access to the town centre, its facilities and train station are up the hill.

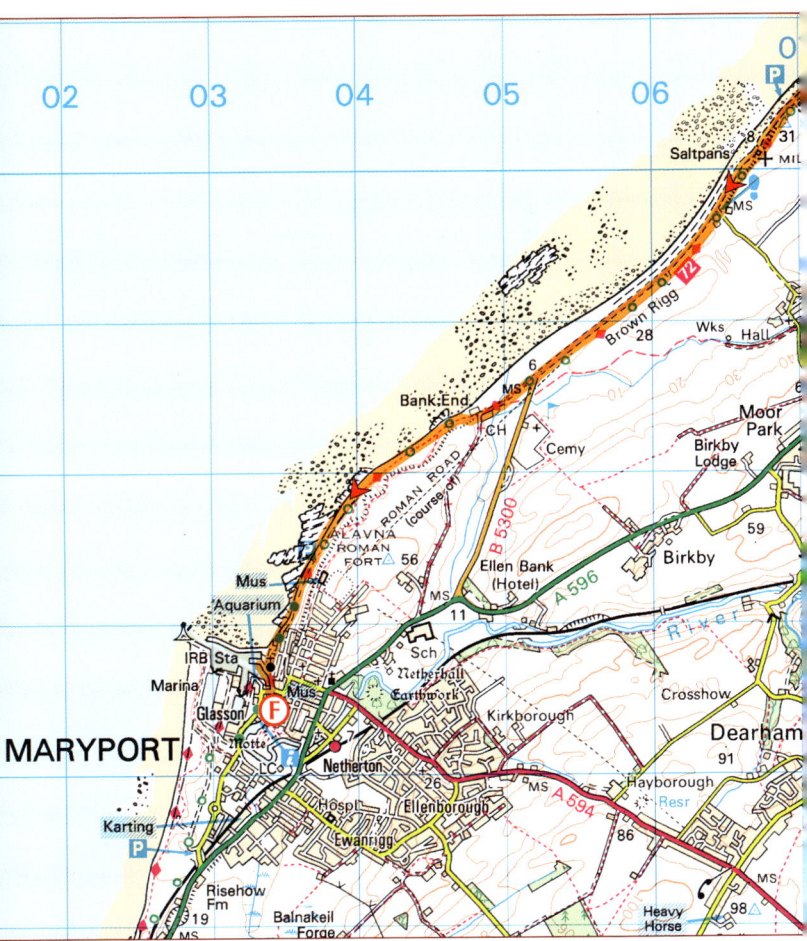

STAGE 6
Maryport to Whitehaven

Start	Maryport old harbour bridge, NY 034 365
Finish	Bransty Row, Whitehaven, NX 974 297
Time	6hr 50min
Distance	25.7km (16 miles)
Ascent	290m
Terrain	Sandy cliffs, beach, urban, fields, cycle path
Refreshments	Cafés in Maryport, various inland at Workington, Harrington and Whitehaven; south Workington KFC
Toilets	Maryport High Street, Irish Street and Aquarium café; Whitehaven railway station and Tesco
Transport	Trains at Maryport, Workington, Harrington, Parton and Whitehaven. Buses 29A, 30, 52 and 60 serve various locations throughout the route
Accessibility	Rugged chairs may manage Maryport Coastal Park; tricky ground past Flimby (use road); steep ground on Workington slag banks; steps from Derwent Howe to Prince's Way (use roads); good on Parton to Whitehaven cycle path. Workington Speedway weekends very loud
Parking	Free on Maryport prom, Workington station and beach, Harrington harbour and Parton beach; paid at Maryport Aquarium (South Quay) and Whitehaven station
Accommodation	Various in Maryport, Workington and Whitehaven including cheaper hotels
KCIIIECP status in 2025	Open

This is a long day with numerous steady climbs, but the arrival of the Cumbrian Coast Line enables easy splits by train. It's a heritage-laden change of scenery with the first large industrial centre looming large alongside Cumbria's maritime history. Beaches, hilltops, easy cycle paths and now-familiar Scottish views provide frequently surprising contrasts to the urban landscapes. Avoid high tides at Flimby – it's a long alternative route on a busy main road.

Stage 6 – Maryport to Whitehaven

MARYPORT

Maryport is an attractive town with historic and working harbours, and a rich cultural heritage. It forms part of the Romans' coastal defences, with its port and fort celebrated at the Senhouse Roman Museum. The Industrial Revolution saw its expansion as a port alongside many other north-west coastal locations, which triggered, courtesy of owners the Senhouse family, the building of the town. Along with Whitehaven, these new grid-based 'planned' Georgian towns are said to have inspired New York. Maryport was one of the Cumbrian coast's 20th-century artistic centres. LS Lowry, famous for his 'matchstick men', enjoyed time in Maryport, producing a number of works depicting the town, alongside fellow local landscape artists Percy Kelly and Sheila Fell. The ECP coincides with part of Maryport's LS Lowry trail.

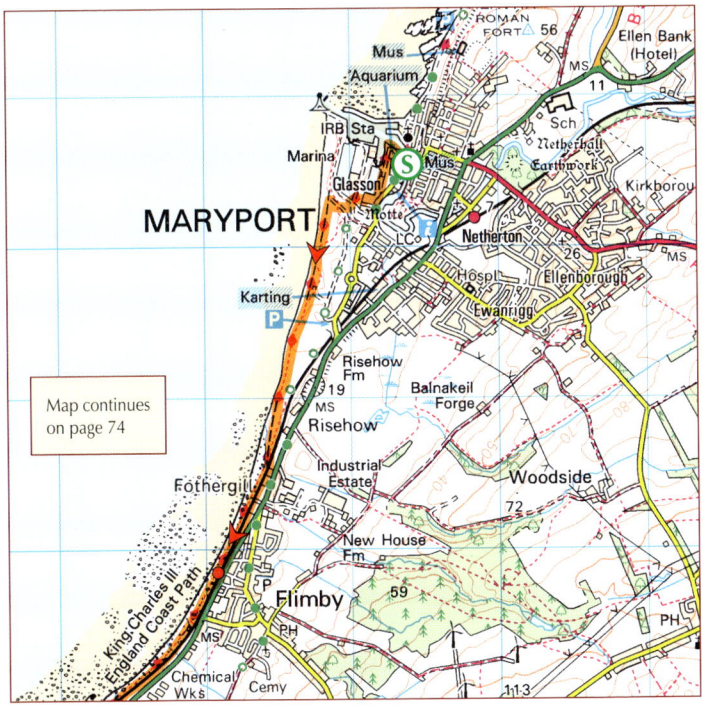

Map continues on page 74

STAGE 6 – MARYPORT TO WHITEHAVEN

Maryport to Flimby (3.6km, 55min)

Cross the bridge to double back down the harbourside to the aquarium car park, then left around a much larger dock to its far right corner. Cross a band of grass then turn left to a road T-junction. Go half-right over the road to pass through a cutting in a large bank. Go right at a fork, following ECP waymarks onto another bank and back to the coast. Erosion hotspot ahead – diversions may apply in future.

In about 1.5km, take a right-hand fork for the route with the view, or the left fork for high tide route access via a low underpass. Keep going on beach and intermittent dune, passing Flimby station. Much of **Flimby's** raised dune has disappeared. The parallel main road is your tide-free alternative, with further links at the station and 400m beyond it.

Flimby to Derwent Howe (Workington) (9.7km, 2hr 40min)

Continue past the **wind farm**, then along the seaward side of sizeable, sometimes steep, slag banks. Pass more turbines and a curved sea defence. After the second-last turbine turn left on an access track, then right, to a large gateway. Access to the Workington Speedway site – busy on some weekends. Turn left on the road and straight on at the roundabout.

Take steps up to cross the road bridge then drop to open greenspace (step-free pavement routes are available either side of the bridge). Continue on road to the stadium entrance to pass Tesco for supplies and toilets. At the field's far end go left between a stadium and railway, to an old iron foundry building by

The trail passes turbines and a distinctive sea defence before turning inland to Workington

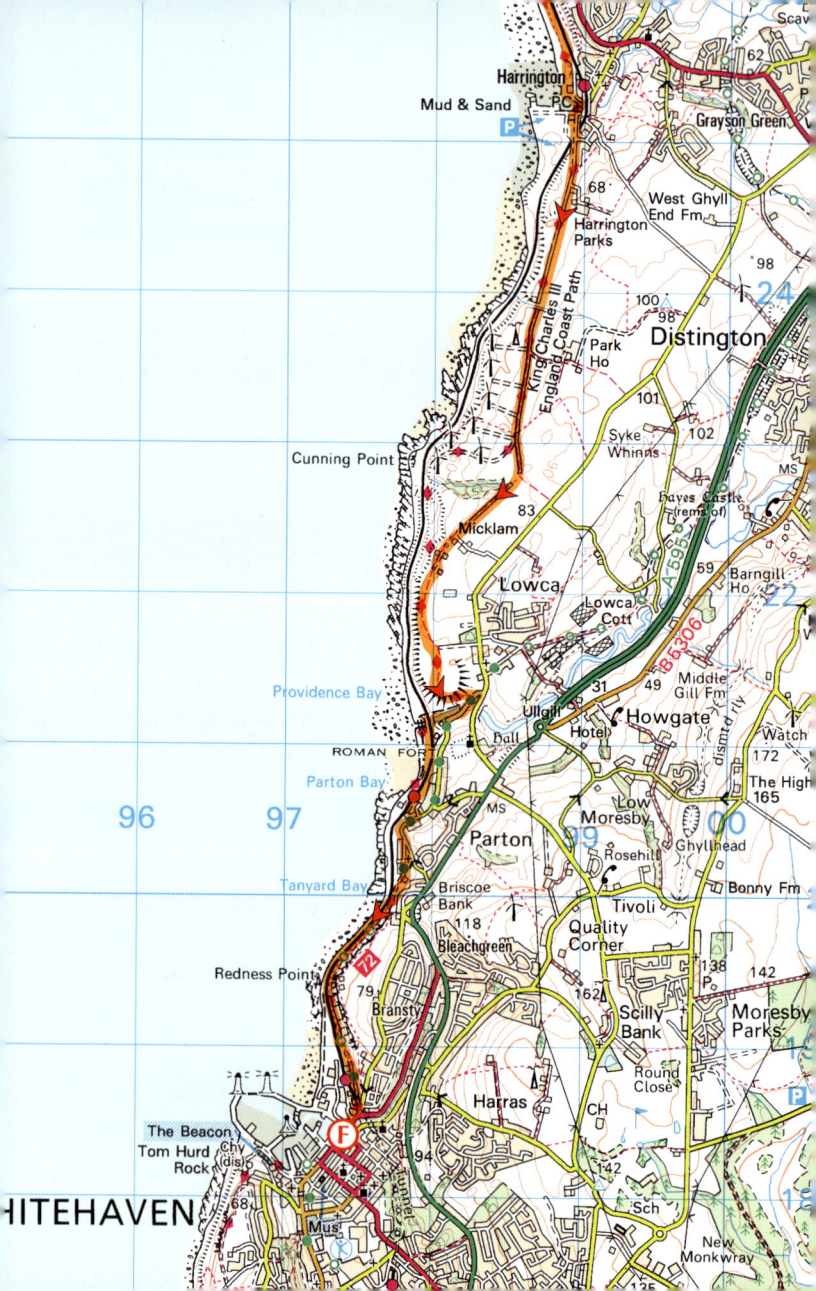

Stage 6 – Maryport to Whitehaven

WHITEHAVEN

Following earlier occupations by the Romans (in nearby Parton) and Vikings, the fishing village of Whitehaven, much like Maryport, rose to prominence through its port. The 'planned' town and attractive stone pier were constructed to further the mining and export of local coal by the Lowther family; transatlantic trade soon led to imports of tobacco, sugar, cotton and coffee.

While other centres overtook Whitehaven's shipping role, the coal industry continued until the 1980s, much of it using a 4-mile long tunnel under the sea. Notable remains include the 'Candlestick' ventilation shaft overlooking the harbour, the restored Saltom Pit building visible beneath the cliffs a little further south, and the modern Haig Colliery just beyond it on the clifftop.

the road. Turn right then right again down to the riverside. Or keep ahead for railway station – note no toilets. Follow the river, circuiting a small marina partway, to its end (and start of the C2C cycle route). Turn left, through a car park, to **The Howe's** crucifix monument.

Derwent Howe (Workington) to Harrington (4km, 1hr)

Soon after, strike left by a boulder to join a fence then descend steps on your left. Continue ahead to the main road by KFC. Turn right, then sharp right after the rail bridge onto a cycle path for 1.7km. Take an underpass beyond a small lake at **Salterbeck**. Follow the lower railway fence path to avoid erosion. Approaching **Harrington**, stay left at a fork to a car park then follow the harbour to its far back corner.

Harrington to Whitehaven (8.3km, 2hr 15min)

Cross the road and take a flight of steps in a retaining wall ahead. Use roads for step-free option. Turn right on the road, which becomes farm track then bridleway, passing the Lowca **wind farm**, before swinging inland to the road above Parton (maps may show the original cliff route, but the ground became too unstable for the path). Turn right, and right again on a track to the beach. Cross a footbridge and continue ahead above the beach. Go through a car park then an underpass.

At the road junction turn right, then right again on Bank Yard Road. Continue on a tarmac track (NCN 72) beneath sandstone cliffs, to **Whitehaven**. Pass an industrial yard entrance, then turn right onto the main road.

Pass the petrol garage for railway access and supermarket. Follow the road around for more town centre facilities and attractions.

STAGE 7
Whitehaven to Seascale

Start	Bransty Row, Whitehaven, NX 974 297
Finish	Seascale beach car park, NY 036 009
Time	7hr 40min
Distance	26km (16 miles)
Ascent	610m
Terrain	Mostly gravel, grass and tarmac cycle tracks and clifftop footpaths; some dune, shingle and road
Refreshments	Various in Whitehaven and Seascale; St Bees beach café and Seacote Hotel
Toilets	Whitehaven Tesco & station; St Bees and Seascale beach car parks; Sellafield station
Transport	Trains at Whitehaven, St Bees, Sellafield and Seascale. The 29 and 30 buses link Whitehaven with Workington
Accessibility	Cycle path Whitehaven to Kells; otherwise trickier terrain with steps, exposed cliffs and kissing gates
Parking	Paid at Whitehaven station and St Bees beach car park; free at St Bees Pow Beck and Seascale seafront
Accommodation	Various in Whitehaven, St Bees and Seascale, including camping at St Bees and Braystones
KCIIIECP status in 2025	Open

The most strenuous day, but again full of contrasts and the option to split or refresh at St Bees. Civilisation is soon left behind on a classic wild clifftop walk to St Bees over the highest point on the north west coast, and a brand-new stretch to Braystones, before the coast levels again. Plan carefully around trains, parking, tides and weather. The Ehen viaduct's underpass can flood during high tides, which can be waited out (same with short sections past Braystones) – but the river may burst its banks after prolonged heavy rain or storms. There's no convenient alternative, so you may wish to postpone or bypass if conditions are bad.

Whitehaven to Birkhams Quarry (4.7km, 1hr 30min)
Past Tesco, turn right down North Shore Road, then left behind the marina (or main

STAGE 7 – WHITEHAVEN TO SEASCALE

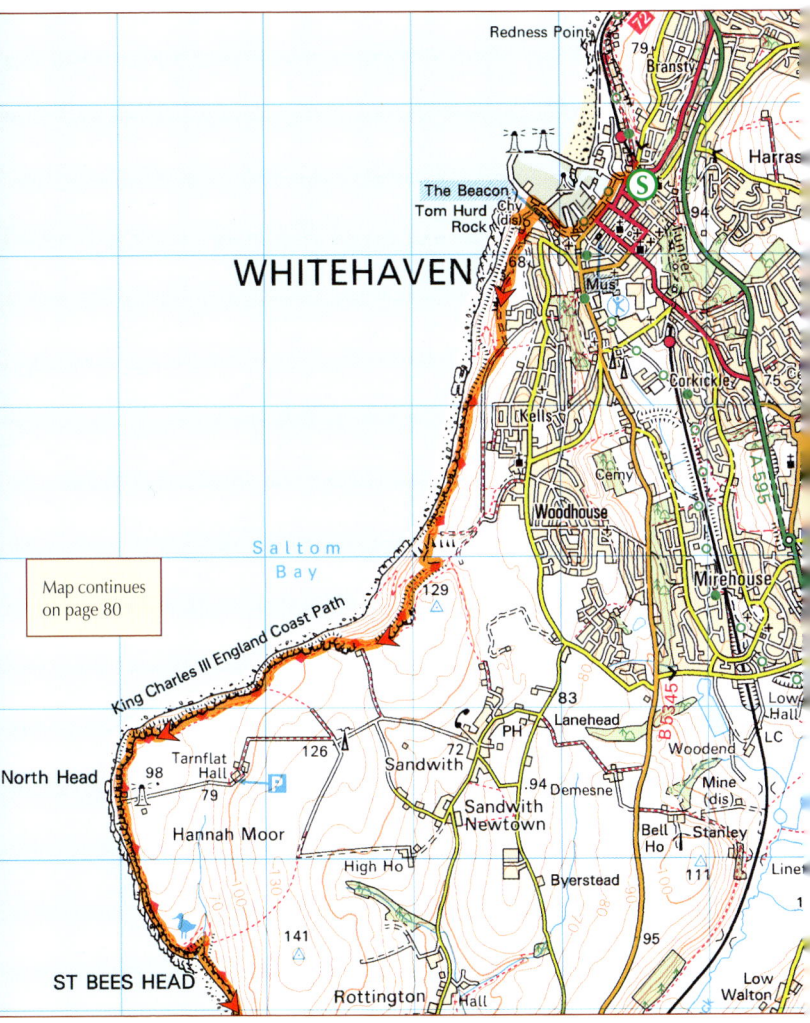

road if events are on). The swirling fish sculpture on the corner is *The Whiting Shoal* by Alan Clark. At the far side, turn right, passing the Beacon Museum (well

*WALKING THE KING CHARLES **III** ENGLAND COAST PATH: NORTH WEST*

worth a visit) and The Edge centre. The old harbour walls are worth walking, otherwise turn left to wind up to the 'Candlestick' colliery chimney.

Oral histories are engraved in the path, and by the Candlestick, **Jonathan Swift House** is debatably claimed to be a childhood home of the 17th–18th century author and satirist.

Follow the gravel path along the cliff and past the Haig Colliery remains. After a length of concrete, take another gravel path – later becoming field edge – along the cliff. Cross a concrete track end, keeping ahead to ascend a heather-covered slope. After some small trees, veer left when the ground levels then right on a path below the uppermost cliffs. After 800m, and the highest point of the entire trail at 115m above sea level, keep right past a house and small quarry with interesting information panels.

Birkhams Quarry to St Bees (6.5km, 2hr)

Stay with the cliff, alternating between cliff and field edge, sometimes narrow, steep or stepped, but always with excellent views. En route, pass the old clifftop foghorn station and **lighthouse**, and three RSPB hides. The best views are from the second and third – allowing safe viewing of the famous cliffs and, in summer, their crowds of nesting seabirds.

Now descend steps and cross a bedrock platform to the back of Fleswick Bay's inlet – do visit the secluded beach if you can! Ascend the south side of the gully and continue on the clifftop, finally dropping steeply to **St Bees**. Cross a footbridge to the prom, then turn left across the green and pass behind the beach café.

For the train station, instead cross the car park and take the road to St Bees village, turning right just after the golf course access road.

Fleswick Bay's sea-sculpted red sandstone is a treat for geology fans

St Bees to Nethertown (5.4km, 1hr 40min)

Behind the café, rejoin the clifftop, rising past a caravan site. Turn inland around the golf course before following, then crossing, Pow Beck to a beach car park, or, if tides allow, the beach is more direct.

Go left through an underpass, then right. At the driveway's end, keep right in field edges. Before long the route begins to traverse stunning gorse-lined slopes above the coastal railway – but expect lots of steps and undulations before rejoining the clifftop fields.

After 2km, cross Sea Lane and continue, passing **Nethertown** station before climbing back up towards the village. Go through two gates and a small field on your right then past houses.

Nethertown to Sellafield (6.4km, 1hr 40min)

Turn right on the road past a green, farm and long field. Over a bridge, turn right through (and up) a field to rejoin the clifftop near a trig point.

Pass a small tarn and drop to a small gully: part of Harnsey Moss and Silver Tarn SSSI. Take an underpass to **Braystones'** beach houses.

Follow the shingle track – mostly easy walking, barring some unavoidable beach sections. Follow waymarking as the trail moves slightly inland and past a motorbike track in dunes to the Ehen viaduct.

Go under the viaduct and up steps to cross it. Follow waymarks inland then turn right up a bank and along the top of the slope on track then field edge. Just before the **Sellafield** boundary, drop down and under a pipe bridge to the station. During emergency or maintenance works, an inland diversion (1km longer) may be waymarked.

FROM NATURE TO NUCLEAR – SELLAFIELD NUCLEAR SITE

After the RSPB's St Bees Head nature reserve, Sellafield feels about as far from natural as it gets, but no less of a spectacle, looking like something from a sci-fi film. Originally a Royal Ordnance factory in World War 2, since the 50s the site, then known as Windscale – and despite one of the world's worst nuclear incidents in 1957 – has been used for nuclear power generation (until 2003), fuel and waste reprocessing and storage, and has now entered a decommissioning phase. You're then dropped straight back into the natural wonders of dunes, flowers and natterjacks on the final stretch to Seascale.

Sellafield to Seascale (3.1km, 50min)

Past the station, take a tarmac cycle path between the railway and security fence.

STAGE 7 – WHITEHAVEN TO SEASCALE

Cross the Calder viaduct footbridge. Pass under it to a path around the edge of a natterjack toad reserve and onwards to Seascale beach car park and road. Flooding and erosion may soon force the ECP onto the golf course footpath, but, whichever route you use, all paths lead to **Seascale**!

The station is above the car park, accessed by the road, or on the path landward of the railway footbridge just before the town. As well as refreshments on the front, there's a Co-op 300m up the hill.

The new path past Sellafield Nuclear Site

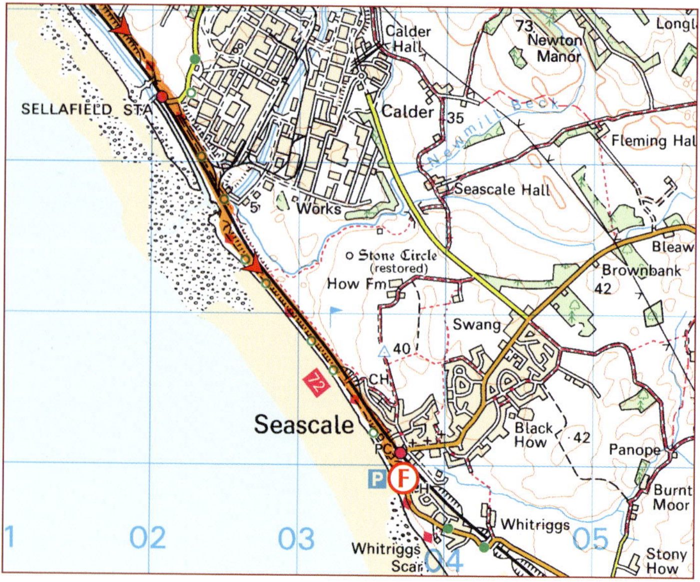

STAGE 8
Seascale to Ravenglass

Start	Seascale beach car park, NY 036 009
Finish	Ravenglass railway viaduct, SD 084 965
Time	3hr 35min
Distance	13km (8 miles); or 10.7km excluding village loop
Ascent	80m
Terrain	Beach, dune, minor road and saltmarsh
Refreshments	Chip shop and ice cream in Seascale; café by Drigg station; pubs in Ravenglass
Toilets	Seascale and Ravenglass main car parks
Transport	Trains at Seascale, Drigg and Ravenglass; no buses as of 2025
Accessibility	Sand and steps south of Seascale; rugged chairs may manage beach or short routes from Drigg beach car park. Steps and narrow bridge at Drigg Holme; okay on road past Hall Carleton and Ravenglass high tide route.
Parking	Free at Seascale car park and Drigg roadsides; paid at Ravenglass.
Accommodation	Various in Seascale; hotels in and around Ravenglass; camping at Drigg, Saltcoats and Ravenglass
KCIIIECP status in 2025	Open

It's time for a gentler day, thanks to Ravenglass's estuary challenges. The ECP currently has no route over the River Esk after Ravenglass. Today's stage will travel as far on the ECP as is possible, but hikers will then need to make their way to the other side of the River Esk by public transport or taxi (see Stage 9). Ambitions for major crossings (or bus reinstatements) may see this stage extended in time; but for now, take the opportunity to explore Ravenglass and its Roman heritage on the main trail/high tide loop from the village; and with attractions including the La'al Ratty miniature railway into Eskdale, and Muncaster Castle, it's a perfect rest day.

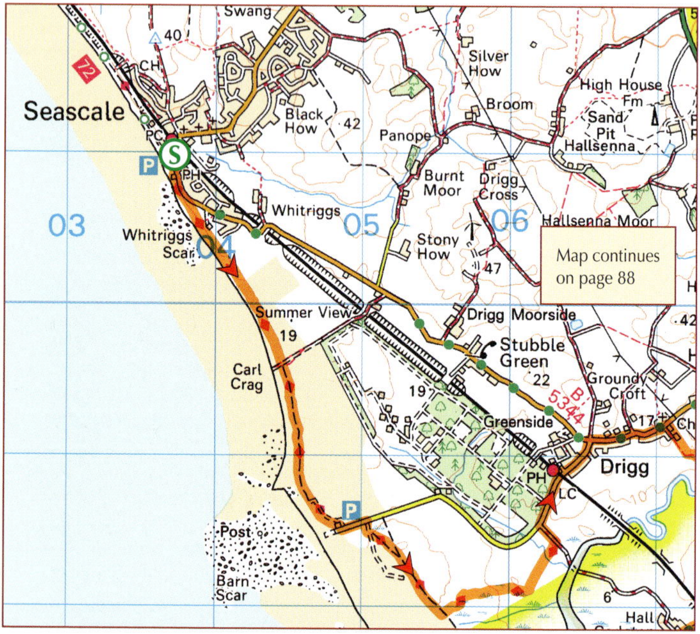

WALKING THE KING CHARLES III ENGLAND COAST PATH: NORTH WEST

The pretty village of Ravenglass, seen across the estuary from Saltcotes

Stage 8 – Seascale to Ravenglass

RAVENGLASS

The Roman bath house remains on the Ravenglass loop are some of the best-preserved in the country.

Ravenglass is a rare double World Heritage Site, in both the Hadrian's Wall and Lake District sites. Originally a fishing village, Hadrian's occupation introduced first a series of smaller fortlets, then the larger Glannoventa fort and well-preserved bath house, at the end of the Roman road between Ravenglass, Hardknott and Ambleside. Muncaster Castle is another historical highlight. Home to the Penningtons since the 11th century, the current castle's construction started in the 1200s and is now open to the public along with its Himalayan gardens, and hawk and owl conservation centre.

Seascale to Drigg (5.5km, 1hr 30min)

Continue south then keep right on a concrete path followed by 575m of beach to some steps. Take these and follow waymarks through dunes then across slightly higher ground with fantastic views up Wasdale to England's highest mountains, to Drigg beach car park. Note the World War 2 observation post seaward of the car park. Head inland up the road for 200m and turn right onto an open, grassy track. After a fence corner, follow waymarks and bridges 1km inland to a lane. In time, the Irt may be bridged; for now go left, then right up the road to **Drigg** station.

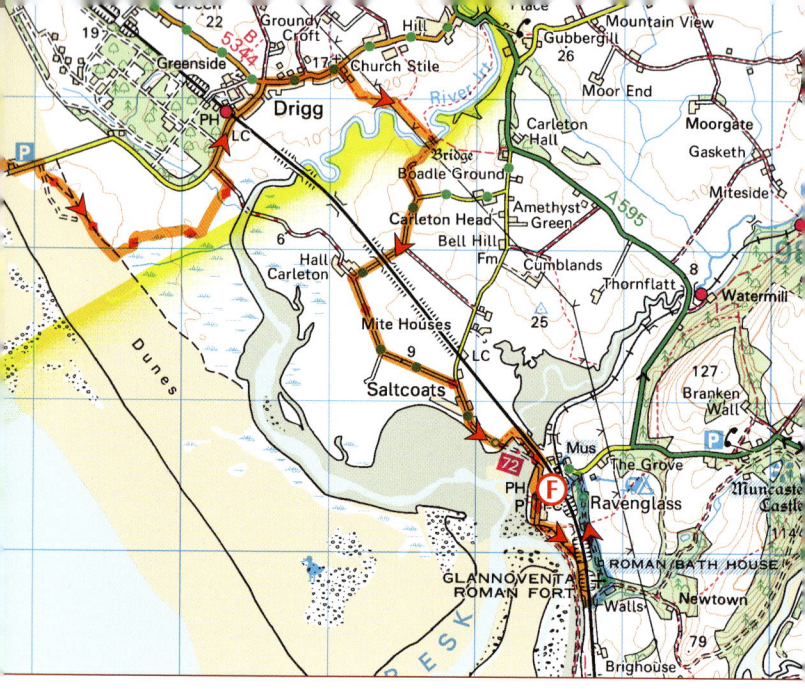

Drigg to Ravenglass (5.2km, 1hr 25min)

Continue to a T-junction. Go right, then right again opposite St Peter's Church into a lane then field. Keep left of a hedge to the packhorse bridge; cross, and climb steps beyond into a lane, then a field on your left. Take the train from Drigg to Ravenglass or Bootle if flooded. Staying above the bank, aim for a gate in the right-hand corner of the field. Go down the lane, then right onto the road, left at Hall Carleton, then right to Saltcoats shore. Head left to cross the Mite viaduct into **Ravenglass**.

(Optional) Ravenglass loop (2.3km, 40min)

Turn right straight through the village, then left on the shore. If flooded, take an out-and-back on the high tide route from the road. Turn right before an underpass onto a grassy path, then descend steps back to the shore (or use beach from Ravenglass to avoid steps). Go left, then left again under the railway. This is the end of the main trail for now. Double back on the high tide route, passing the Roman bath house. Turn left after the caravan site to the railway footbridge.

You can exit the bridge to either the La'al Ratty or main stations, or continue down to the car park, pub, toilets and village. To continue the route as described in Stage 9, take the train from Ravenglass's main station to Bootle station at Hycemoor.

STAGE 9
Bootle to Silecroft Beach

Start	Bootle railway station, Hycemoor, SD 093 893
Finish	Silecroft beach car park, SD 121 312
Time	3hr 55min
Distance	14.4km (9 miles), or 16.1km (10 miles) from Eskmeals viaduct; plus 1.3km to Silecroft station
Ascent	160m
Terrain	Grassed cliffs and fields, short shingle section, some short but strenuous climbs
Refreshments	Tarn Bay Treats honesty shack; Silecroft beach café and Miners Arms (inland)
Toilets	Silecroft beach car park
Transport	Trains between Ravenglass, Bootle (inland) and Silecroft (inland); no buses as of 2025
Accessibility	Loud firing on Eskmeals operational days; kissing gates; steps (many at Hyton Marsh and Summer Hill), steep terrain
Parking	Free on roadsides at Bootle station and Stubb Place; donations at Silecroft beach car park
Accommodation	Various in Ravenglass; motorhomes and self-catering at Tarn Bay; camping at Selker Farm
KCIIIECP status in 2025	Open

As described in Stage 8, there is no reliably safe crossing of the River Esk, either on mapped fords or the A595. Public rights of way and minor roads can be used between Waberthwaite and the Eskmeals Viaduct on the south bank, but even if you're tempted to connect on foot, taxis from Muncaster to Waberthwaite on the A595 are recommended. Otherwise, take the train from Ravenglass to Bootle station. You can take a 7km out and back to Eskmeals viaduct where the ECP officially restarts, but it's all road, behind an MOD firing range.

Described here is an easier option from Bootle station to join the ECP at Stubb Place. From there, Tarn Point is eroding rapidly, so allow plenty of time, and check tide times in case you get unlucky – the beach is much quicker than any inland options but you'll need to leave space to avoid any cliff slumps from above. On a clear day the mountainous backdrop to Tarn Bay is spectacular.

The rest of the stage is similarly attractive and relatively tide-free, although Hyton Marsh can get very wet. An new stretch of clifftop trail between Annaside and Silecroft avoids the shingle beach – although if the tide's far enough out, the beach can be a gloriously wild and secluded, as well as avoiding livestock if preferred.

Hycemoor to Hyton Marsh (5.5km, 1hr 25min)

Take the road for 2km from Bootle station to the sea at **Stubb Place**. Turn left along field edges around Tarn Point then on a gravel track past **Selker Bay**, soon swinging left. Allow time for unexpected diversions, as described above. There's also a direct bypass from the station to Selker Bay past Broadwater Farm.

Past Selker farm, a short fenced corridor returns you to the clifftop, then a large flight of steps down to Hyton Marsh, another of Cumbria's natterjack toad strongholds. Watch out for toadlets underfoot in summer, and keep dogs away from the water. Follow waymarks between ponds to cross a large footbridge.

SEA TO SUMMIT – BLACK COMBE AND ANNASIDE & GUTTERBY BANKS SSSI

Behind the remote, undulating cliffs sits the ever-present hulk of Black Combe, the only 600m peak in England walkable as a one-day sea to summit route. It often has a 'hat' of cloud as warm air rises from the sea, but on the clearest days it's possible to see Scotland, Northern Ireland, Wales, England and the Isle of Man from the top – as also celebrated by Wordsworth and Alfred Wainwright. Rather than the chaotic volcanics of central Lakeland, Black Combe is formed of metamorphic Skiddaw slates and shales. Below, the sea-bitten cliffs show off the glacial red deposits of the narrow coastal plain – in themselves a geological SSSI from Annaside to Gutterby.

Hyton Marsh to Silecroft Beach (8.9km, 2hr 30min)

Keep ahead through some narrow fields then, after a short floodbank, cross a track and climb again on clifftop field edges. A track merges from the left then leads onwards, veering landward through more narrow fields. When the track moves away, stay on seaward field edges to the Gutterby Lane End beach access track and continue along the cliff, alternating left and right of the fence, for 3km. Whilst occasionally strenuous, the climbs are short-lived with long stretches of level high ground and consistently great views.

Drop to the shore to pass **Summer Hill**; then take a large flight of steps back up. (It's OK to cheat and use the beach!) Another 1.5km gradually drops you to

STAGE 9 – BOOTLE TO SILECROFT BEACH

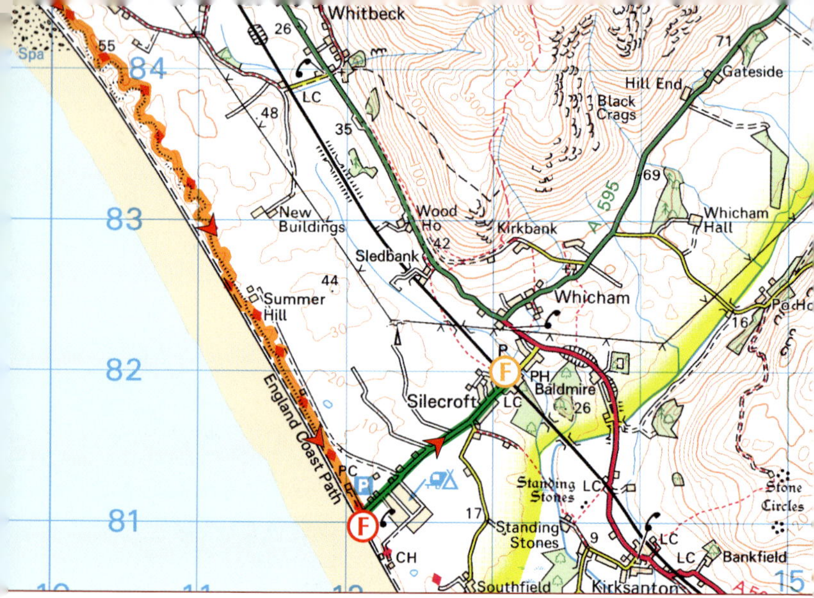

Silecroft beach car park. In the second field there are faint remnants of a World War 2 decoy arrow in the grass.

There's a café and toilets in the car park. Silecroft station and Miners Arms pub are 1.3km inland – just follow the road.

Silecroft beach, with Gutterby Banks beyond, is popular for various forms of recreation

STAGE 10
Silecroft Beach to Green Road

Start	Silecroft beach car park, SD 121 312
Finish	Green Road railway station, SD 189 839
Time	4hr 50min
Distance	18.6km (11½ miles) plus 1.3km from Silecroft station
Ascent	25m
Terrain	Hilly grassed and sandy dunes; flat fields, gravel, beach and floodbank
Refreshments	Silecroft beach café; cafés and ice cream at Haverigg beach and holiday park; café, pubs, supermarket and station café in Millom
Toilets	Silecroft and Haverigg beach car parks, Millom town centre
Transport	Trains between Silecroft, Millom and Green Road; buses M1 from Haverigg to Millom;and 7 from Millom to Barrow-in-Furness
Accessibility	Kissing gates and loose dune to Haverigg Point; wheelchair potential to Green Road but with 2 RADAR gates and some tricky latches
Parking	Donations at Silecroft beach car park; free at Haverigg beach car park and Millom roadsides
Accommodation	Various in Haverigg and Millom including campsite at Haverigg
KCIIIECP status in 2025	Open

On this stage, occasionally strenuous sandy dunes between Silecroft and Haverigg contrast with more efficient level walking around Hodbarrow and Millom to the Duddon Estuary.

The Black Dub and Haverigg Bents dune section may change. Described here is the original route past Haverigg's World War 2 airfield (now wind farm) and prison, avoiding a deep gully, but do follow any future diversions in response to developing winter flood issues and land management changes.

Coastal Access rights cover all the dunes by default, but dogs are excluded, apart from on the trail (unless flooded) to prevent conservation grazing patterns being displaced. Dog-free walkers may avoid the most strenuous terrain by using a vehicle access track to Stoup Dub any time of year, but expect to climb a gate.

Walking the King Charles III England Coast Path: North West

Silecroft Beach to Kirksanton Haws (2.5km, 40min)

From the car park, pass through a small heath behind the beach houses, then take the lane to the golf club. Go through the entrance gate and turn left, soon entering a fenced corridor around the course and through farmland with lovely views inland.

Past the farm, turn right through a kissing gate around a field corner to another gate. Now stay on the fence's seaward side for 450m. After a final few metres in an enclosed lane, turn right to the beach at **Kirksanton Haws**. Don't try to shortcut – there's no way out and the golf course plays right up to the cliff edges – use the beach for a direct route.

STAGE 10 – SILECROFT BEACH TO GREEN ROAD

Kirksanton Haws to Haverigg (4.8km, 1hr 20min)
Turn left on the dune edge. Where it narrows, a short bypass is available in the field around a natterjack toad pond. Follow waymarks to a gate at the far end of the dune bank. Turn left over a footbridge, then aim half-right to the enclosure's far corner.

Follow the **wind farm** and prison boundaries, meandering a little when waymarked. At the far end, turn right through a gate, following waymarks back to the coast. Follow its outer fence for 1km to a kissing gate. Go through and drop to the shore when directed, or stay behind the dune ridge at high tide. Follow a compacted path (watch out for toadlets and spawn in path ruts), then beach, to Haverigg's beach café, car park and toilets.

Haverigg to Green Road (11.3km, 2hr 50min)
Follow the road to a bridge. Cross it and follow the byway to Hodbarrow sea wall just before the holiday park. Sample Riva Gelato's excellent ice cream at the campsite to the left.

Circuit the lagoon then turn right behind the ruined windmill into trees. Cross a small clearing to its far corner then follow the seaward edge of a long enclosure

The ECP follows Hodbarrow Lagoon's sea wall – once an iron mine, now in part a nature reserve

Walking the King Charles III England Coast Path: North West

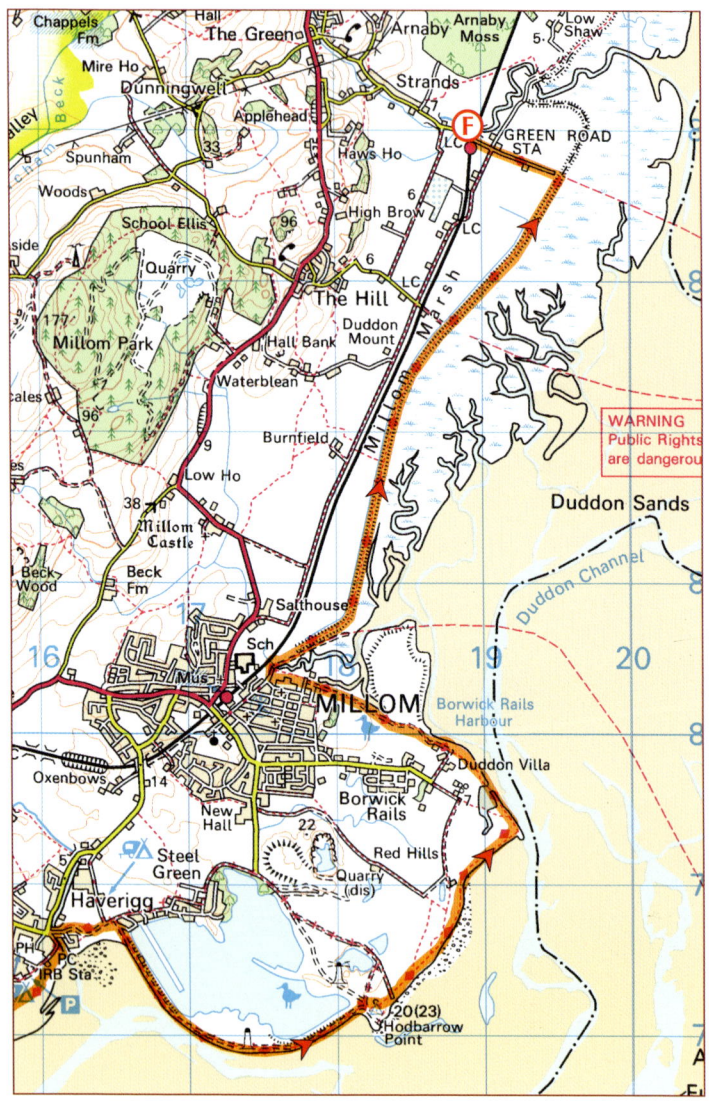

Springtime on the Millom Marsh floodbank, with stunning views of the Coniston and central Lake District fells

to the far end. The ECP stays within this field to protect sensitive 'embryonic dunes' developing outside the fence.

Emerging on the old **Millom** Docks, turn left along its edge to another gate then a gravel track. Some of the coast's best views are here, across Duddon Sands to the Coniston fells. You'll pass between the former Millom Ironworks site and the huge (and ecologically sensitive) Borwick Rails slag bank to your right. After the water treatment works, a grassier path drops you at the corner of Millom Marsh.

Walking the King Charles III England Coast Path: North West

IRON LINES – MILLOM & HODBARROW

150 years ago, Hodbarrow sea wall was built to protect an iron mine from the sea, and was strengthened over time. It's now a byway containing a lagoon, watersports centre and RSPB reserve favoured by breeding terns and waders, which can be seen from a hide near the lighthouse. Plants such as bee orchid grow on the banks. Iron ore was processed in Millom – between the two sites once sat a network of rail tracks and workings; the only remnants being raised banks through Hodbarrow Mains, and Millom's old dock wall. A project called Iron Lines aims to further improve access to this area in the near future.

An underpass links to the station and town centre if needed. Otherwise keep right over a bridge and walk north on the floodbank for 4km to the next boundary and turn inland to Green Road station. You'll need to take the train from here to Foxfield to begin Stage 11.

Gazing across the Duddon Estuary at high tide from Millom's old quay wall

PART 2 – MORECAMBE BAY

In 2024 shifting sands re-exposed the historic Collins Weir with its construction cart track, originally intended to channel deep waters closer to Canal Foot (Stage 14)

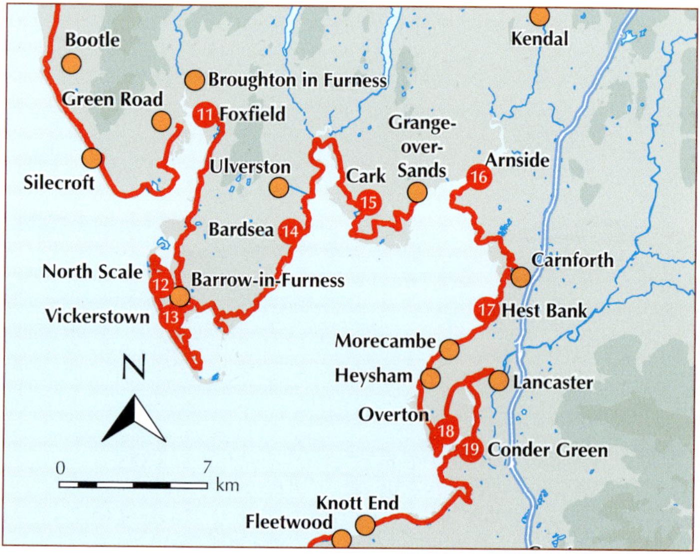

WALKING THE KING CHARLES III ENGLAND COAST PATH: NORTH WEST

Small boats in Walney Channel with northern Vickerstown, the island's main settlement, beyond (Stage 11)

STAGE 11
Foxfield to North Scale

Start	Foxfield railway station, SD 208 854
Finish	North Scale, Walney Island, SD 183 696
Time	6hr 15min (plus train)
Distance	23km (14¼ miles)
Ascent	150m
Terrain	Saltmarsh, fields, dune, woodland, cycle path, road and promenade
Refreshments	Askam Co-op and Platform One Café (off-trail); Dock Museum café, Barrow; the Ferry and Crown pubs, Walney
Toilets	Platform One café, Askam (public toilet); Sandscale Haws; Dock Museum
Transport	Trains between Foxfield, Kirkby-in-Furness, Askam and Barrow-in-Furness (off-trail). Bus X7 serves Foxfield, Askam and Barrow, 2 links Barrow Dock Museum to Vickerstown and Earnse Point and 5 links Barrow, Vickerstown and North Scale
Accessibility	Alternative level crossings help with Kirkby to Dunnerholme (steps from station); good on Ormsgill to North Scale cycle path and pavements
Parking	Free at Askam beach car park and roadsides at Foxfield (very limited), Kirkby, and Walney Promenade; paid (free for NT members) at Sandscale Haws
Accommodation	Various in Broughton-in-Furness (off-trail), Askam, Kirkby, Walney Island and Barrow
KCIIIECP status in 2025	Expected to open 2025/6. Use minor roads for Foxfield to Kirkby, and beach on other sections in the interim, but check tides, especially at Roanhead near Askam.

The eastern shores of the Duddon combine dune, marsh and geological interest, and intriguing views of Walney Island across the channel. It's another well-connected and adaptable stage. Attention to tides would be wise, although equally enjoyable alternative routes are waymarked, other than one or two pinch points described below.

Foxfield to Kirkby-in-Furness (4.2km, 1hr 5min)

From Foxfield station, cross the road and turn right. Re-cross with care – the road floods and visibility isn't the best – to take a level crossing and then a marshside minor road. Or continue to the next right for high tide route or safer crossings. Re-cross the railway and turn right alongside it, through a field then Duddon Mosses NNR. Keep dogs close, the peat bog is deep. At the end, follow doglegging field edges left to a narrow road. Turn right, then back over the railway to veer left through a farmyard and field. Take another crossing to a footbridge over Kirkby Pool river channel. Cross the field and turn right to **Kirkby-in-Furness** station.

Kirkby to Askam-in-Furness (5.4km, 1hr 25min)

On the seaward platform, steps drop to the marsh where the ECP continues seaward of the railway. Follow waymarks for the driest route to **Dunnerholme**, overlooked by the limestone promontory of Dunnerholme Rock. The better high tide escape routes are waymarked from various points and offer excellent raised vistas, but expect stiles – some can be avoided on a minor road. On the marsh, beware a slippery shore section until remedial rock armour works are completed by Network Rail.

Through the golf course boundary, keep right past houses and up a slope onto the Rock, soon doubling back above an old quarry, or explore the foreshore at low tide – traces of huge ammonoid fossils can be found in the limestone cliffs. Follow waymarks through dune to a raised bank between marsh and golf club (avoiding ground-nesting birds on the beach), finally taking the seaward edge of a golf tee to reach a gate. Head left onto the clifftop past caravans, then in fields, to cross **Askam-in-Furness** beach car park.

Trains, toilet, café and shop are 600 metres up the road.

Askam-in-Furness to Scarth Bight (5.2km, 1hr 30min)

Continue above the bank, dropping to the shore after the Inshore Rescue building, and take the underpass. If flooded, take the high tide route on your left; access to the pier is on a slope just before the pier.

Enter the dunes (the high tide route rejoins you shortly) then continue towards and through trees. Climb a steep bank up and over Roanhead Crag then through trees to **Sandscale Haws**. Use the beach until ECP opens – aim well ahead of high tide past Roanhead Crag. Pass the natterjack toad ponds then continue ahead, turning left in dunes just beyond the car park turn-off. The 'Red Hut' information shack is sometimes open in the car park; toilets are just up the road.

Follow a fence to a gate. From here, the waymarked route is driest, but a firmer track to the left is available during dry spells.

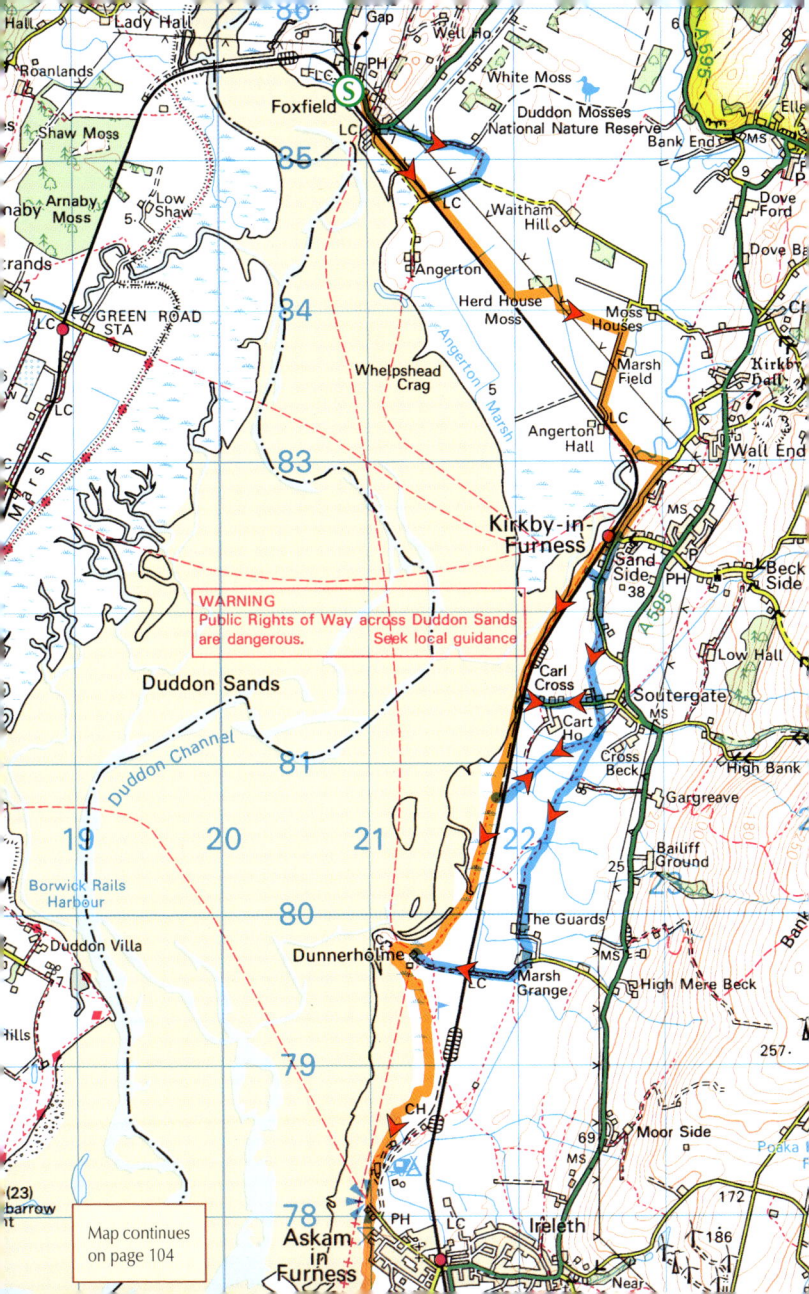

STAGE 11 – FOXFIELD TO NORTH SCALE

DUNE RESTORATION AT SANDSCALE HAWS

The trail passes landward of the looser dunes at Sandscale Haws, through vegetated areas rich with scrubby plants and wildlife

The north-western sand dunes between them host wildlife such as great crested newts, insects like rare northern dune tiger beetles, nesting and wintering birds, and plenty of rare and delicate dune plants. Sandscale's specialities are the natterjack toad and coralroot orchid. These need space to exist, including loose sand and shallow ponds, but the spread of dominant marram grass stabilises dune systems and slowly causes over-vegetation. Farm animals mimic prehistoric herds by trampling the marram and creating space. The ECP follows the easiest line between Sandscale's dunes and the marsh behind, but you can explore the dunes or beach if preferred.

At the far end of the reserve, turn left through a gate, soon joining a shingle track to a concrete pillbox at **Scarth Bight** bay. The highest tides may flood the track temporarily.

Scarth Bight to North Scale (8.1km, 2hr 15min)

Keep right along the boundary fence and through an enclosure towards Sowerby Woods. Cross the gully to a primarily clifftop path, for 1.75km. Use the beach until ECP opens. Past the solar farm, zigzag up the slope ahead onto **Barrow-in-Furness**'s slag banks – a fabulous viewpoint.

One of many wartime 'pillbox' lookouts now succumbing to coastal erosion north of Barrow

Cross the hills, veering briefly inland around the first main dip. After a steeper second descent, take the second then first rights on tarmac back to the clifftop. Continue above the Walney Channel, then on promenade, to the Dock Museum, well worth visiting. Cut past the museum for the main road and buses. Use the cycle path to avoid large flights of steps.

Cross the metal lock bridge and keep right on an enclosed path, then promenade. Keep right around gardens at the far end. If bypassing Walney, cross the road and turn left on the Stage 13 route. Turn right over Jubilee Bridge, and right on Walney Island's promenade to **North Scale**. The bus stop can be found where the road turns inland and the Crown Inn just beyond.

STAGE 12
North Scale to Vickerstown

Start	North Scale, Walney Island, SD 183 696
Finish	Jubilee Bridge, Vickerstown, SD 186 686
Time	6hr 25min
Distance	24.6km (15½ miles)
Ascent	50m
Terrain	Shore, saltmarsh, field, dune, gravel, cycle path, minor road
Refreshments	Pubs at North Scale, Biggar village and Vickerstown; Earnse Point Surf School snack bar; Roundhouse Café, Biggar Bank; Vickerstown Tesco (off trail)
Toilets	Earnse Point car park; Roundhouse café; South Walney nature reserve (off-trail)
Transport	Buses 1 (Biggar Bank), 2 (Earnse Point), and 5 (North Scale) connect with Vickerstown and Barrow. Trains and buses link nearby Barrow-in-Furness with other stages.
Accessibility	West of airfield good, with NNR access due to be improved; south end to Jubilee Bridge is on road but no pavement till Vickerstown
Parking	Free on Walney promenade, Earnse Point, Biggar Bank north, west of Thorney Nook Lane; various lay-bys and roadsides from South End to Vickerstown
Accommodation	West Point House self-catering hostel and glamping, north Walney; South End caravans; motorhome parking options throughout Walney; various B&B options throughout Walney and Barrow
KCIIIECP status in 2025	Open

Another easily adaptable day as Walney is rarely more than a mile wide – splitting in two helps facilitate an optional extension in Cumbria Wildlife Trust's South Walney reserve (small fee, no dogs allowed). Due to sensitive wildlife in Walney Channel, from September to March you'll need to use the road options past North Scale and the Biggar peninsula (both of these double as high tide routes, along with another short length at South End). Summer will therefore reduce the amount of road walking, but either way you will have a glorious mix of mountain, castle, sea and saltmarsh views, nature, World War 2 and maritime history, throughout.

Walking the King Charles III England Coast Path: North West

North Scale to Earnse Point　　　　　　　　　　　　　　　(7km, 1hr 50min)

From April to August, take the shore path past the village, then a raised lane (offering a high tide escape through houses), then saltmarsh until you meet a flight of steps on your left. Above these, turn right through the woods.

From September to March and during high tides, follow the road for 1km, then turn right down a public footpath before the airfield, to the woodland path junction.

Continue east of BAE's **Walney Island Airport** then through remnants of World War 2 concrete aircraft dispersal pads. Follow the fence around two fields – these are important nesting grounds for wading birds. At the far-left corner go through a gate and follow waymarks leading west then south. For an excellent viewpoint, go right through a gate just before you turn south and aim north west to the highest dune ahead.

After meandering around ponds (old gravel pits) and heathland west of the airfield, passing the 'One for Sorrow' camouflage birds artwork en route, you'll reach the park home, car park, toilets and surf school snack bar at Earnse Point. Expect diversions over time due to erosion.

WALNEY'S NATURE

Walney is a 'barrier island' formed of post-glacial deposits, protecting Walney Channel and Barrow from the Irish Sea. While the island's habitation rapidly expanded during the Vickers shipbuilding era (hence 'Vickerstown'), the northern and southern ends retain natural dune systems and saltmarshes, with all the wilderness and wildlife benefits they bring, from natterjack toads to flocks of migrating waders and waterbirds, the north west's only population of breeding grey seals on South Walney (often swimming close to the ECP at high tide), and even the endemic Walney Geranium, found nowhere else in the world. This pale pink mutation of the bloody cranesbill grows on Walney's dunes and western shore in summer.

Earnse Point to South End　　　　　　　　　　　　　　　(8.5km, 2hr 15min)

Follow the sea defence beyond the car park then continue on the beach past the golf course (extreme tides may need waiting out) to the start of the Bay Cycle Way at Sandy Gap. Through a gap in the wall ahead, follow a good path for 2km down the Biggar Bank amenity grasslands.

At the end, cross a car park and continue on crumbly, undulating clifftops for around 4km, passing through fields, and an informal motorhome parking area. Take care and keep dogs close in spring and summer. Birds may be nesting

Easy walking around North Walney NNR provides excellent views back over the Duddon to Haverigg wind farm and Black Combe

on sea-thrown shingle in the dips. After the triangular tower at Walney's highest point, drop down and left to the road.

South End to Jubilee Bridge (9.1km, 2hr 20min)

During the highest tides, turn left; otherwise turn briefly right on road then left, doubling back on the shore beyond the caravan park – or continue to the nature reserve if you wish. Rejoin the coastal road for 3km, with views of the 14th-century Piel Castle in the channel. Don't try to walk to Piel Island unless on an official guided walk – the marsh and tides are treacherous.

At the Biggar peninsula, from April to August, turn right around the peninsula then inland again before the village.

From October to March (and at high tide), use the winter road route. Far preferable for walkers as well as birds – it gets very boggy in winter.

Continue on road for another 2.3km, past **Biggar** village, to the junction with the A590 through **Vickerstown**.

STAGE 12 – NORTH SCALE TO VICKERSTOWN

Turn right and right again with the coast, then follow the road inland to a T-junction. Go right, left at the end then right, to follow Walney Channel back to Jubilee Bridge.

Bus service 1 stops by the handy King Alfred pub, and 1, 2 and S2 near the bridge.

111

STAGE 13
Vickerstown to Bardsea

Start	Jubilee Bridge, Vickerstown, SD 186 686
Finish	Bardsea beach car park, SD 302 742
Time	5hr 55min
Distance	22.3km (14 miles)
Ascent	115m
Terrain	Cycle path, road, fields, woodland and shore
Refreshments	Pubs at Walney, Concle, Rampside, and Bardsea; Morrisons, Buccleuch Dock; The Milk Hut, Goadsbarrow; Moat Farm tea rooms; ice cream van and café, Bardsea beach
Toilets	Morrisons, Buccleuch Dock; Aldingham car park; Bardsea beach car park
Transport	Trains and buses to Barrow. Buses 1 for Walney, Hindpool (Morrisons) & Barrow Island; 6, 6C, X6 & X12 Barrow to Ulverston; X7 Barrow to Roa Island; and 11 for Barrow, Roa Island, Coast Road, Bardsea and Ulverston
Accessibility	Road, cycle path and promenade to Newbiggin, but expect some grass verges, potholes, pinch points and parked cars; then kissing gates and steps to Sea Wood
Parking	Free on Walney promenade, west of Cavendish Dock, Concle and Rampside roadsides, Aldingham car park and various lay-bys and informal parking areas on Coast Road including Bardsea
Accommodation	Various in Barrow and Ulverston (off-trail); pubs in Rampside and Bardsea; others on booking sites
KCIIIECP status in 2025	Expected to open 2025–26, in meantime use beach past Moat Farm and Aldingham

This stage is far more enjoyable than the map's urban appearance suggests. There's a bit of road to start, but you're soon back with the channel then an almost-complete loop of Barrow Island – really a small cycle-tracked peninsula surrounded by docks and shipyards. From there it's water and wildlife rich by the docks, surprisingly subtle gasworks and road to Bardsea.

Stage 13 – Vickerstown to Bardsea

There are optional detours from Rampside down the causeway road to Foulney Island, Roa Island and the summer ferry to Piel Island, making it a good place for a split route or rest day. In summer, the area is a haven for nesting terns, plovers and eider ducks, the latter of which can be seen frequently from the ECP.

Vickerstown to Cavendish Dock (5.5km, 1hr 25min)

Cross Jubilee Bridge, and at the main junction ahead, turn right down Bridge Road, past metal BAE buildings, to a small roundabout. If you're in a hurry, simply continue 400m to the bridge to bypass Barrow Island. Turn right onto Michaelson Road, veering left at a roundabout, and left again just before a third roundabout onto a cycle path through a stone gateway. Keep right, following the path along BAE's fence. Cross a road end. After another 370m, after a pillbox, turn left up the bank and inland past allotments. Keep left along Buccleuch Dock Road then right, rejoining Michaelson Road. Cross the bridge, doubling back down steps to the Buccleuch Dock promenade. Step-free option via roads ahead. Pass Morrisons (toilets and refreshments), then keep right on the dock road alongside rail tracks.

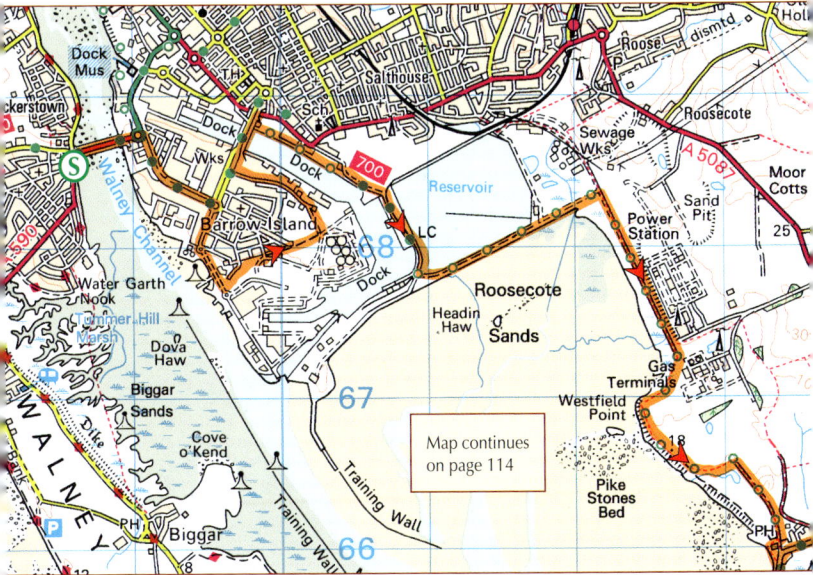

BARROW'S SHIPBUILDING STORY

The latter half of the Barrow section follows dockside paths including Cavendish Dock and here, Devonshire Dock

Barrow-in-Furness was a small, marshside village until the iron, steel and then shipbuilding industries arrived. Passing through various hands, including Barrow Shipbuilding Company and Vickers, the shipyards are now owned by BAE Systems and involved in production of the UK's nuclear submarines. The numerous docks are a reminder of various prominent families with stakes in Barrow's industries – Ramsden, Devonshire, Buccleuch and Cavendish. A narrow tower on the marsh at Rampside is the last one standing from a series of beacons once guiding ships into port. Find out more at the free Dock Museum in Barrow, passed on Stage 11.

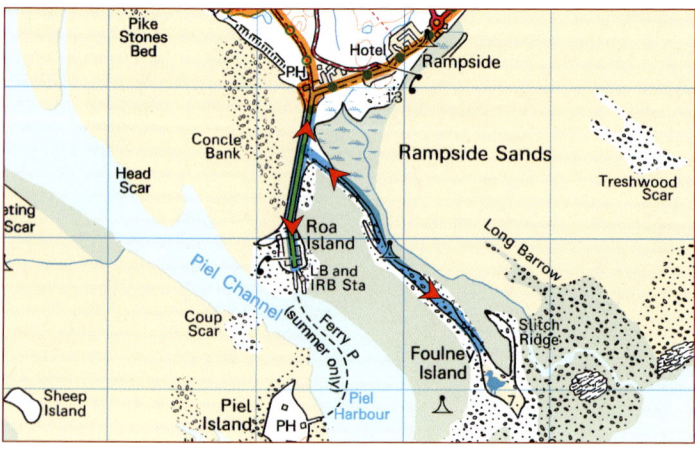

STAGE 13 – VICKERSTOWN TO BARDSEA

Cavendish Dock to Aldingham
(12.5km, 3hr 15min)

At the Port of Barrow turn left between Cavendish Dock and the shore, then right at a junction. Follow the cycle path past the gas works for 2.5km. At a path junction, keep right; approaching houses, go right again to the shore. If flooded, use the last section of cycle path. Turn left, then left again on road to a roundabout. Continue on for Roa and Foulney islands. Turn right for 4km of Coast Road to **Newbiggin**, on a mix of grass verges, pavements and promenades.

Keep right with the coast when the road diverges, on gravel then field, turning left at the remains of a medieval motte and bailey castle site (visible over the fence), to the road. After 200m of verge, turn right again through **Moat Farm** – with another medieval moat on the right as you enter, and the café on the left. Drop to the shore briefly (or use road until ECP opens), soon climbing back to field edges then raised shore to **Aldingham**.

Rampside's 'leading light' – the last remaining of a series of historical beacons guiding ships into Barrow

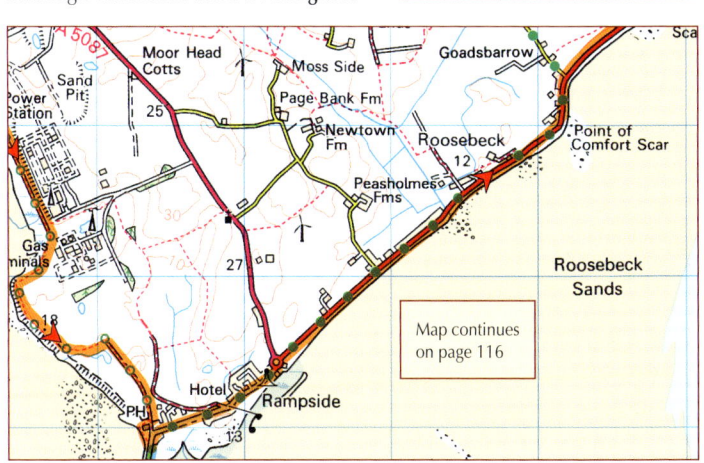

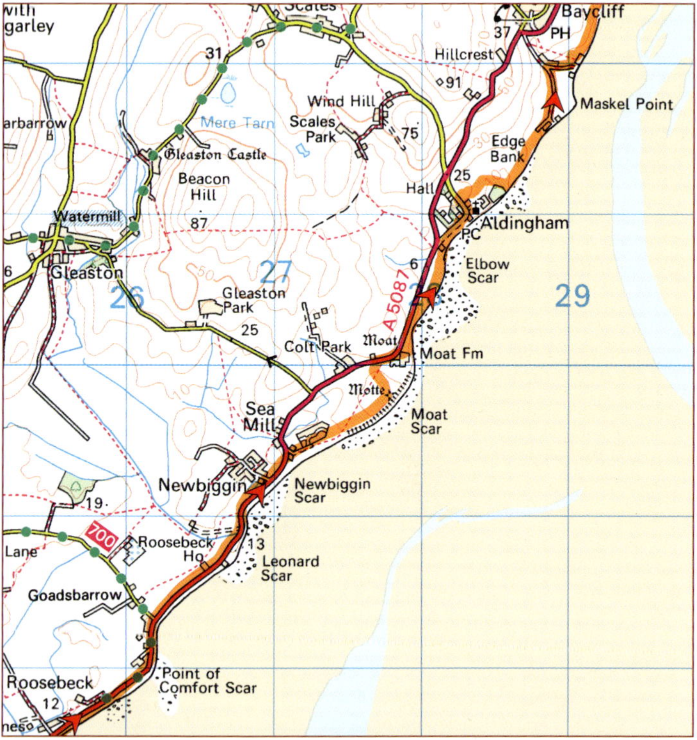

WALKING THE KING CHARLES III ENGLAND COAST PATH: NORTH WEST

The beach at Newbiggin, on the Barrow to Ulverston Coast Road

STAGE 13 – VICKERSTOWN TO BARDSEA

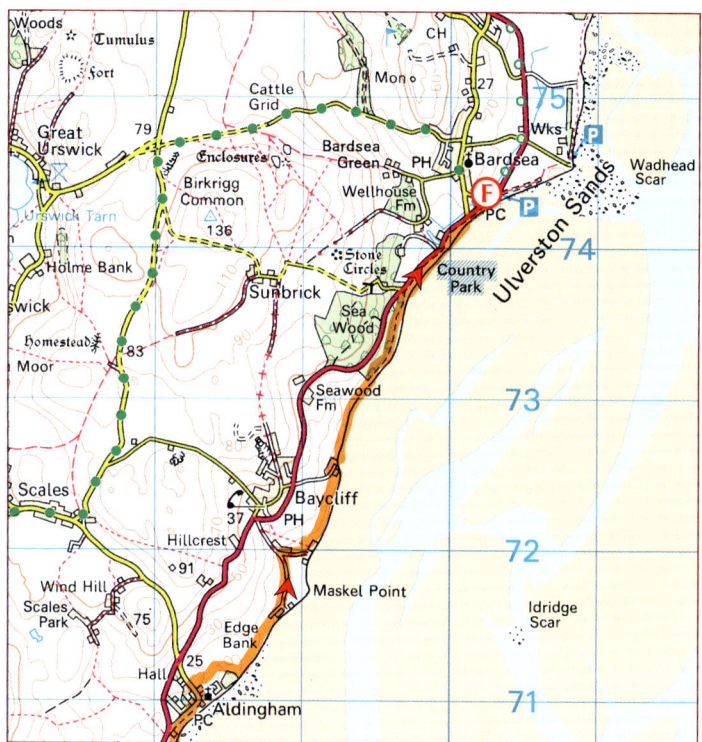

Aldingham to Bardsea (4.2km, 1hr 15min)

Head left through a car park. Or continue on shore to next houses (at Leythey Lane) until ECP opens. Turn right on road past the toilets, church and houses, then right into a field. Follow waymarks around seaward field edges to a small lane behind bungalows. Continue up Leythey Lane. Go right at the junction; just before more cottages, turn left along more field edges. Detour briefly behind more properties before dropping to the shore again, east of **Baycliff**. Look for art works and information QR codes in a garden-like area on the shore.

Stay behind reeds then take steps into **Sea Wood**. The shore is step- and root-free but sometimes wet. At the end, return to the shore and soon into the first beachside parking area and bus stop. At the second parking area you will find the the road to **Bardsea**, toilets, a small café and frequent ice cream van.

STAGE 14
Bardsea to Cark

Start	Bardsea beach car park, SD 302 742
Finish	River Eea bridge, Cark, SD 360 765
Time	6hr 20min
Distance	24.2km (15 miles)
Ascent	90m
Terrain	Field, shore, gravel, woodland, road, floodbank
Refreshments	Ice creams and café, Bardsea beach; Conishead Priory café (off-trail); Greenodd chip shop and bakery; pubs at Bardsea, Canal Foot and Cark
Toilets	Bardsea beach car park
Transport	Trains at Ulverston and Cark. Bus 11 links Bardsea to Barrow and Ulverston; X70 links central and southern Ulverston (near trail); 530 and 532 serve Cark; 6, 6C, X6 & X12 link Barrow, Ulverston and Greenodd.
Accessibility	Roudsea Wood has off-road mobility scooter routes
Parking	Free at Bardsea beach car park, Canal Foot, Greenodd rest stop, Cark roadsides and station. Free permit needed for Roudsea – search 'Roudsea NNR' on www.gov.uk
Accommodation	Ship Inn, Bardsea; Bay Horse, Canal Foot; various in Ulverston (off-trail); Engine Inn, Cark
KCIIIECP status in 2025	Bardsea to Greenodd expected 2025–26; Greenodd to Cark expected later

This stretch will be a real highlight, with long lengths of brand-new access over limestone cliffs and through woodland. However, as one of the most complex, there may be a wait. The Plumpton peninsula route will soon save a trek alongside the A590, but until the through route from Roudsea Woods & Mosses NNR to Cark opens, you'll need to take footpaths over Cartmel Fell, or public transport. Either way, it's worth looping around Roudsea for ancient woodlands, lowland bogs and nesting ospreys in summer. Check tides as the Mearness peninsula can be affected, but there's an easy bypass. The descriptions below reflect the anticipated ECP route, but check nationaltrail.co.uk in advance, and adapt your plans accordingly in the meantime.

STAGE 14 – BARDSEA TO CARK

Bardsea to Canal Foot (4.6km, 1hr 10min)

Continue along the coast, keeping right above a concrete retaining wall, right again over a small cliff, and through a car park. Go left through trees to avoid erosion, then right on road. Follow the coast again through trees and shingle, past **Conishead Priory**'s grounds. The grounds and Priory are usually open – it's now a Buddhist monastery with a café and gift shop. Cross a car park then more shingle, to re-enter the trees on a disused railway. In the channel, look for eider 'creches' in spring and summer – groups of chicks whose care is shared between adult females. Keep going, then continue on tarmac to a small roundabout. Turn right to Ulverston's historic Canal Foot and pub, or left then right for the nearest bus.

CANAL FOOT AND THE HOAD MONUMENT

As the name suggests, the village of Canal Foot sits at the end of the Ulverston Canal. Opened in 1796, the 2km long canal linked the sea with Ulverston's railway, and facilitated the transportation of goods and development of industries around coal, charcoal, timber, paper, gas, chemicals and shipbuilding. The ECP crosses the site of the old sea lock gate, now replaced by a concrete wall retaining the canal waters.

Ulverston's most famous seafaring resident was Sir John Barrow, the son of a tanner who went on to lead the British Navy. The lighthouse-inspired monument on Ulverston's Hoad Hill, known locally as the Hoad Monument, is officially named the Sir John Barrow Monument having been erected in his memory.

Ulverston's lighthouse-inspired Hoad Monument is a striking landmark above the Leven Estuary

Walking the King Charles III England Coast Path: North West

Stage 14 – Bardsea to Cark

Canal Foot to Greenodd Rest Stop (6.2km, 1hr 40min)

Cross the lock. Continue past houses, then along the back of the shore. At high tide or to avoid wet limestone, use the waymarked high tide route up a lane before the shore. The path moves into trees, leading to a junction near **Plumpton Hall**, where the high tide route returns. Although the ECP is due to open soon after publication, the only alternative from Plumpton Hall to Greenodd in the meantime is the former Cumbria Coastal Way route on the A590 dual carriageway, which should only be used with great care. Keep ahead on the track. Go under the railway, then right through fields.

Keep right around a small bump, and left after the next up the hill. Follow ECP waymarks through a length of undulating gorse-covered ground. Turn right inside a field to Ashes Wood. Wiggle around a disused quarry (watch out for hidden edges!) then drop to a floodbank. Follow this to its end.

From April to August, continue around the coastal edge. From September to March, turn left. This protects winter bird roosts at Nab Point.

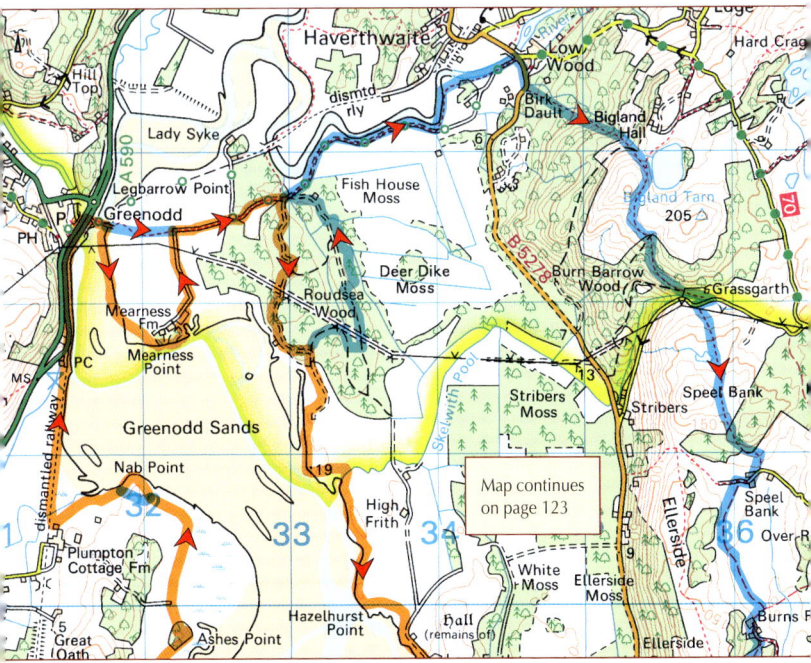

Rounding Mearness Point, with Roudsea Woods & Mosses NNR over the water

Continue with the coast to Plumpton Cottage Farm then turn right on the old railway line to **Greenodd Rest Stop**.

Greenodd Rest Stop to Cark (13.4km, 3hr 30min)
Follow the channelside fence, rising to the roadside just before the footbridge. Cross and turn right on a marsh path which leads you around the rocky **Mearness Point** (aim well ahead of high tide). At high tide or in a hurry keep ahead 450m to bypass Mearness Point. Cross a creek then turn left through a farmyard and right onto a track. At the end turn right, back onto the public footpath from Greenodd to Roudsea.

After 850m, turn right through a small permit car park into Roudsea Woods and Mosses NNR. Follow the main path, keeping right at two splits, and to a ruined building (once a bark store for Ulverston's tanning industry).

Until the ECP opens, the recommended link route is mapped here, looping around Roudsea then following the former Cumbria Coastal Way over Cartmel Fell, and still waymarked as such in places.

STAGE 14 – BARDSEA TO CARK

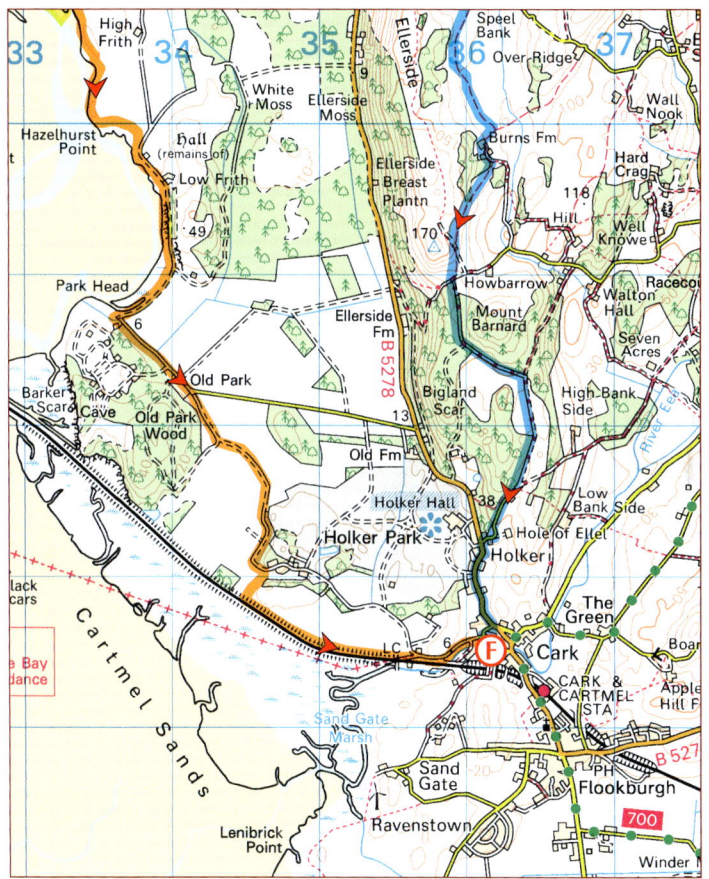

Once the ECP opens, turn right beyond the ruined bark store to a gate. Follow the floodbank ahead, then waymarks through trees and field edges to a track, then road. Follow this past Low Frith to a car park (permits only) at Park Head.

Turn inland with the road for 700m then right after a farm. Keep left on the main track, then right towards the railway just before Holker Farm. Follow field edges for 1.2km alongside the railway then continue on road to a small bridge approaching **Cark**. Trains and facilities are up ahead in the village centre.

STAGE 15
Cark to Grange-over-Sands

Start	River Eea bridge, Cark, SD 360 765
Finish	Grange-over-Sands railway station, SD 412 781
Time	4hr 55min
Distance	18.1km (11¼ miles)
Ascent	160m
Terrain	Floodbank, gravel, field and promenade
Refreshments	Engine Inn, Cark; shop, bakery & chip shop, Flookburgh (high tide route); shops, pubs and cafés in Grange
Toilets	Cark village; Grange prom
Transport	Trains at Cark, Kents Bank and Grange. Bus 530 serves Cark, Flookburgh, Allithwaite, Kents Bank & Grange-over-Sands, 532 extends to Lakeland Leisure Park; X6 links Barrow, Ulverston, Greenodd and Grange
Accessibility	Good on Grange prom, still to be confirmed elsewhere
Parking	Free at Cark and Kents Bank roadsides and stations, Flookburgh, and Humphrey Head (SD 390 740); paid at Grange station & prom car parks
Accommodation	Engine Inn, Cark; Lakeland Leisure Park; various in Grange
KCIIIECP status in 2025	Not yet open but mostly walkable (including Cark to Sandgate). Take high tide route around Lakeland Leisure Park; bypass Kirkhead via Allithwaite or shore

Stage 15 is a must-do for keen naturalists. After birding by the marsh and muds, the dramatic grass-topped limestone cliffs of Humphrey Head are home to rare butterflies and limestone plants including green-winged orchid, peregrine falcons and extensive views over the plains you've just crossed and the onward journey around Morecambe Bay. Humphrey Head is said to be where the last wolf in England was killed in the late 14th century. There's more limestone and woodland at Kirkhead, once the ECP opens, before reaching Grange-over-Sands' seaside attractions. The pretty parks, mountain views and Victorian hotels remain, even if the sandy beach has long since succumbed to saltmarsh!

STAGE 15 – CARK TO GRANGE-OVER-SANDS

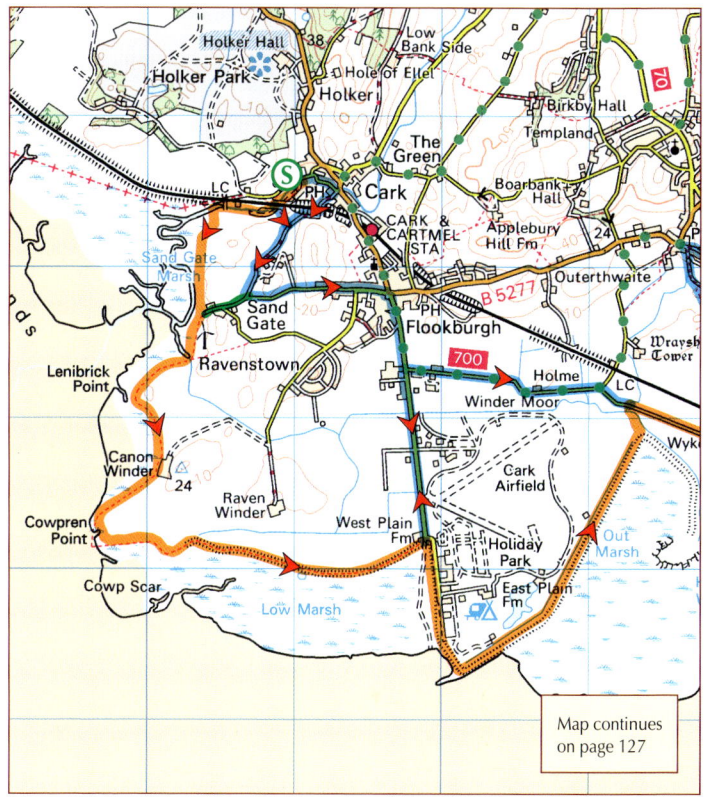

Cark to Humphrey Head (9.7km, 2hr 30min)

Cross the bridge, doubling back on road then gravel to return to saltmarsh. Or use high tide routes from Cark to Flookburgh and Humphrey Head, with connections at Caton Lane, Sandgate Farm and West Plain. Pass under the railway back to open saltmarsh. Follow the boundary track around, passing the Sandgate car park (with high tide link route), **Canon Winder** farm, and continuing east on a large floodbank. At the end, turn right on **Lakeland Leisure Park**'s floodbank (or left for another high tide route). Around the corner, drop behind the floodbank (to protect birds) then left at the end to a road and the high tide route end. Turn right on road to **Humphrey Head** Outdoor Centre.

Morecambe and Heysham feel tantalisingly close from the point of Humphrey Head

Around Sandgate and Flookburgh, you'll likely see trailers with nets and ropes lining the path – evidence of the **traditional fishing and netting methods** still well-practised by fishing families around the Bay. Cockles and mussels are fished, along with shrimping, the main activity. Although the industry has vastly declined, you can still treat yourself to plenty of local potted shrimp in shops around the Bay.

Humphrey Head to Kents Bank (5.2km, 1hr 35min)

Turn left on the track then right inside Humphrey Head's clifftop perimeter fence, passing through ancient woodland with large coral fossils underfoot on the return. You can bypass Humphrey Head if in a hurry but you'll miss a highlight! Rise with the path, passing left of the outdoor centre, to join a walled path (until open, access via the road). Turn left on the marsh, rising into a small field just after **Wyke Farm**. Continue under the railway and ahead on a public footpath.

Once the ECP opens, turn right past the waterworks to access, then climb inland on the Kirkhead outcrop, before turning right through a field then down past trees to join the road to **Kents Bank** station. Until open, use public rights

STAGE 15 – CARK TO GRANGE-OVER-SANDS

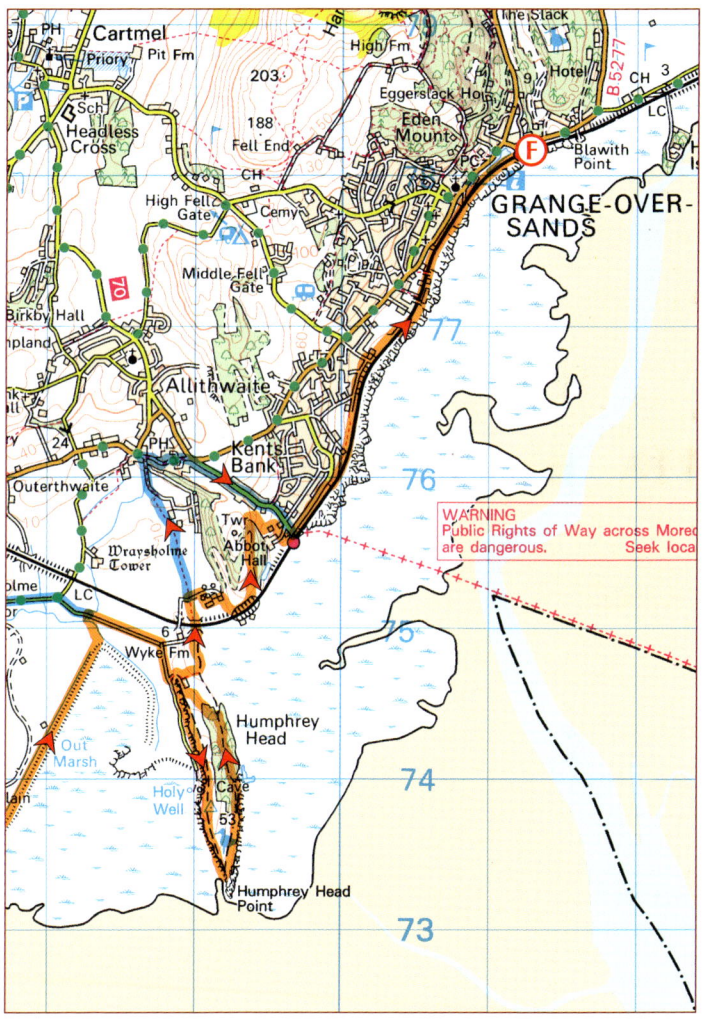

of way via Allithwaite, as mapped here, or use the shore at low tide (rough and waterlogged in places).

Grange-over-Sands must surely have one of the most picturesque station views in the country

Kents Bank to Grange & Arnside (3.2km, 50min)
Follow the road past Kents Bank station. Cross the railway for a lovely rest stop overlooking the Bay. After 400m, descend steps to a narrow railside path and past meadows. Use roads for step-free route.

Keep ahead on a track which becomes Cart Lane. At the end turn right down Carter Fold (can flood, but shallow on left), past houses and a skate park then under the railway to the promenade. Pass various playgrounds, cafés, public toilets and the famous Grange Lido, currently under restoration, to Grange station and your train to Arnside. While waiting, explore the ornamental gardens or head up the road into town for refreshments.

STAGE 16
Arnside to Hest Bank

Start	Arnside railway station, SD 460 788
Finish	Hest Bank beach car park, SD 468 665
Time	6hr 45min
Distance	23.6km (14½ miles)
Ascent	270m
Terrain	Promenade, limestone shore, woodland and cliffs, floodbank, road, saltmarsh
Refreshments	Arnside chip shop, cafés and pubs; New Barns café; Co-op and pub in Silverdale; Wolf House café, Lindeth; various in Carnforth including Brief Encounter station café (off-trail); Archers Café, Bolton-le-Sands; Shore Café, Hest Bank
Toilets	Silverdale (off-trail opposite Co-op)
Transport	Trains at Arnside, Silverdale (off-trail), Carnforth (off-trail) and Bare Lane (off-trail, Stage 16). Between them, buses 5, 49, 50, 51, 55 & 755 serve Arnside, Silverdale, Warton, Carnforth and Hest Bank
Accessibility	Shore and cliff routes can be rough and tricky; but high tide routes more road-based. Silverdale's cliffs especially require sure footing and head for heights
Parking	Free at Arnside station (limited roadside), Arnside prom and beach car parks, Quaker's Stang (RSPB), Carnforth Shore Road, Bolton-le-Sands and Hest Bank beach car parks
Accommodation	Various in Arnside, Silverdale and Carnforth: numerous holiday parks, some with camping; others off-trail in Bolton-le-Sands and Hest Bank
KCIIIECP status in 2025	Not yet open, but mostly walkable or linkable

Another complex day requiring some planning, including the train connection to Arnside if you've stayed in Grange overnight, but very rewarding. Until the ECP is open, you'll need to use the road from Silverdale to Jack Scout, the shore past Jenny Brown's Point, and the road below Warton Crag. Once open, it'll be one of the more challenging stages. Steep, rugged cliffs with rocky limestone underfoot are mostly fenced (Jack Scout) or have close alternatives (Jack Scout and Arnside), but if you're wary of narrow, exposed paths use the high tide route past the Silverdale Cliffs section (Shore Road to Jack Scout) which offers the excellent Wolf House café and craft shop instead. Approaching Warton, check tide times – it's a long way to retrace your steps from the marsh for the high tide route. From the Carnforth area, it's virtually all walkable, but expect some channel-hopping on the marsh until new sleeper bridges are installed.

ARNSIDE & SILVERDALE NATIONAL LANDSCAPE

This highly distinctive landscape crosses the Cumbria/Lancashire border at Silverdale, extending towards Milnthorpe, Carnforth and the A6. Geology is everything here, influencing soil types, plants, woodland, wildlife and the wider landscape and walking terrain. The Carboniferous limestone bedrock is fossil-rich, particularly entrancing in water-worn limestone by the sea. Human histories abound too, such as the copper smelt chimney and rapidly disappearing dock walls at Jenny Brown's Point.

Arnside station to Far Arnside   (5.6km, 1hr 40min)

Turn right on road then promenade past shops, a stone pier and through a car park. Keep right on a concrete path above the shore. Continue past a lifeboat station onto the beach. The high tide route is just before it. Just past a boatyard ramp, enter trees to cross a meadow within Cumbria Wildlife Trust's **Grubbins Wood** reserve, then drop back to shingle. Continue around the back of the marsh, where the high tide route returns, to **New Barns** café. The access track floods temporarily on highest tides – after that there's another high tide route past the café. Pass New Barns on the marsh then go left into the woods. The ECP/public footpath can be tricky and precipitous, but easier parallel paths exist if preferred – or hunt for fossils on the beach path.

After 700m, drop briefly to the shore to bypass a hidden garden. Back in the trees, keep right for more of the same around Arnside Point and Park Point, to **Far Arnside**.

Far Arnside to Jenny Brown's Point   (5.1km, 1hr 45min)

Take the left-hand path through the holiday park. Turn right and downhill at the T-junction, then take a roadside path back up past trees to **Silverdale**, passing another holiday park, a cricket pitch and the county boundary – you're now in Lancashire! Continue on road, turning right onto Cove Lane, to Cove Well Bay.

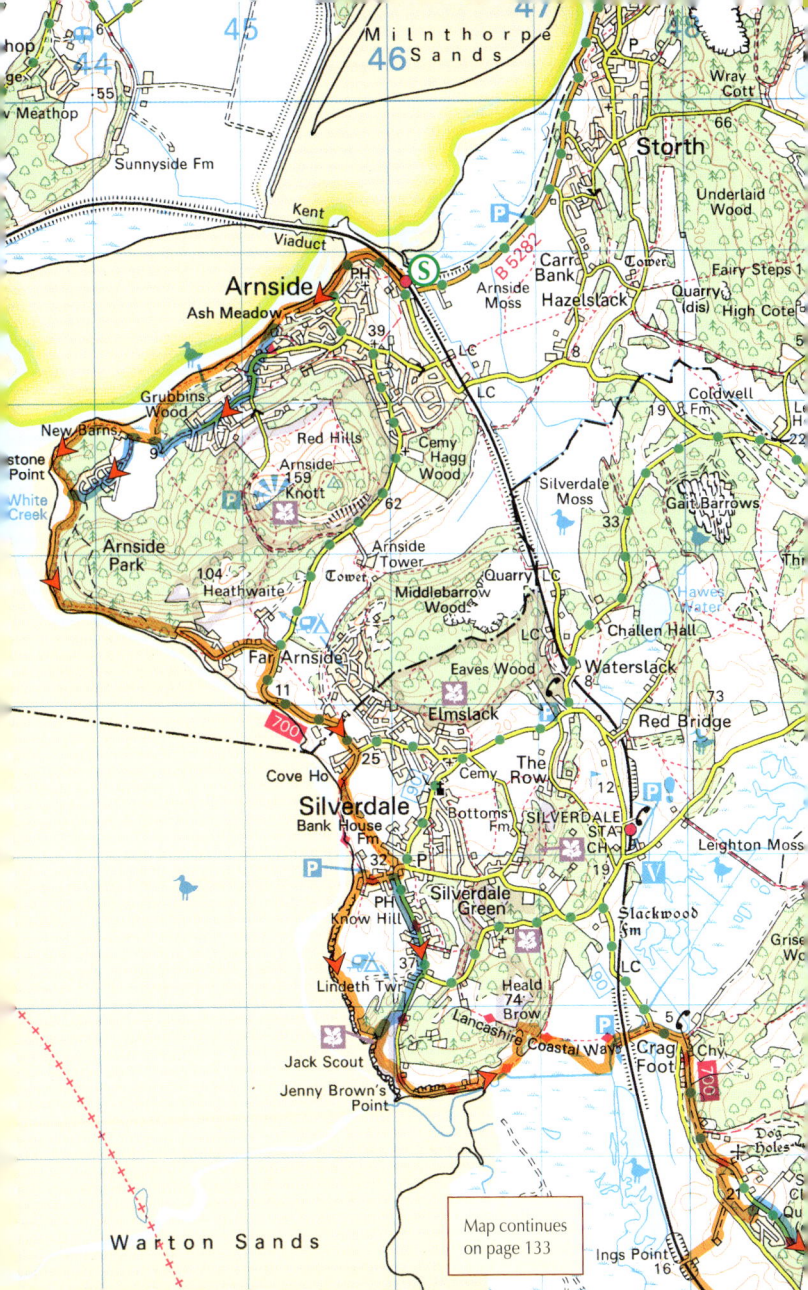

Arnside beach during one of the Bay's many cultural festivals

Go left on the cliff path, then through trees and fields to another road (Silverdale's centre is up the hill to your left). For the high tide and more accessible route, take Lindeth Road ahead, past Gibraltar Farm, to Jack Scout. Turn right down Shore Road, then left along the shore. This is the tricky section referred to above – rocky bands provide an early taster of the terrain, especially useful if wet. Don't try to reach Jack Scout on the shore – there's no suitable exit until the ECP opens.

Beyond these cliffs, steps in the gully to your left will access the National Trust's **Jack Scout** nature reserve, soon rejoined by the alternative route. Turn right and follow the cliffs, then a minor road to **Jenny Brown's Point**.

Jenny Brown's Point to Cote Stones (5.6km, 1hr 35min)
Follow field edges behind and beyond Brown's Houses then descend woodland steps – or use the rocky shore path past the old chimney. Both meet at a path junction – take the flood bank. Over a bridge, turn left under the railway. There's also an optional extension to the RSPB's coastal hides just after the bridge.

Turn right at the end of the lane to a road junction at **Crag Foot**. Cross carefully onto Crag Road (the lower road isn't safe).

STAGE 16 – ARNSIDE TO HEST BANK

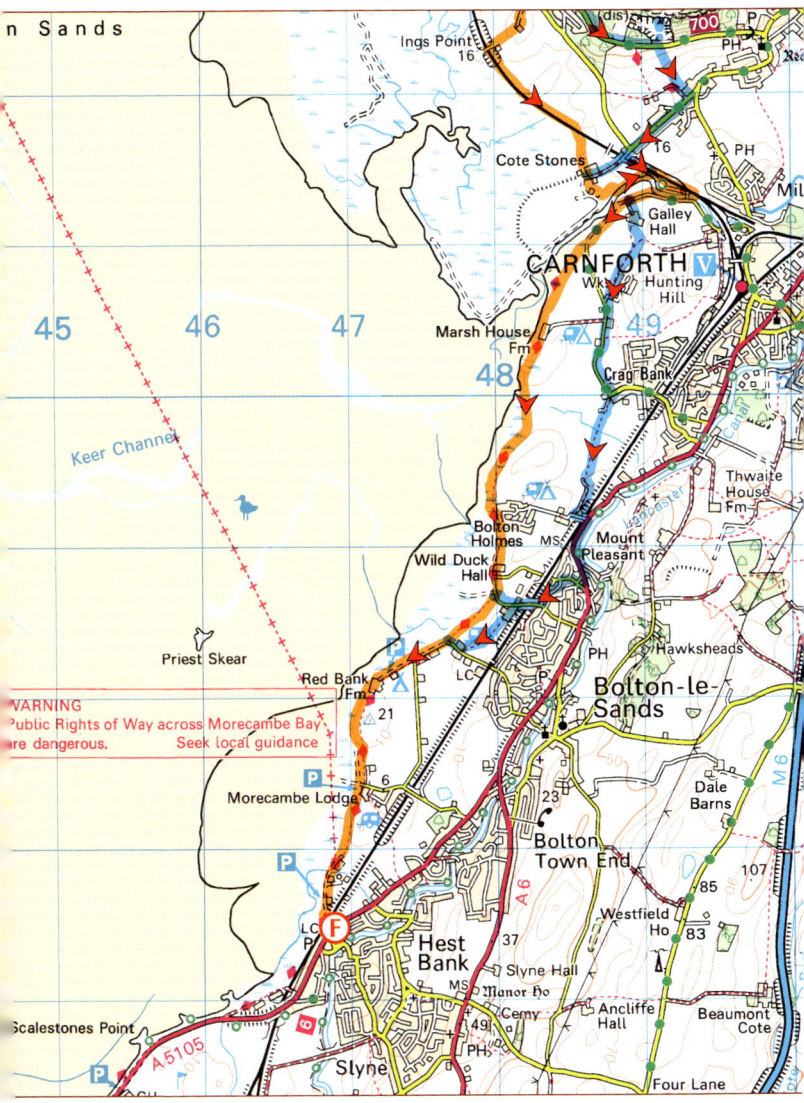

133

Walking the King Charles III England Coast Path: North West

After 350m join a parallel path in the woods, eventually taking a large zigzag to a lower field edge. Until ECP opens, stay on the road. At a junction, turn right. Pass a quarry (now caravan site). Cross the main road, with care, into the field below. Join a farm track to the railway. Cross, turning left to the farm and road end at **Cote Stones**.

High tide routes, Crag Foot to Cote Stones and Carnforth (same distance)
At high tide, and until the ECP opens, continue along Crag Lane (keep going on road for Warton facilities) then down fields to Warton and right to Cotestones Farm. An extension from Cotestones to Carnforth avoids further flooding on the Keer riverside.

Cote Stones to Hest Bank (7.4km, 1hr 55min)
Keep ahead (or left if accessing from road). Pass a building, turn left through a gate, then drop to follow a reedy riverside path, soon lifting to a tarmac cycle path. Follow this right, then across a footbridge, then right on a narrow road for 800m. Now follow the marsh for 2km (with one short field-edge section once open). More high tide options link Galley Hall, Wild Duck Hall, Red Bank and Sandside Caravan Park near Bolton-le-Sands. At the Bay View holiday park, join the track past **Wild Duck Hall** to Red Bank Farm. Pass the café, keeping right through the farmyard then between caravans. Follow field edges then shore to a café and car park by the level crossing at **Hest Bank**.

Cross for bus stops and facilities.

Windswept trees on steep limestone cliffs are one of the Arnside and Silverdale coast's most striking natural features

STAGE 17
Hest Bank to Overton

Start	Hest Bank beach car park, SD 468 665
Finish	Overton, near Globe Hotel, SD 432 578
Time	5hr 35min
Distance	21.2km (13¼ miles)
Ascent	80m
Terrain	Marsh, field, floodbank, promenade, road
Refreshments	Hest Bank Shore Café; copious in Morecambe; cafés at Half Moon Bay and Heysham; Globe Hotel, Overton
Toilets	Various on Morecambe prom; Sunderland Point
Transport	Trains at Bare Lane (off-trail), Morecambe and infrequently Heysham port. Between them, buses 1, 1A, 2X, 5, 55 and 755 serve Hest Bank, Carnforth, Morecambe, Heysham and Lancaster. 1, 1A & 5 extend to Overton; 755 to Ocean Edge
Accessibility	Urban areas good; expect kissing gates and possible steps elsewhere
Parking	Free at Hest Bank, Bolton-le-Sands and Potts Corner shore car parks and opposite the Globe in Overton; various in Morecambe and Heysham
Accommodation	Plentiful in first half including caravan parks; for Overton, buses to Morecambe or Lancaster may be easiest
KCIIIECP status in 2025	Not yet open but all linkable. Use public footpaths or tidal marsh road from Sunderland Point to Overton.

Some adaptation is required until the ECP opens, but the only real weak spot is south of Heysham, and it's offset by the joy of Morecambe itself, namesake of both the entire Bay and its most famous resident, Eric. The fast going buys time to enjoy the many sights (and ice creams), with glorious views across the Bay to Cumbria. Beyond Heysham power station, development in the Middleton Sands area means the future ECP route is yet to be confirmed; in the meantime, you'll need to tackle the shore or road to Potts Corner.

Walking the King Charles III England Coast Path: North West

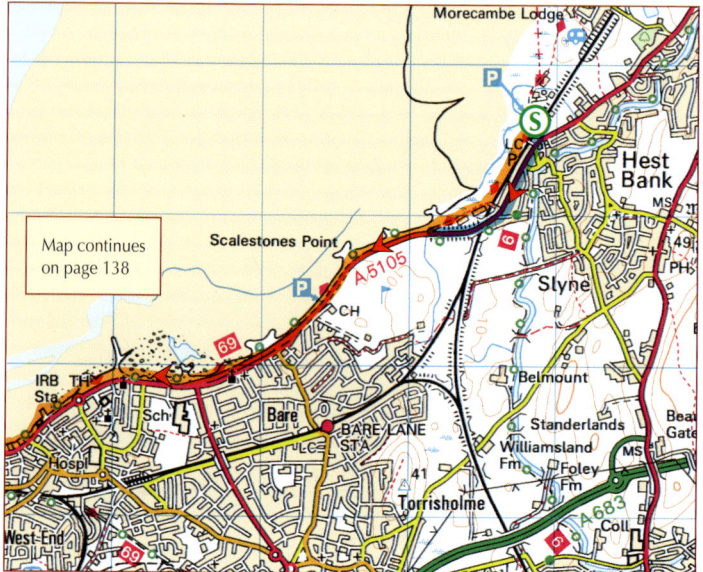

Hest Bank to St Patrick's Chapel (8.7km, 2hr 15min)
From the beach car park by the recently-exposed 19th-century quay, continue on beach then in front of houses and through a car park, to the main road. To avoid tides or shingle use the road from Hest Bank.

Follow the pavement and promenade all the way through **Morecambe**. Underfoot engravings contrast with mountain views, and don't miss the Eric Morecambe prom-side statue as you fully enter British Seaside territory.

You'll pass the future Eden Project North site, the Stone Jetty with great views and sculptures, and the Art Deco Midland Hotel. Tourist Information is in an old railway building, with the train and bus stations a little inland.

Beyond the town, and some small paddocks, keep left up to **Heysham** village. Turn right, left and right again on road to St Patrick's Chapel.

The 8th-century ruin is accompanied by 11th-century carved graves – also famous from Black Sabbath's 'Best of' album cover.

St Patrick's Chapel to Potts Corner (6.6km, 1hr 45min)
Follow the coastal edge through the National Trust site then straight ahead past Half Moon Bay and up the road.

STAGE 17 – HEST BANK TO OVERTON

Turn right on Penrod Way, left on Port Way, and right on Princess Alexandra Way (A683). Turn left opposite a site entrance. Follow the fence-side path then drop through a visitor area with nature reserve information. Turn right just beyond a large building. At the far end, cross another access road onto gravel; keep right on good paths along the final power station fence to the shore. Turn left, following waymarks past a green and through a series of holiday parks to **Potts Corner** shore car park. Until ECP opens, use roads or drop to the shore after the green, but expect hidden obstacles and rocky sections. Don't stray if walking in reverse – there's a hidden tidal channel at the north end.

Potts Corner to Overton (6km, 1hr 35min)

Take a track through the marsh (not the raised bank on the left), continuing ahead when the track turns inland. A path junction accesses Sambo's Grave and artist Chris Drury's 'Horizon Line Chamber'. Turn left here to bypass the Point at high tide. Continue around Sunderland Point to the village, initially on the shore then partly in fields once open.

On Morecambe prom, looking across the Bay to the Lake District fells

Walking the King Charles III England Coast Path: North West

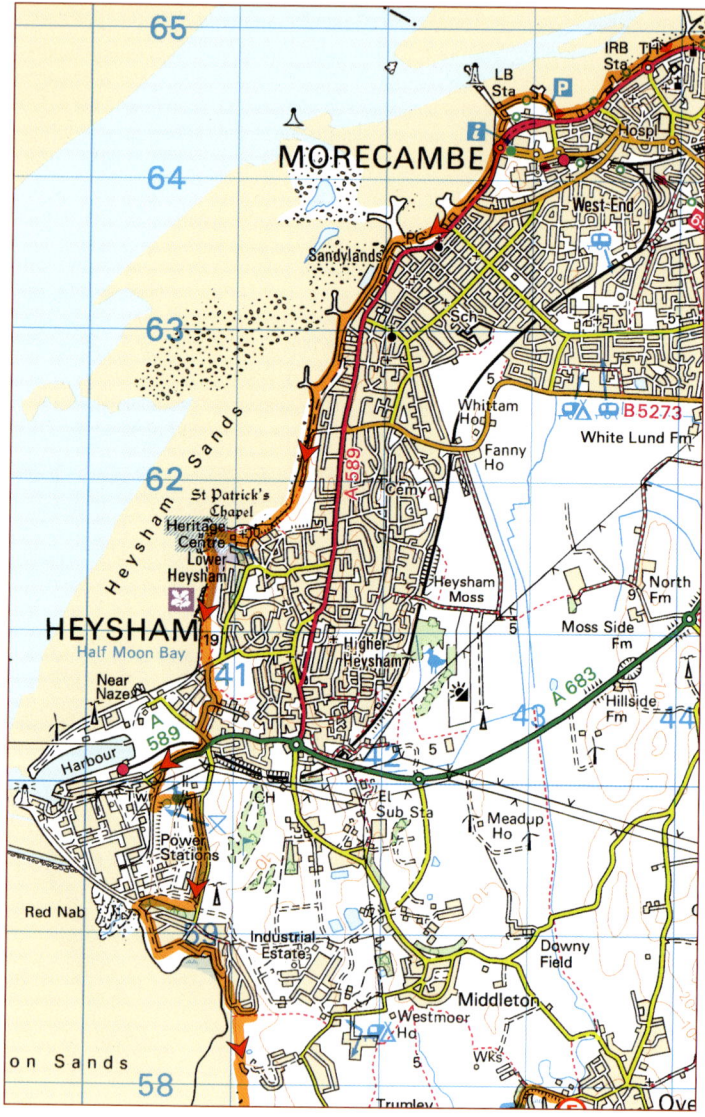

Stage 17 – Hest Bank to Overton

SUNDERLAND POINT AND SAMBO'S GRAVE

Sunderland Point was an 18th-century port until Glasson Dock took over. Inevitably, many of the traders were complicit in the slave trade. A young Black boy known as Sambo (now an offensive slur), who died on a ship docked at Sunderland Point in 1736, was buried by the shore. A plaque added 60 years later asking that 'worth of heart' be judged above 'man's color' was funded and written by the former head of Lancaster Grammar – and brother to a Lancaster slave trader. It's well worth a visit as a reminder of the complexities of Britain's coastal wealth and continued racial inequalities.

From April to September, use the summer route: just after the causeway junction pass into fields on a public footpath, becoming a lane beyond a farm, near **Trailholme**. Keep right on road, then floodbank, to **Overton**. You can walk the causeway directly, but heed warnings and allow lots of time around tides.

From October to March (once open), follow the coast on field edges and floodbanks to Overton.

The pub and main village road are straight ahead.

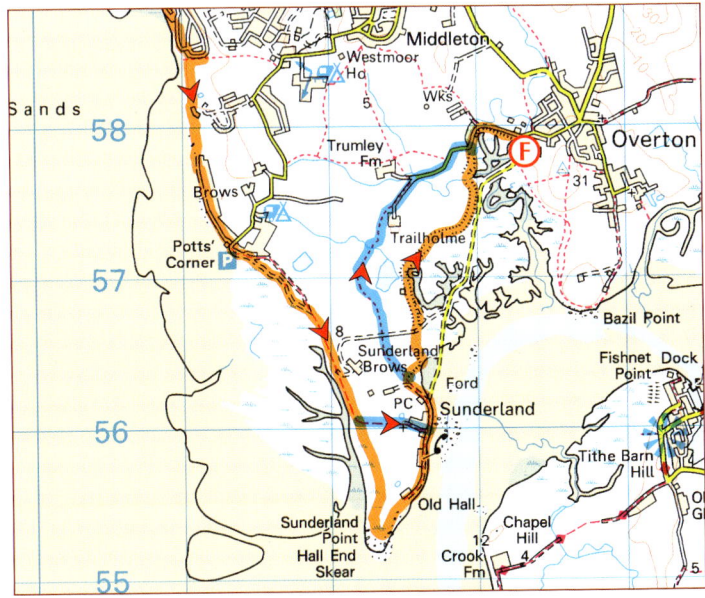

STAGE 18
Overton to Conder Green

Start	Overton, near Globe Hotel, SD 432 578
Finish	Corricks Lane, Conder Green SD 456 560
Time	4hr 55min
Distance	19km (11¾ miles)
Ascent	40m
Terrain	Fields, shore, floodbank, tarmac and gravel cycle paths
Refreshments	Pubs at Overton, Snatchems and Conder Green; various inland at Lancaster
Toilets	Lancaster Sainsburys and city centre (off-trail); Conder Green car park
Transport	Buses 1 & 1A Overton to Morecambe, Heysham & Lancaster, 2X Lancaster to Morecambe & Heysham, 88 & 89 Lancaster & Conder Green to Glasson Dock, Cockerham, Pilling and Knott End
Accessibility	From Heaton, all road or cycle path; step-free route via Millennium Bridge, Lancaster
Parking	Free opposite the Globe, Overton and roadsides at Snatchems and Lancaster (Lune south bank); Conder Green low-cost car park
Accommodation	Various in Lancaster; Golden Ball pub and pods, Snatchems; Ashton Hall, Stodday; Stork Hotel, Conder Green
KCIIIECP status in 2025	Not yet open but all walkable using shore around Bazil Point and road to Heaton

After rounding Bazil Point, today's walk is a full out-and-back on the River Lune via Lancaster, finishing on the opposite shore at Conder Green. After 4km of new access to start, it's mostly easy and enjoyable walking on tree-lined river- and estuary-side paths, with waders and waterfowl on the banks throughout. Lancaster also makes an excellent split or rest day.

STAGE 18 – OVERTON TO CONDER GREEN

Overton to Snatchems (8.4km, 2hr 15min)
Turn right over a cattle grid. Follow the back of the marsh to steps into fields above. Turn right along field edge, floodbank, then shore; circuiting **Bazil Point** and passing some houses. Go straight ahead from the steps at high tide. Turn inland past a church to the road, then right, zigzagging back to the coast. Until open, use the road from Overton to Heaton, with care. Follow floodbank and field edges for 3km then go left on a lane. Turn right on tarmac and right again at three junctions, passing **Heaton**, to the Golden Ball Inn at Snatchems.

Snatchems to Conder Green (10.6km, 2hr 40min)
After a road corner, turn right onto the riverside cycle path for about 2km, keeping right at the only tarmac junction, to **Lancaster**. Go under the railway viaduct and up steps to its attached footbridge. The Millennium Bridge upstream is step-free; access the city centre from either.

The Lune's railway footbridge enables access to and impressive views of Lancaster

Walking the King Charles III England Coast Path: North West

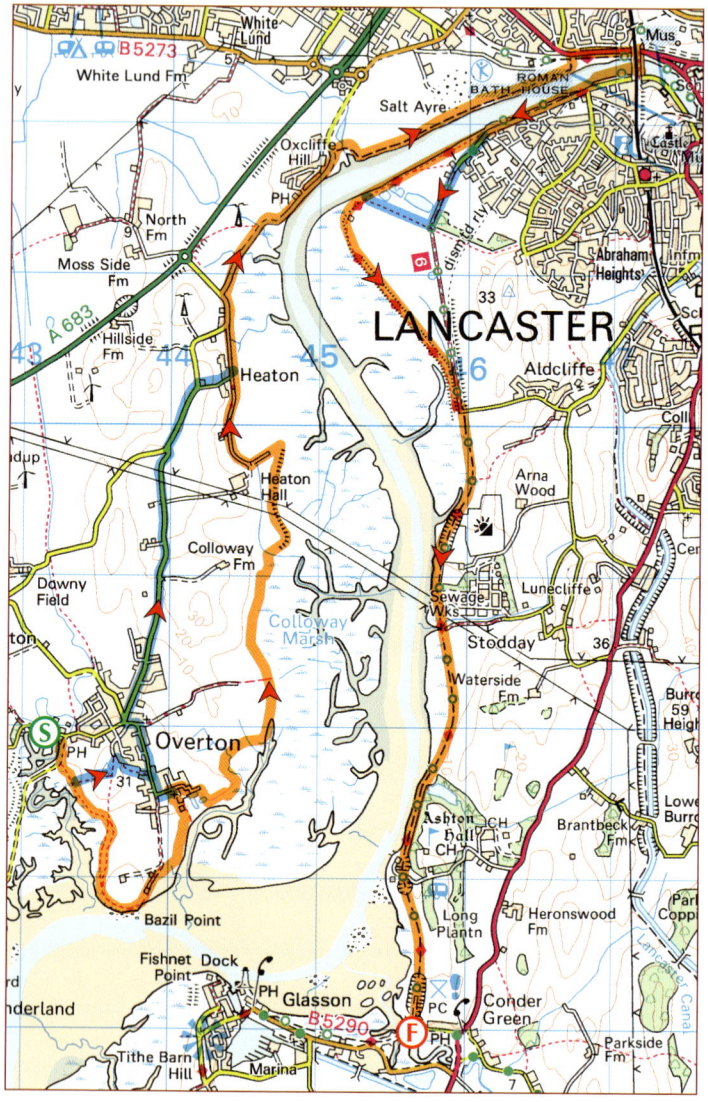

STAGE 18 – OVERTON TO CONDER GREEN

Lancaster is a small and very attractive city, with long royal, industrial and social histories. As the 'caster' name suggests, it has Roman roots, and later flourished with the Industrial Revolution and a port on the River Lune. **Lancaster Castle** originates in the 11th century with the Normans, and has since seen everything from royalty to the occult: the famous Pendle 'witches' were held and tried there in 1612; and the latest Duke of Lancaster, in a line stretching from John o' Gaunt, son of Edward III, is King Charles III.

Return to the riverside to head downstream. After 1km a short wooded riverside section can be bypassed at high tide. Join the floodbank, swinging south with Aldcliffe Marsh for 1.7km. At the end, join the Millennium Park cycle path just inland, for 4km, to **Conder Green**.

There's benches, a car park, toilets, parking and fabulous views over the bend in the Lune to Glasson Dock. Turn left at the road for bus stops and Stork Hotel.

Looking ahead to Glasson Dock (Stage 19) from Conder Green

STAGE 19
Conder Green to Knott End

Start	Corricks Lane, Conder Green, SD 456 560
Finish	Knott-End-on-Sea ferry dock, SD 346 485
Time	5hr 40min
Distance	22.6km (14 miles)
Ascent	30m
Terrain	Fields, floodbank, cycle path
Refreshments	Stork Hotel, Conder Green; various in Glasson Dock, Cockerham (off-trail); Pilling, Knott End and Fleetwood
Toilets	Conder Green car park; Glasson Dock and Knott End
Transport	Buses 88 & 89 Lancaster & Conder Green to Glasson Dock, Cockerham, Pilling and Knott End; 5c Knott End to Blackpool; 1, 14 & 24 Fleetwood from Blackpool; 74 Fleetwood from Preston
Accessibility	To Cockerham, expect wet fields and possible kissing gates and narrow spots; to Fluke Hall, summer route may be okay; to Knott End, good (cycle path).
Parking	Paid at Conder Green and Glasson Dock; free at Pilling Lane Ends Amenity Area, Knott End car park and Fleetwood prom
Accommodation	Best options are Stork Hotel, Conder Green, and various offers in Fleetwood
KCIIIECP status in 2025	Not yet open but walkable by adapting winter routes past Pilling

Today is essentially the last of Morecambe Bay, ending at the mouth of the River Wyre after passing Glasson Dock and circuiting the Cockerham and Pilling sands and marshes, key roosting grounds for migrating and wintering birds. As such, even once the ECP opens, you'll need to use the inland route in winter, and the summer route is aligned behind the floodbank – but the pathside greenery will remain welcome ahead of tomorrow's change of scenery. Where you overnight might depend on tide times – Fleetwood boasts more accommodation, but the Wyre Ferry from Knott End only runs from 7.45am to 5.45pm (half-hourly), and can't cross at low tide. Otherwise, buses connect the towns from Monday to Saturday.

Stage 19 – Conder Green to Knott End

Conder Green to Cocker Bridge (10km, 2hr 30min)

Resume the cycle path to **Glasson**. Pass the marina and turn left over a swing bridge. On your right now are the shop, café, and pub. Go up the road past the café and right down Ten Row to an industrial area.

> **Glasson Dock** took over from Lancaster and Sunderland Point after the Lune became difficult to navigate in the late 18th century, soon linking instead with the city via the Lancaster Canal's Glasson Branch. The dock is still in use, mostly serving the onsite grain and fertiliser business.

Turn left up Bodie Hill, and straight on at a T-junction. At a sharp bend, turn right down Marsh Lane and onwards through fields. Keep left of a hedge to reach and pass **Crook Farm** to the shore. Take the sea wall road to Lighthouse Cottage then a grassy floodbank. The lighthouse in question is just off Plover Scar, where the bank curves south. Pass the remains of **Cockersand Abbey**.

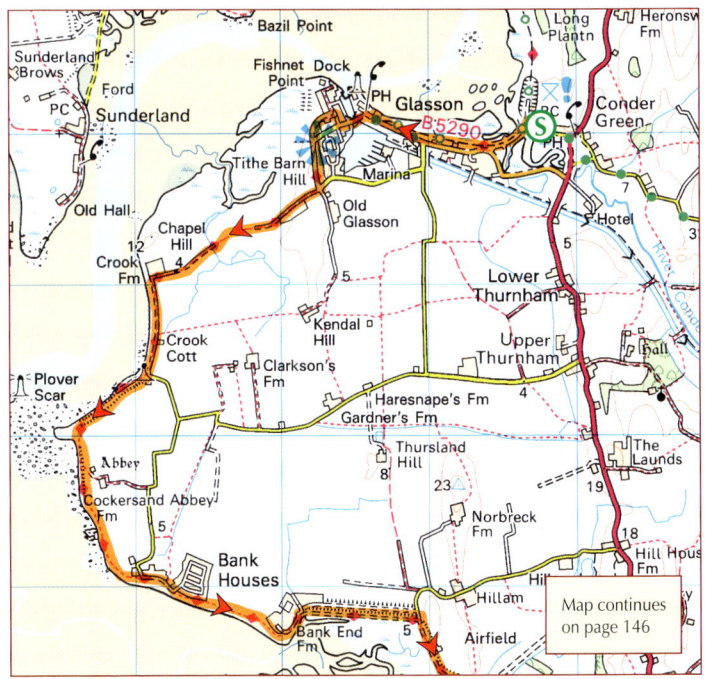

145

Walking the King Charles III England Coast Path: North West

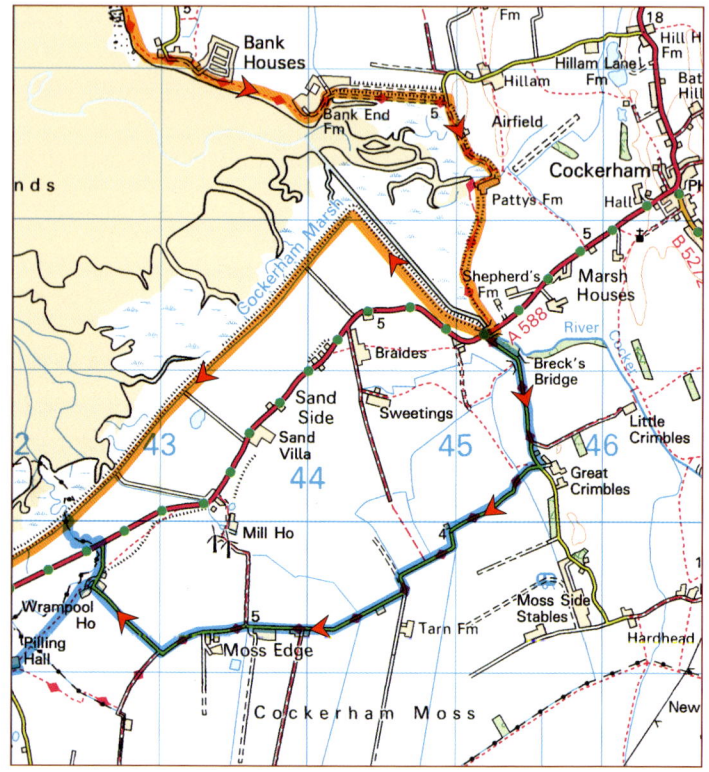

The late 12th-century **Hospital of St Mary** became an abbey around 1192 under the Premonstratensian Order, until its dissolution in 1539. The ruins are accessible from the path, although the only intact section is the Chapter House, which survived due to its use as a mausoleum by a local family until the 19th century.

As the floodbank turns west again, drop briefly onto a concrete slope then road seaward of **Bank Houses** and a caravan park. A track then circuits the marsh, passing a giant memorial seat and table, to **Patty's Farm**. Stay on tarmac below the farm, turn left after the buildings onto more floodbank, then cross Cocker Bridge. Cockerham and its bus stops are 1.5km up the road to your left.

STAGE 19 – CONDER GREEN TO KNOTT END

Boats at Glasson Dock, beyond the Lancaster Canal extension's final lock gates

Map continues on page 148

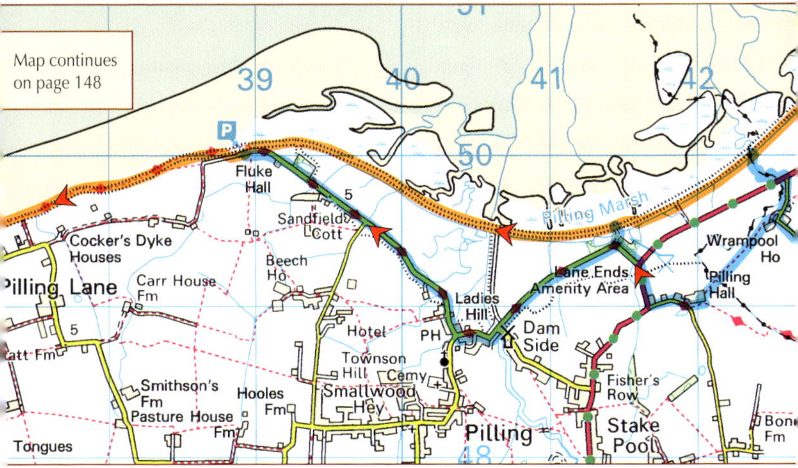

WALKING THE KING CHARLES III ENGLAND COAST PATH: NORTH WEST

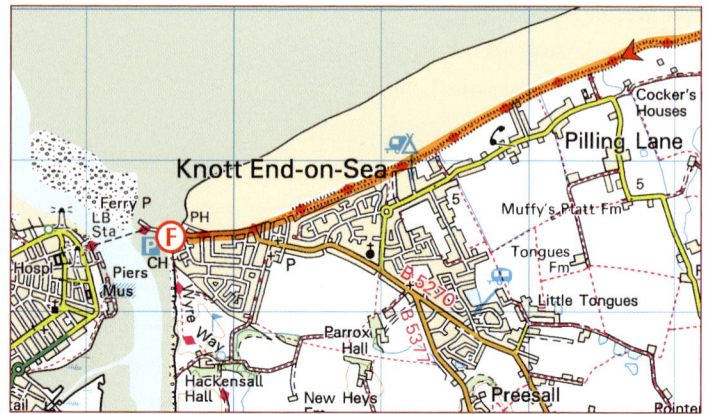

Cocker Bridge to Knott End
(12.5km, 3hr 10min)
This section is a really important refuge area for birds, including the fields in winter, so please follow instructions on signage and keep to the waymarked path.

April to August: Turn left up Crimbles Lane then right on Gulf Lane. Once the ECP is open, cross the A588 to rejoin the coast beyond **Wrampool House**. In the meantime, take public rights of way from Wrampool House to Pilling Hall and Lane Ends. Turn left behind the floodbank. Climb steps onto the floodbank just before Lane Ends car park and continue to **Fluke Hall** car park. Until the ECP opens you may need to drop to marsh at the far end so check tide times. You can also unofficially reach Pilling on a floodbank running directly south from the trail to Broadfleet Bridge.

The Wyre Ferry links Knott End and Fleetwood – but don't forget it can't run at low tide!

September to March: From Cocker Bridge drop to the landward side of the floodbank for 5km to **Lane Ends**. Climb steps onto the floodbank to Lane Ends car park. Use the road to Pilling, keeping right at junctions after a bridge to rejoin the main trail at **Fluke Hall**.

Another 4.5km of floodbank transitions gently from rural to urban. At **Knott End**, pass left of the Bourne Arms for the bus stop, café and toilets (in the car park). The ferry to Fleetwood for Stage 20 is straight ahead.

PART 3 – WYRE TO WALES

Part of New Brighton's Mermaid Trail, based on the 18th-century local legend of the Black Rock Mermaid who was spotted on what is now Fort Perch Rock (Stage 26)

Walking the King Charles III England Coast Path: North West

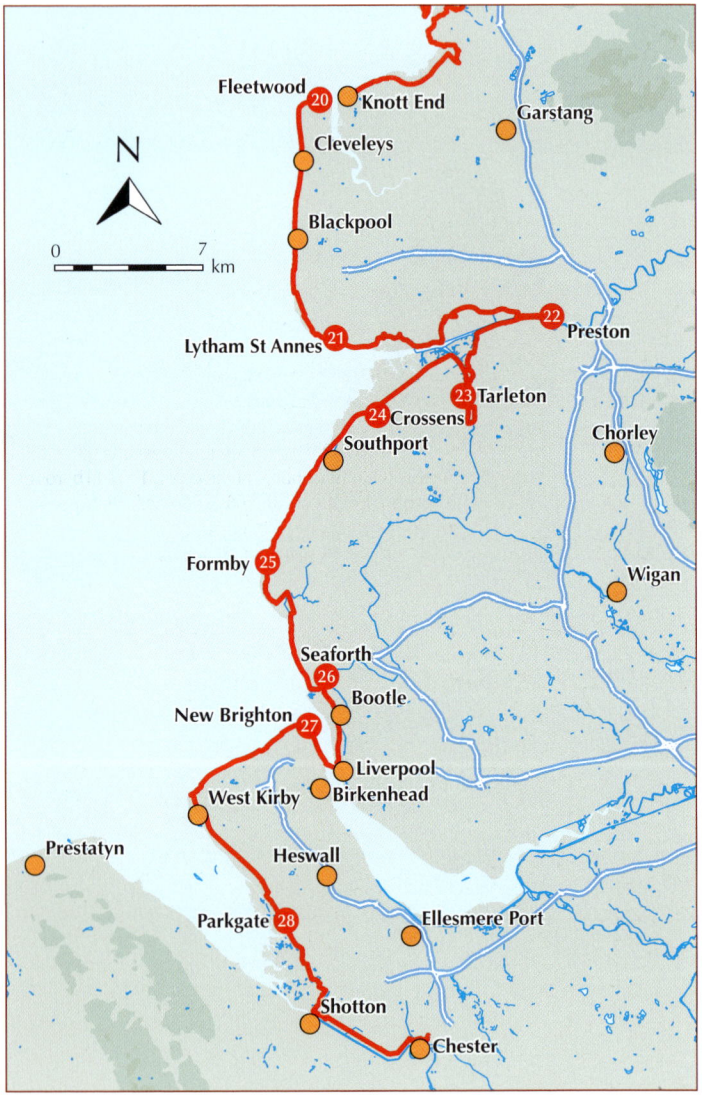

STAGE 20
Fleetwood to Lytham

Start	Fleetwood ferry dock, SD 339 484
Finish	Lytham, car park west of Lifeboat Station, SD 365 269
Time	7hr 15min
Distance	28.6km (17¾ miles)
Ascent	65m
Terrain	Promenade, short beach sections
Refreshments	Various in Fleetwood, Cleveleys, Blackpool, St Anne's, Fairhaven and Lytham prom
Toilets	Options on or near trail throughout
Transport	Trains between Blackpool North and Lytham. Trams between Fleetwood & Starr Gate. Various buses cover the route – the most useful services are 1 from Fleetwood to Blackpool via the coast, 11 & 11b from Blackpool to Lytham, and 68 & 68c from Blackpool to Preston via much of Stage 20 and 21
Accessibility	Good – shore sections can be bypassed on roads
Parking	Free on Fleetwood and Lytham proms; copious other free and paid options throughout the stage
Accommodation	Lots throughout via booking sites, including some motorhome sites and budget hotels
KCIIIECP status in 2025	Expected 2025, but all walkable sooner

This is the second-longest day in the book, on account of easy mileage on the prom, but also adaptability thanks to copious accommodation and eateries, and excellent public transport. It's surprisingly varied, with options to alternate the walking surface in adjacent parks, gardens, dunes and beaches; alternately the amount of prom enables some excellent (if occasionally crowded) all-abilities wheeling. Why not stay over in Blackpool and indulge in some classic seaside nostalgia?

Stage 20 – Fleetwood to Lytham

Fleetwood to Gynn Square (13km, 3hr 20min)

Turn right off the ferry, passing maritime memorials and a clock tower, keeping right after a patch of dune. Continue for 9km past **Rossall Point** (the technical end of Morecambe Bay) and **Cleveleys**. When the road moves inland at **Little Bispham**, take the cycle path for 3km of pleasant clifftop parkland to a roundabout just past the Gynn Square tram stop.

Gynn Square to Starr Gate (6.7km, 1hr 40min)

Drop back to the promenade. The ECP takes the 'middle' prom towards the North Pier, but any level will do. Pass **Blackpool Tower** (labelled Tower on map) and the Comedy Carpet. After **South Pier**, veer right around the casino to continue past rollercoasters and public artworks to Starr Gate, where both prom and trams end.

BLACKPOOL – THE QUINTESSENTIAL SEASIDE HOLIDAY

Blackpool's fame began in the 18th century, as sea bathing for health became popular, and primarily provided holidays for Lancashire's factory workers. In the 19th century, the three piers were built, and electric lighting installed on the promenade – a world first, and precursor to the modern Blackpool Illuminations. The town's entertainment scene became world famous, with venues like the Royal Palace Gardens, Winter Gardens and of course Blackpool Tower hosting music hall and variety shows throughout, alongside the 20th and 21st century's most-loved television performers and comedians, as celebrated in the prom's 'Comedy Carpet' mosaic, and the new Showtown Museum.

The unmissable Blackpool Tower – and a more unusual means of transport on your fairytale journey!

Walking the King Charles III England Coast Path: North West

Stage 20 – Fleetwood to Lytham

Starr Gate to Lytham (9km, 2hr 15min)

Officially, the ECP turns inland then right on road then dune, but thanks to dune access improvements, the parallel beach now makes a better walk with plenty of high tide escape routes.

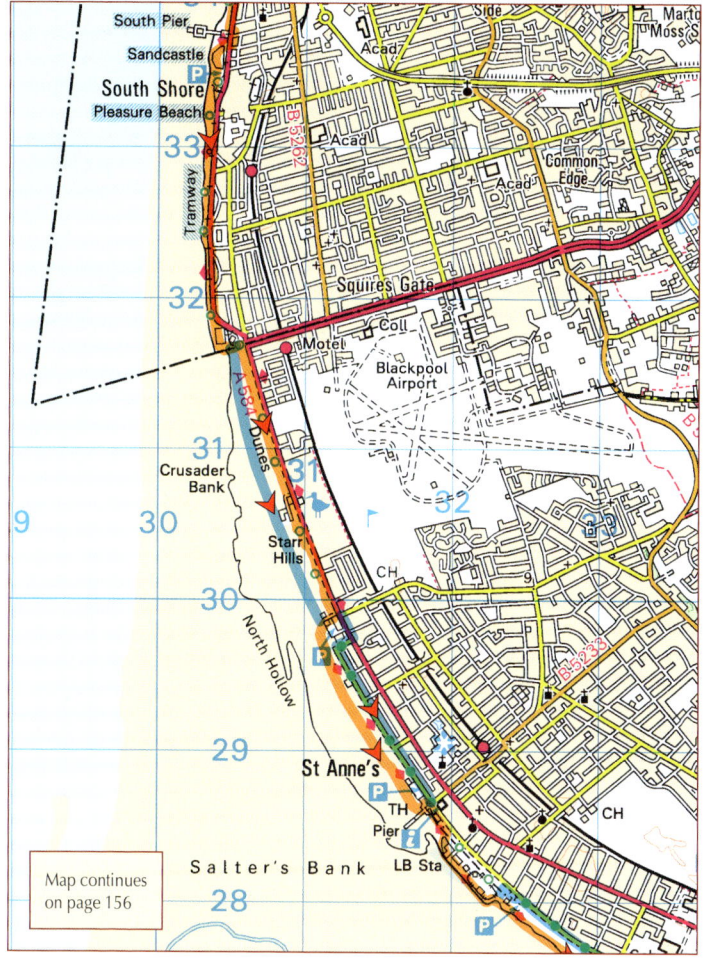

Beyond Starr Gate the St Anne's dunes and beach are a welcome change for concrete-weary feet

If taking the road, drop into the dunes where stable enough, bypassing a red-brick building on pavement. Continue in the dunes then turn right on a track past a café then left on a firm, sandy beach. Use the high tide route behind buildings and dunes if needed.

Turn left just before **St Anne's Pier**. Pass its entrance to join the prom, keeping right of a small boating lake, then past chalets to more dunes. Descend steps onto the beach. Stay above for high tide/step-free route. Follow the shore as it turns from beach to saltmarsh. Take steps onto the promenade past Fairhaven Lake, which continues to **Lytham** through a public green.

At a car park 150m before the lifeboat station, turn left for trains and town centre via Dicconson Terrace.

STAGE 21
Lytham to Preston

Start	Lytham, car park west of Lifeboat Station, SD 365 269
Finish	Penwortham Bridge, Preston, SD 528 288
Time	5hr 45min
Distance	22.1km (13¾ miles)
Ascent	40m
Terrain	Fields, marsh, pavement and cycle path
Refreshments	Various in Lytham centre; McDonalds near Lytham Dock; Costa and garage shop, Savick Bridge (A583); various in Preston (off-trail)
Toilets	Lytham prom; Preston Ashton Park (off-trail); Penwortham Recreation Centre
Transport	Trains to Lytham and Preston. The 68 & 68c buses serve most of this stage.
Accessibility	A-road pavements and cycle path should be okay for wheels; rest to be confirmed. Very loud when airfield and motocross are operational.
Parking	Various options on the green at Lytham and approaching Preston; free at Holme Road end, west end of Penwortham Bridge
Accommodation	Various in Lytham, Freckleton and Preston; a handful elsewhere
KCIIIECP status in 2025	Expected 2025; all walkable using high tide route

Stage 21 jumps straight back into estuary territory. The Warton section passes between airfield and wild marsh – a curious juxtaposition when fighter jets are operating at close range. The public footpath past the airfield is due for major improvements; until then expect some wet terrain.

Due to significant obstacles on the riverbanks including sewage works and landfill, the next section is on main roads with no through routes in the Coastal Margin. The wet fields host many rare wintering and breeding birds, which are sensitive to disturbance and a major risk to jets if put up unexpectedly. If 6.5km of pavement doesn't appeal, the number 68 buses are on hand. Thankfully, the docks and cycle path into Preston are an enjoyable compensation.

Walking the King Charles III England Coast Path: North West

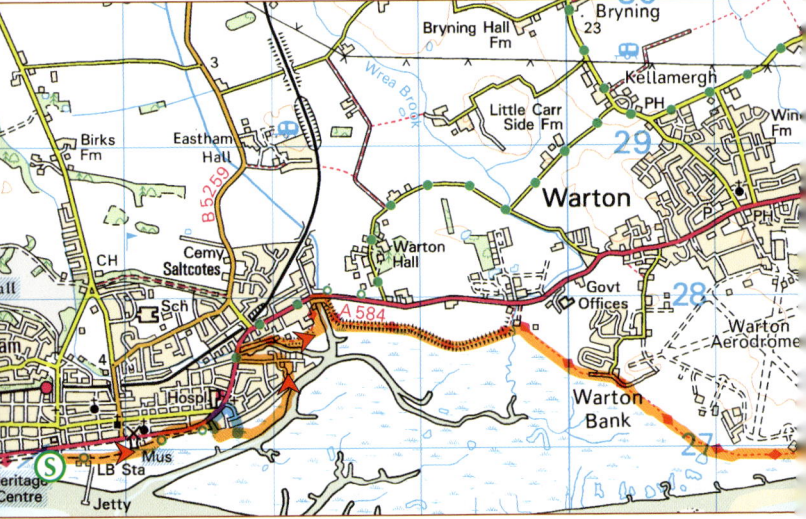

Lytham to Warton Bank (5.8km, 1hr 30min)

At the end of the promenade turn right onto the shore, or left for a high tide route behind buildings. Climb steps beyond the retaining wall, and continue through a grassy park. At the end, turn inland through black metal gates into a housing estate. At junctions, go right, left, and right again onto the main road. Cross the bridge and turn immediately right on a floodbank, then through trees. Continue back inland past a boatyard to cross another road bridge. Turn right for 2.4km of floodbank, passing Brook House partway. Until the ECP opens, a short detour inland crosses Wrea Brook at the road.

Warton Bank to Freckleton (A584) (6km, 1hr 40min)

Drop onto a lane past **Warton Bank**; at the end turn right in a corridor past animal pens. Follow field edges then the airfield fence.

> Should one of Warton's jets take off over your head, it'll definitely be memorable. The **Warton Aerodrome** was created in early World War 2, during which it became a US Air Force base. Postwar, it became an aircraft development and testing site, and continues to do so under BAE's ownership. Its most famous creation is the Eurofighter Typhoon – which at close range feels more apt to Star Wars than rural Lancashire!

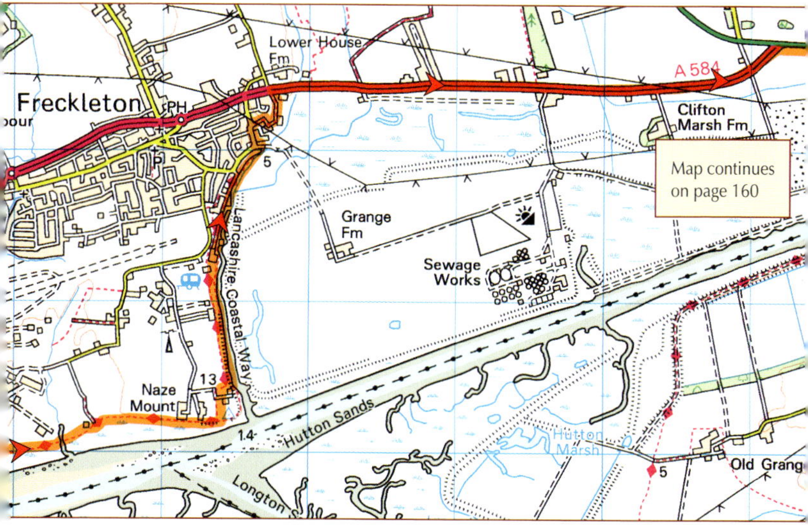

STAGE 21 – LYTHAM TO PRESTON

Map continues on page 160

Lytham's windmill and final length of prom

Cross a large footbridge then follow the back of the marsh for 1km. The very highest tides may need waiting out. The path heads left into trees 150m before Dow Brook meets the Ribble near **Naze Mount**.

Turn right at the next junction, then left, parallel with Dow Brook. After 1km, descend a concrete then gravel path between houses to the riverside. When the track turns inland, keep ahead, to the right of gardens and fences, to pop out on a road. Turn left, then soon right down Lower Lane.

After 150m turn right on a grassed lane, becoming the tarmac Brades Lane, then right on the A584 dual carriageway, or cross and turn left for the bus.

Freckleton (A584) to Penwortham Bridge (10.3km, 2hr 35min)
Follow the A584 for 3.5km then keep right on the A583.

Once open, the path should turn seaward before a service station, but the route is under review so you'll need to follow waymarks accordingly.

At high tide, and until ECP opens, keep going on the A583, then right on Nelson Way, to meet the cycle path into Preston by the **Ribble Steam Railway** & Museum.

Take the cycle path upriver. At the docks, keep going to the roadside swing bridge then right to circuit Bullnose Point. If you're in a hurry, cross a lock bridge straight onto Bullnose Point, or bypass Bullnose from the swing bridge. Continue on the riverside cycle path for nearly 2km, passing under the first road bridge, to Penwortham Bridge.

For the city centre and trains, turn left for 700m up Fishergate Hill. There are bus stops near the trail.

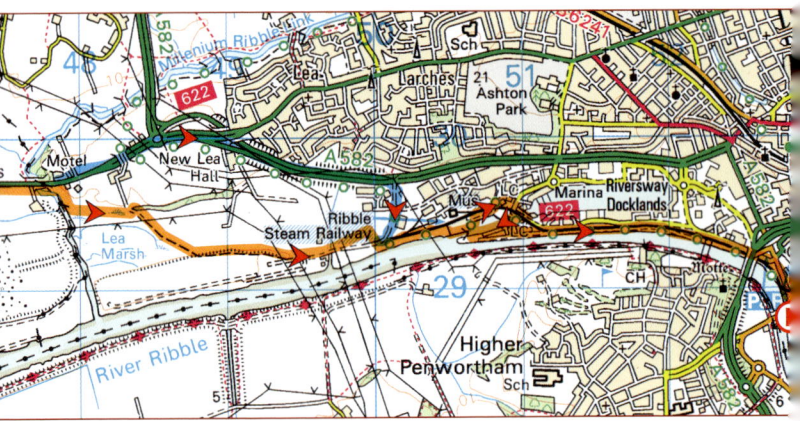

STAGE 22
Preston to Tarleton

Start	Penwortham Bridge, Preston, SD 528 288
Finish	Tarleton Lock, SD 455 214
Time	4hr 40min
Distance	18.4km (11½ miles)
Ascent	20m
Terrain	Cycle path, fields, floodbank
Refreshments	Various in Preston and Penwortham (off-trail); Dolphin Inn, Longton; various in Tarleton
Toilets	Penwortham Recreation Centre; Dolphin Inn for customers; Church Road and cafés in Tarleton (off-trail)
Transport	Trains to Preston (off-trail). Bus 2 links Preston, Penwortham, Longton, Walmer Bridge, Much Hoole and A59 (for Tarleton) with Southport and Liverpool
Accessibility	Cycle path and floodbank may be wheel-friendly, dependent on infrastructure upgrades. Very loud opposite motocross and jets from Stage 21
Parking	Free at Holme Road end (Penwortham Bridge); Marsh Lane and Station Road ends, west of Longton and Much Hoole; Plox Brow and roadsides in Tarleton
Accommodation	Various in Preston; a handful of self-catering options in Hesketh Bank (start of stage 23) and other off-trail villages
KCIIIECP status in 2025	Expected 2025, but all walkable

A quicker, smoother journey today, mostly on floodbanks. From close-up urban nature to boatyards, open marshes and sweeping skies, the interest changes constantly. It should be tide-free, so your main consideration is a gap in the trail at the day's end, pending aspirations for safer river or road crossings, but you can get round it on the A59 pavement – just take great care crossing the road, especially at rush hour. The no. 2 bus is also a good option. The statistics listed in this stage assume that the link is walked on the most direct 'local' route, but do plan for up to 1.6km extra in case the river is high, or the lane from Plox Brow is unavailable.

Walking the King Charles III England Coast Path: North West

Penwortham Bridge to Station Road (Walmer Bridge) (11.4km, 2hr 45min)

Over Penwortham Bridge, turn right onto 6.5km of riverside, transitioning from tarmac to wide grassed floodbank. Information panels just after the A582 road

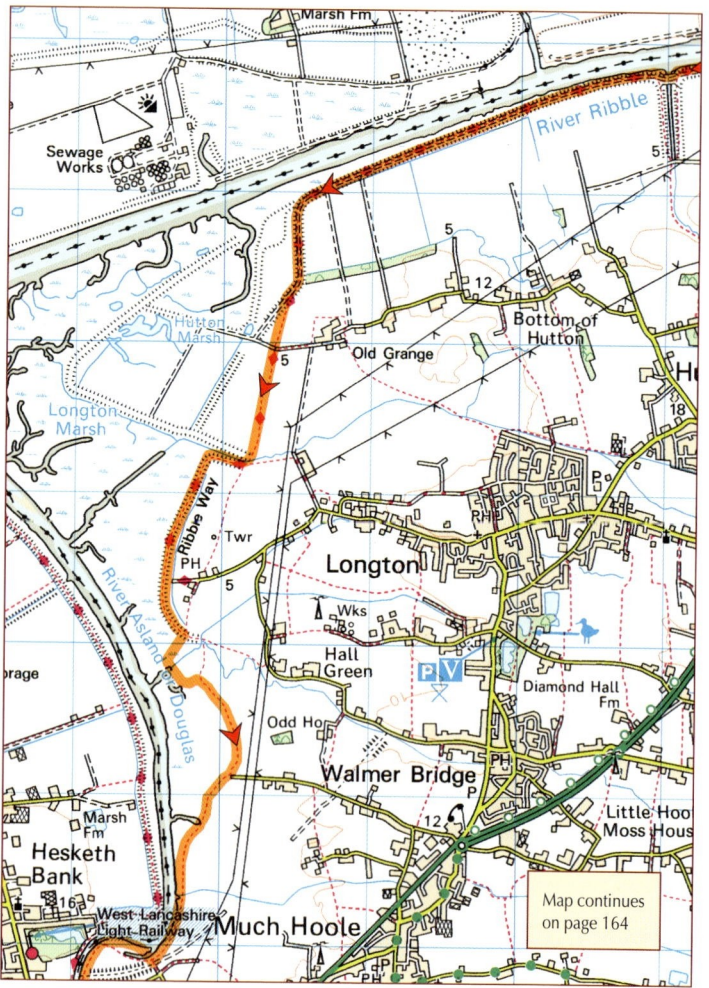

STAGE 22 – PRESTON TO TARLETON

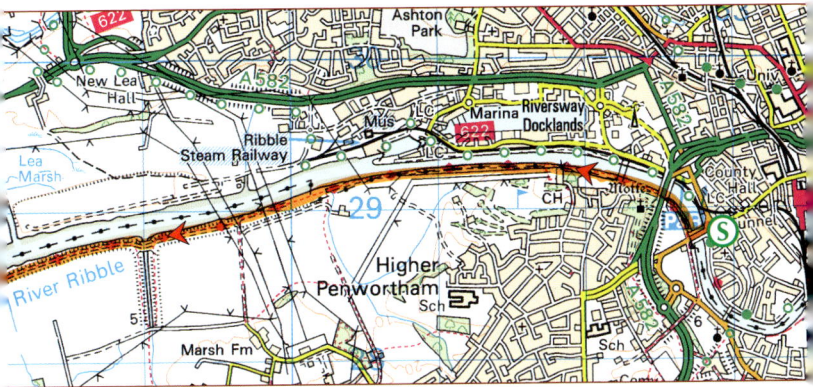

PRESTON

'Preston' derives from the Old English for 'Priest's Town'. It was passed by major Roman roads, and became a market town in 1179. Woollen textiles were produced there from the 13th century, leading up to its being one of Lancashire's industrial centres. Situated on the banks of the tidal River Ribble, it also has a dock, passed on the ECP, which operated until 1981. In 2002 Preston was granted city status to mark Queen Elizabeth's Golden Jubilee.

bridge highlight an adjacent motte and bailey castle. When the bank splits near a large old tank, go left.

After the next bend in the bank, turn left through a field, across a track, then along a second field edge. Now take the second of two floodbanks on your right, turning left at its end for 1.3km. A path junction partway leads to the nearby Dolphin Inn. At the end, take another right on more floodbank, then into an initially wooded corridor between fields to a road end.

Station Road to A59 east　　　　　　　　　　　　　　　(4.2km, 1hr 10min)
Cross, and keep right on more banking in the field, then on marshside becoming riverside. 2km beyond a sharp bend opposite a boatyard, you'll reach the current end of the ECP near the A59.

A59 to Tarleton link routes　　　　　　　　　　　　　　(2.8km, 45min)
If preferred, take the 2 or X2 bus which stops a short way down the A59 to your right.

Boats returning to Preston marina on the Ribble near Hutton

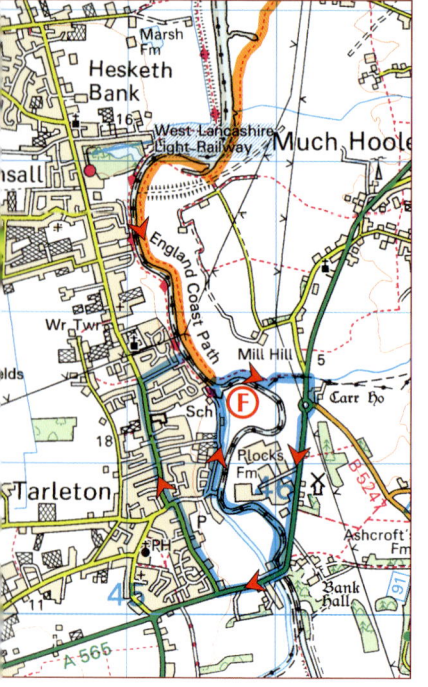

Otherwise, carefully cross the road and turn right on pavement for 1.3km until you've crossed the river. For the most direct route, at your own risk, turn left through a gateway to cut under the A59 road bridge (muddy and floodable) between the river and canal and walk down the riverside to cross the canal at Plox Brow. From there, locals usually continue on a canalside track to Tarleton Lock where the ECP restarts at the canal and river confluence. However, this lane is private land and not always open – if closed, join roads through the town between Plox Brow and Sutton Avenue.

If you're more comfortable taking the 'legal' route – or if the river is too high – continue to traffic lights at the next road junction. Right turns down Coe Lane, Hesketh Lane (the main road through the town) and Sutton Avenue will return you to the ECP for Stage 23.

STAGE 23
Tarleton to Crossens

Start	Tarleton Lock, SD 455 214
Finish	Fiddler's Ferry road bridge, Crossens, SD 376 206
Time	3hr 55min
Distance	15.3km (9½ miles)
Ascent	15m
Terrain	Riverside path and grassed floodbank
Refreshments	Various in Tarleton centre and off-trail in Hesketh Bank, Banks and Crossens, but none en route
Toilets	Church Road and cafés in Tarleton (off-trail)
Transport	Buses 2 & X2 serve Preston, Tarleton, Crossens and Southport; 40, 44, 47, 49 & 347 link Crossens and Southport
Accessibility	Pushchairs and smaller mobility scooters may be able to access the RSPB floodbank from the car park. Benches available near RSPB car park and Douglas/Ribble confluence. Loud jets from Warton airfield
Parking	Free roadside parking near either end, space for a couple of cars at the path end in Fiddler's Ferry
Accommodation	Somewhat sparse other than some off-trail AirBnBs and campsites; using buses from Southport may be easier
KCIIIECP status in 2025	Open

This stage could mainly be described as 'follow the floodbank' – all 13km of it. But that would betray the constant attractions: the Douglas's heritage trail, the marsh restoration projects and nature reserves, and the sheer sense of openness and freedom without devoting too much energy to navigation or terrain. However, although there are plenty of escape routes, it's some distance inland to buses and there's no facilities en route, so do go prepared for a full day's expedition with no shelter. And definitely don't forget the binoculars!

Tarleton Lock to RSPB viewpoint (7.8km, 2hr)

From Tarleton Lock, head downstream for 1.6km, then continue through the middle of the Douglas Boatyard. At the far-right corner, exit onto 3.7km of floodbank to the mouth of the Douglas. After another 2km, back on the Ribble now, drop

WALKING THE KING CHARLES III ENGLAND COAST PATH: NORTH WEST

briefly through the RSPB's **Hesketh Out Marsh** car park at SD 421 250 and back to the bank. Benches and information panels make for a good lunch stop.

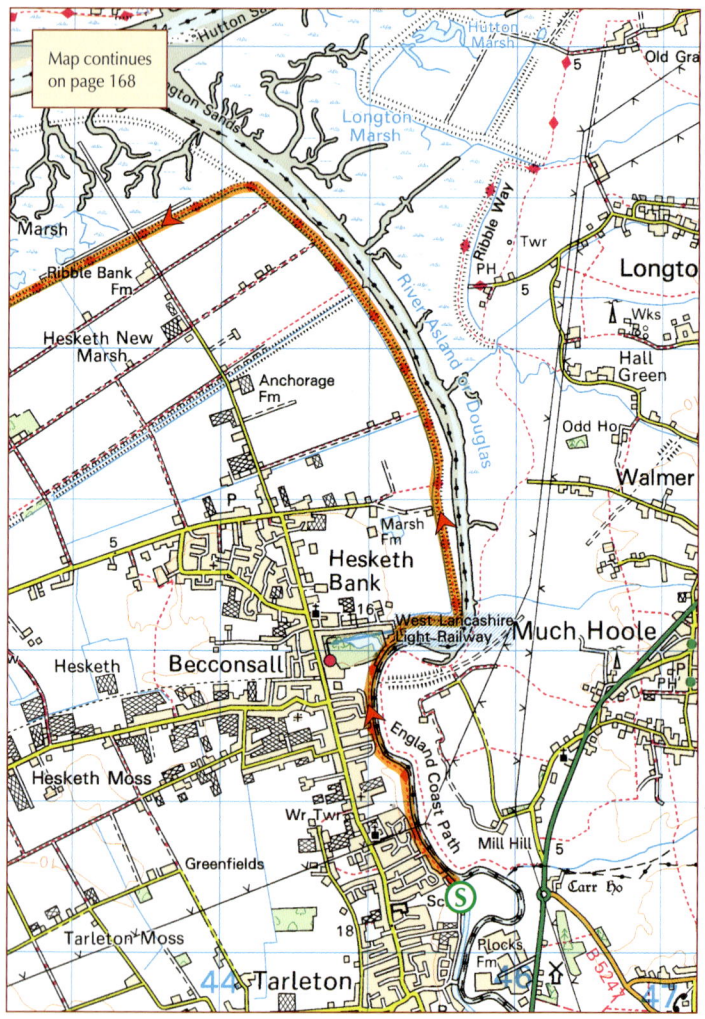

There's every chance part of your packed lunch started life right next to the Ribble

The Arctic Tern sculpture 'One Wing Among Many' marks the restoration of Hesketh Out Marsh in 2016

Thanks to a **saltmarsh restoration project** between the RSPB, Environment Agency and Natural England, Hesketh Out Marsh has seen massive changes here. By breaking through the outer floodbank, this 'managed realignment' has allowed saltwater to re-flood the area, rapidly returning it to saltmarsh. It's home to waders, egrets, ducks and geese year-round, plus swooping marsh harriers; and in summer, avocet and terns breed on artificial nest islands. Saltmarsh is also a natural flood defence, slowing the tide, and creating more floodplain space to accommodate rising sea levels.

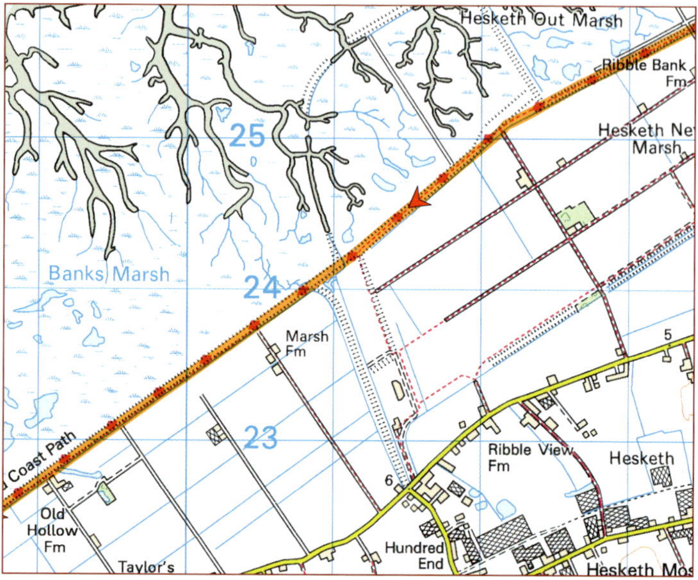

WALKING THE KING CHARLES III ENGLAND COAST PATH: NORTH WEST

Idyllic skies and vast views from the Ribble Estuary NNR near Old Hollow Farm

Stage 23 – Tarleton to Crossens

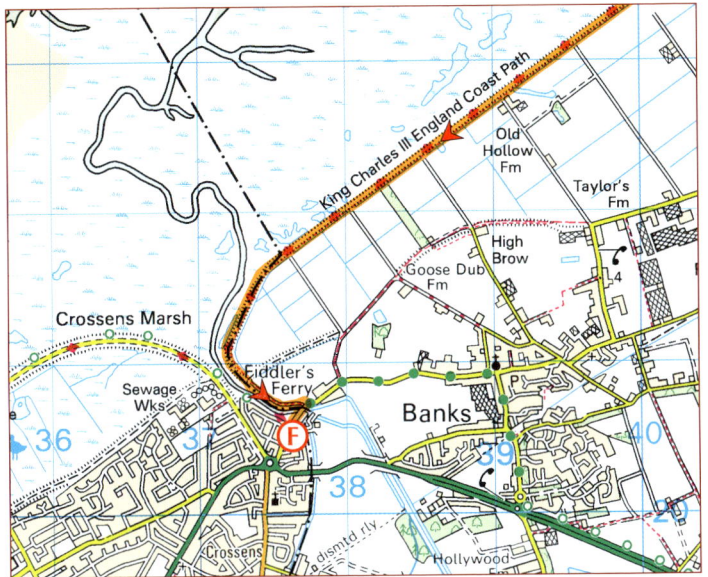

RSPB viewpoint to Crossens (7.5km, 1hr 55min)

Keep going. When the outer floodbank returns north of Hundred End, you're leaving the RSPB site, but still within the wider NNR. At **Old Hollow Farm**, pass through two kissing gates either side of a marsh access track. These are tighter than usual due to space constraints, and mark the end of the buggy accessible length.

After another 2km the floodbank starts to curve, and soon after follows the riverside to a small parking area by the road at **Fiddler's Ferry**. Turn right on pavement opposite Crossens Pumping Station to cross the road bridge.

Congratulations: you've completed Cumbria and Lancashire – welcome to Sefton!

Follow the road ahead for Crossens and bus stops on Rufford Road or Preston New Road.

STAGE 24
Crossens to Formby

Start	Fiddler's Ferry road bridge, Crossens, SD 376 206
Finish	Formby National Trust site, Freshfield, SD 277 082
Time	5hr 10min
Distance	18.6km (11½ miles); plus 1.3km to station
Ascent	20m
Terrain	Promenade then mainly soft dune
Refreshments	Various via detours into Southport, Ainsdale and Formby, but none guaranteed on the route
Toilets	Southport centre, Ainsdale Shore Road and National Trust car park, Freshfield
Transport	Railway is roughly 1.5km inland with stops at Southport, Birkdale, Hillside, Ainsdale, Freshfield and Formby. Various buses link Crossens and Southport, with the 2X extending to Formby and Liverpool; 300 links Southport and Liverpool; F4 shortens the link to Formby centre
Accessibility	Dunes beyond Southport can be tough going; path width varies depending on vegetation growth and footfall erosion
Parking	Various paid car parks in Southport; National Trust site at Freshfield. Free on Weld Road near Birkdale station and beach car parks at SD 320 164 (Birkdale) and SD 297 126 (Ainsdale)
Accommodation	Hotels including budget Travelodge in Southport; holiday parks, motorhome sites and B&Bs in Southport and the Ainsdale area
KCIIIECP status in 2025	Open

After a swift start on pavement between marshes, then Southport prom, you'll reach the north-west's biggest dune system. Although your muscles might disagree as you battle soft terrain, it's highly varied and extremely enjoyable, with wetlands, scrub, and the Formby pines; home to red squirrels, the National Trust, and in 2019, crashed Martians courtesy of the BBC's War of the Worlds filming. You could do Birkdale to Crosby in a day,

STAGE 24 – CROSSENS TO FORMBY

avoiding the detour into Formby, but splitting the commitment is wise – the sand makes for much slower going; even stable paths will erode to sand over time. It's also well worth swapping at least part of it for the seemingly endless wild, dune-backed beach if the tide's out.

Crossens to Southport Pier (6.1km, 1hr 35min)

Turn immediately right back onto riverside, which soon joins a cycle path on pavement alongside Marine Drive between the landward and seaward marshes of the RSPB Marshside reserve, before taking in **Southport**'s promenade.

Trains, buses and facilities are in the town centre, slightly inland from the pier, behind Marine Lake and Princes Park.

A mixture of vegetation, loose sand and wet dune slacks create a perfect balance of habitats for different wildlife species

Alongside the inevitable Adventure Coast and Splash World resorts, you'll find the Marine Lake and lovely gardens to explore and relax in, between **Southport**'s town centre and the prom; plus attractive Victorian architecture and the Iron Pier. It's a good base for the whole Sefton and Mersey coast thanks to regular trains on the Southport and Liverpool line – you could even combine with the annual Southport Flower Show or Air Show in summer.

Southport Pier to Ainsdale Shore Road (6.4km, 1hr 50min)

Continue down the prom and, shortly after leaving Southport, a waymarked path drops slightly onto marsh and dune, soon passing the seaward end of a car park to continue straight ahead. From here, follow the waymarks as best you can. Desire lines on the ground can vary rapidly as local access patterns change, and there are few distinct landmarks, so the waymarked route may not always feel like the most intuitive. GPS may be helpful here. Generally, the route goes straight ahead, keeping just landward of a series of dune slacks, marshy areas and a line of trees. Beyond those, keep landward of another marshy area for about 1km, then look for a waymark pointing you left. Follow the path slightly inland, over a footbridge, then a little more inland towards a large building. The former nightclub now boasts Paul Curtis's full-building sand lizard mural.

STAGE 24 – CROSSENS TO FORMBY

Walking the King Charles III England Coast Path: North West

Ainsdale Shore Road to Formby NT site (6.2km, 1hr 45min)

Take the road in front of the hotel, passing public toilets and a former holiday park. Re-enter the dunes at the far end. Keep right along a fence and through the next gate. Now turn left, keeping right at a fork just ahead. Once again, follow the waymarks, but be aware that other, easier routes may present themselves over time. You'll pass through scrub, summer flowers, natterjack toad pools and bare sand. After passing a large marsh or pond (depending on time of year), you'll enter the **Ainsdale Sand Dunes** NNR. Follow a fence for 650m. Shortly beyond its far corner, turn left to the pine forest. The path now winds through trees for 600m before reaching the Fisherman's Path (after the Old Fisherman's Path!), a beach access track. Cross it half-left to the onward path. In another 2km you'll meet the National Trust's access track to **Formby** beach.

Toilets and refreshment vans are just left; Freshfield station is 1.3km straight up the track then Victoria Road; the F4 bus stops slightly closer on Squirrel Green and Shireburn Road.

STAGE 25
Formby to Seaforth

Start	Formby National Trust site, Freshfield, SD 277 082
Finish	Potters Barn, Seaforth, SJ 324 974
Time	4hr 35min
Distance	16.5km (10¼ miles); plus 1.3km from Freshfield station
Ascent	40m
Terrain	Dune, woodland, cycle path
Refreshments	Mobile ice cream and coffee vans at National Trust car parks and Crosby promenade; cafés at Crosby Leisure Centre and behind Marine Lake
Toilets	National Trust car park, Freshfield; Crosby Leisure Centre
Transport	Railway is 300m to 1.5km inland at Freshfield, Formby, Hightown, Hall Road, Blundellsands, Waterloo and Seaforth. Bus X2 links Formby, Seaforth, Southport and Liverpool; 300 links Southport and Liverpool; 53 & 54 link Seaforth and Liverpool; plus local F3 bus around Formby
Accessibility	Dunes are tough going and loose in places, path width varies depending on vegetation growth and footfall erosion. Prom from Hall Road is good for wheels with plenty of rest stops. Book beach wheelchairs at NT Formby.
Parking	Paid at National Trust site, Freshfield; free roadsides near Hightown station; free at Crosby Leisure Centre; paid at Burbo Bank/Hall Road prom and Marine Lake
Accommodation	Most B&B and self-catering offers are centred on Crosby; but public transport links easily to Southport or Liverpool options too
KCIIIECP status in 2025	Open

Another very enjoyable, if occasionally hard-going, day. The last section on cycle path and promenade is much easier than the continued dune system, and Anthony Gormley's famous 'Another Place' sculptures will undoubtedly draw you beachwards. The day ends at Seaforth, where Liverpool's docks

Walking the King Charles III England Coast Path: North West

begin. A final curiosity is Potter's Barn, a never-completed replica of La Haye Sainte – the farmhouse on the Waterloo battlefield. From here, buses (on the A565) and trains (at Waterloo station) link you to Liverpool and Southport.

Formby NT site to south Formby (5.9km, 1hr 40min)

After turning left for 50m on the NT's track, turn right. Keep right, left then right again at the main path junctions ahead, as you pass through more forest, sand and fields. A gravel track then leads through open grassland to the NT's Lifeboat Road car park.

Keep right on tarmac to another dune path at the far seaward corner. Go left at a path split, then cross another sandy track to enter trees again briefly. Follow waymarks through more dune, overlapping in places with the Lost Resort and Devil's Hole trails.

AINSDALE & FORMBY DUNES

While much of the ecological importance of dune habitats and their wildlife are shared between the Sefton, Fylde and Cumbrian coasts, the Sefton dunes have an entirely unique character. The product of ten thousand years of post-glacial blown sand, this 21km stretch of dune is a SSSI and almost all managed as nature reserve between the National Trust, local authorities and Ainsdale Sand Dunes NNR team. A number of themed trails celebrate the unique features, such as the Asparagus Trail where the land was reclaimed for asparagus crops; the Lost Resort – as the name suggests, an attempt to create a seaside resort long since abandoned to the mercy of the dunes; and the Devil's Hole – a dune blowout thought to be created by a wartime bomb. The Formby Pines are an unmissable curiosity – originally planted to try to stabilise the dunes, they are now a habitat in and of themselves. Sefton's specialist dune species include sand lizards and the northern dune tiger beetle, one of the fastest beetles in the world!

Passing through Formby's famous dune forest

Walking the King Charles III England Coast Path: North West

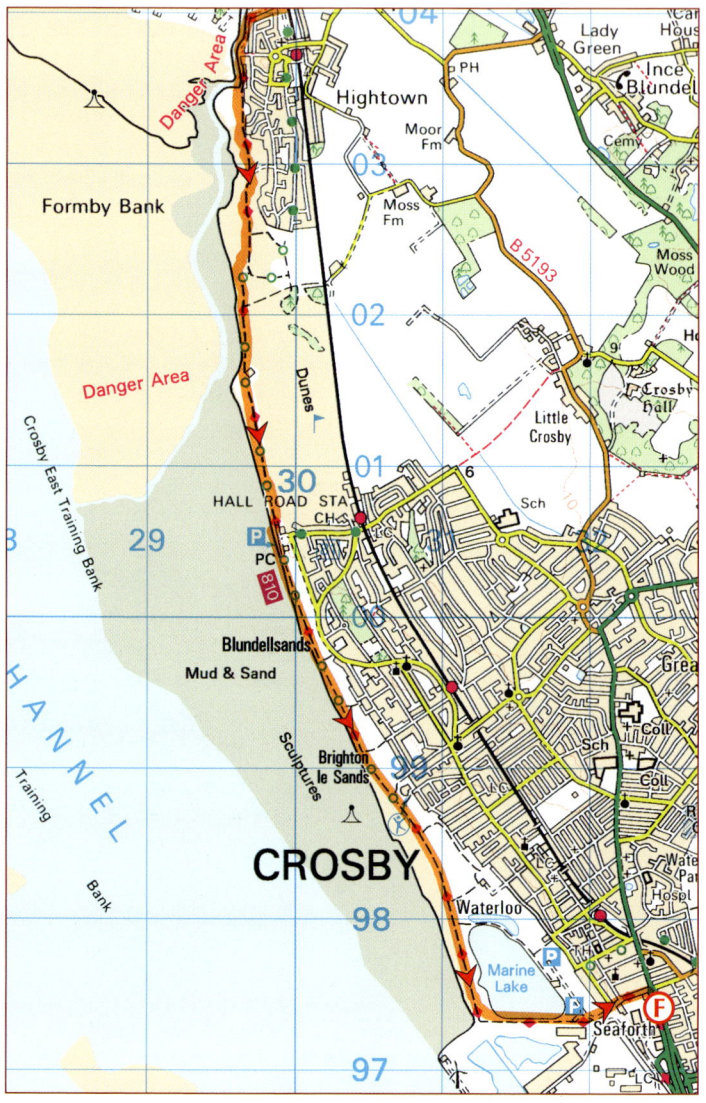

Anthony Gormley's 'Another Place' installation comprises 100 cast-iron figures over 3km of beach.

After about 1km, pass seaward of a house, where views towards the Liverpool Docks begin to open up, then cross a sandy track into the Ravenmeols Sandhills Local Nature Reserve. Continue on the Devil's Hole trail for another 1km or so, then turn left for 1.4km between the small Cabin Hills NNR and MOD's Altcar Rifle Range boundaries.

South Formby to Blundellsands Sailing Club (3.4km, 55min)

At a junction, turn right with the MOD fence on 2km of cycle path. Or keep left (ahead) in fields for the F3 bus to Formby centre from Park Road.

Turn right past the rifle range entrance, still following the boundary, then left along the River Alt.

Keep right onto the riverside marsh path, then straight ahead when the river curves right. Continue through dune for 650m to the **Blundellsands Sailing Club** car park. Remains of an ancient submerged forest can be accessed from the car park.

Blundellsands Sailing Club to Potter's Barn, Seaforth (7.3km, 2hr)

Cross the car park and continue through about 1km more dune, then the Sefton Circular cycle path to Crosby. Continue past Anthony Gormley's famous 'Another Place' beach installation. The cycleway is losing its battle with the dunes – expect loose sand, or bypass on beach or adjacent grassland.

Finally, follow the cycle path inland past the Crosby Marine Lake then a car park. Follow the path round to the left, then keep right on pavement to the A565 road junction, passing a park and the Potter's Barn ruins on the corner.

STAGE 26
Seaforth to New Brighton

Start	Potters Barn, Seaforth, SJ 324 974
Finish	New Brighton Pumping Station, SJ 312 941
Time	2hr 55min (plus ferry)
Distance	11.7km (7¼ miles)
Ascent	35m
Terrain	Pavement and cycle path
Refreshments	The Lake House, behind Marine Lake; occasional shops through Bootle and Liverpool; Bramley Moore pub, Regent Road; Pier Head and Seacombe ferry terminal cafés; The Ferry, Egremont; various in New Brighton
Toilets	Ferry terminals
Transport	Trains at Waterloo, Seaforth, Bootle New Strand, Bootle Oriel Road, Bank Hall, Sandhills, Moorfields, Liverpool James Street, Hamilton Street and New Brighton. Buses 53 & 54 link Seaforth and Liverpool centre; 136 runs parallel to ECP to James Street Station, near Pier Head and Albert Dock; 101 sightseeing bus links Liverpool centre and Pier Head; various services link Liverpool centre, Seacombe and New Brighton
Accessibility	Pavement and cycle path throughout; Mersey Ferry is wheelchair accessible.
Parking	Paid at Crosby Marine Lake, Albert Dock, roadsides near Pier Head, and Seacombe ferry terminal; free at New Brighton Marine Lake and various side streets including near New Brighton station
Accommodation	Available throughout – budget options include Liverpool and New Brighton Travelodges and similar, and Albert Dock YHA
KCIIIECP status in 2025	Open

Your enjoyment of today's first part depends how intrigued you are by the Liverpool docks. It's potentially a fascinating walk with closer (albeit well-fenced) views of the cranes you'll later see across the Mersey, and interesting

STAGE 26 – SEAFORTH TO NEW BRIGHTON

old buildings along the way. Football fans may delight, depending on loyalties, at passing the new Everton stadium, but expect it to be busy on match days. If 8km of urban pavement is too much, take a semi-rest day using the 136 bus to James Street, and explore the north-west ECP's cultural highlight, the Albert Dock, before the Mersey Ferry drops you in Seacombe for a much more serene walk on the Wirral. Either way, this is a shorter day to allow time for the Mersey crossing. If neither the ferry or replacement bus are running, ECP signage maps link walks via James Street and Hamilton Street stations.

Seaforth to Pier Head (8km, 2hr)

Turn right on the A565 then keep right to the Port of Liverpool entrance. Turn left on pavement along its fence, and straight on for 2.4km after the A565 rejoins you. You'll pass a Go Outdoors if any kit is due a replacement. Turn right down Millers Bridge (the A5058) then left on Regent Road. Pass more docks, industrial sites, the new Everton stadium, and the old docks' turreted stone gateways for 3.5km. At a roundabout turn right then cross the next one, rejoining the Mersey on Princes Parade. Pass the cruise terminal gates. A short inland diversion bypasses the terminal when in use – but you'll need to backtrack for a step-free version. Pass left of the Titanic Memorial then cross open ground to the Gerry Marsden (Pier Head) Mersey Ferry terminal.

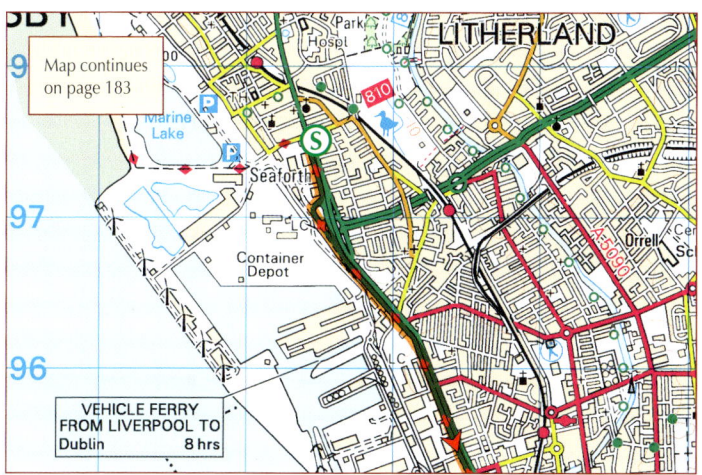

181

The ferry terminal at Seacombe, where the Wirral section starts

PIER HEAD AND ALBERT DOCK

Best seen from the ferry and east Wirral, the iconic Liverpool skyline centres around Pier Head, where the Liverpool length of the ECP gives way to the famous 'Ferry Cross the Mersey'. Most striking from a distance are the early 20th-century Liver Building, built as an insurance company headquarters and featuring sculptures of the mythical Liver Bird, Liverpool's cormorant-like mascot; the Cunard Building hosting the ship company; and the Port of Liverpool Building, home of the Docks and Harbour Board; collectively known as the 'Three Graces'. Alongside Pier Head are the Beatles statues, the Museum of Liverpool, featured in the 2021 Doctor Who series, and the Albert Dock, now home to a Tate Modern gallery, a Beatles museum, restaurants and much more.

Seacombe to New Brighton (3.7km, 55min)

Take the ferry to Seacombe. Turn right out of the terminal on 4km of promenade to the north eastern corner of the Wirral peninsula at **New Brighton**. The quickest route to the train station and town centre is left up Victoria Parade opposite the Art Deco-style concrete pumping station, although you could access via Atherton Street from the north shore to reduce the distance on Stage 27.

STAGE 26 – SEAFORTH TO NEW BRIGHTON

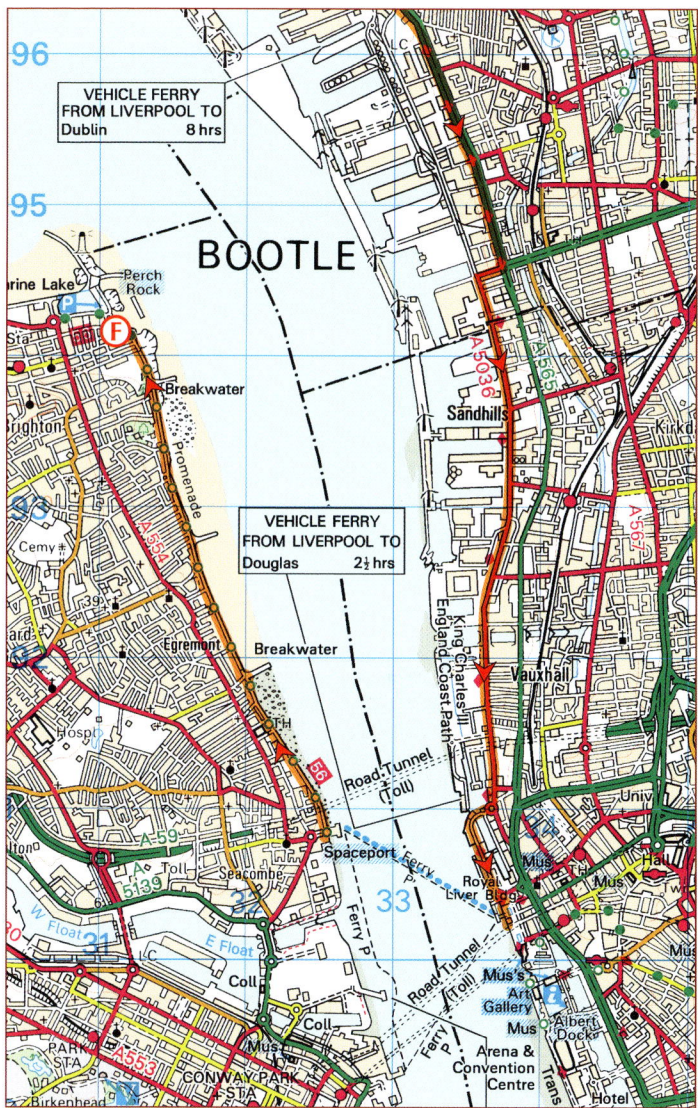

STAGE 27
New Brighton to Parkgate

Start	New Brighton Pumping Station, SJ 312 941
Finish	Old Quay pub, Parkgate, SJ 280 778
Time	7hr 20min
Distance	28.4km (18¼ miles)
Ascent	100m
Terrain	Cycle path, pavement, dune, saltmarsh, beach, fields, promenade
Refreshments	Various in New Brighton; cafés, ice creams and Morrisons in West Kirby; cafés at Wirral Country Park, Thurstaston; the Boathouse, Old Quay and others in Parkgate; various others en route
Toilets	Morrisons, New Brighton; Leasowe (before lighthouse); Meols Parade; West Kirby; Wirral Country Park, Thurstaston; School Lane, Parkgate
Transport	Trains to New Brighton, and between West Kirby and Neston. Various buses link New Brighton & Wallasey to Seacombe and beyond; the 407, 38A & 38B link Meols, Hoyland and West Kirby; and the 22 links West Kirby and Parkgate
Accessibility	Prom and pavements then cycle path with plentiful benches. Rocks and sand between Hilbre Point and West Kirby – high tide route on road. Use Wirral Way cycle path to avoid crumbly clifftops and marsh south of Wirral Country Park, and a narrow path and steps south of Gayton Cottage
Parking	Free at New Brighton Marine Lake, Leasowe Gunsite car park, North Wirral Country Park, Hoylake prom, Banks Road and Parkgate Old Baths; paid at West Kirby and Wirral Country Park, Thurstaston
Accommodation	B&B and self-catering options throughout including New Brighton, Hoylake, West Kirby and Parkgate; motorhome site at Wirral Country Park
ECP status in 2025	Open

Stage 27 – New Brighton to Parkgate

This penultimate stage – the last you'll spend wholly on ECP – is also the longest, so you'll feel suitably accomplished by tomorrow! It takes in the majority of the Wirral peninsula stretch, so like the Blackpool stretch has options for splitting the route, especially at West Kirby. You can also finish Stage 26 a little further around New Brighton or Wallasey to get a head start, assuming your Mersey Ferry crossing runs smoothly. Bear in mind the Neston and Shotton trains run on separate lines to West Kirby and New Brighton, so there's no direct link between the start and finish. You'll also need to bear the tides in mind at West Kirby and Heswall. There are sections of the trail which move inland to avoid tidally affected and ecologically sensitive areas, but the shore does sit within unrestricted coastal margin so can be used with care. Enjoy some easy walking and a satisfying combination of promenade, dune and rurality around this stunning corner of England, with plenty of appetite-whetting views to north Wales!

THE WIRRAL PENINSULA

The area of land between the River Mersey and the River Dee has been inhabited since the Neolithic era, with Meols in particular producing many finds proving its importance as a historical international trading port. The ever-present Romans have their place in Wirral's history, as do the Celts, Anglo-Saxons and Vikings. Like Cumbria, many place names allude to this Norse influence – including Meols itself, named for its dunes. Agriculture, fishing and shipping were key industries in the Medieval period – Hoylake is named for the former 'Hoyle Lake', a natural deep-water channel formed by sandbanks in the Dee Estuary. Like Blackpool, tourism arrived with the 18th century trend for sea bathing, and saw the development of New Brighton as a popular holiday and entertainment destination. Originally wholly within Cheshire, the majority of the peninsula was redesignated as part of Merseyside in 1974.

New Brighton to West Kirby   (15km, 3hr 45min)

Past the pumping station, keep right past **Marine Lake** and left before Fort Perch Rock.

> The current **defensive structure**, designed to protect the Port of Liverpool, replaced the earlier Perch Rock lighthouse in the 1820s. It now hosts a café and escape rooms.

Walking the King Charles III England Coast Path: North West

Leaving Hilbre Point for the Red Rocks Nature Reserve and West Kirby beach

Follow 8.5km of promenade cycle path, passing beach, golf course, dunes, Leasowe Lighthouse, saltmarsh, the 'Wader's Walk' artworks and an RNLI station, to the prom's end at The King's Gap. A car park before the lighthouse leads to a snack bar. Turn left, then zigzag right on Cromer Road, left on Curzon Road and so on, to Stanley Road. Go straight ahead on The King's Gap for the high tide route to West Kirby – the pinch point is at the far end, so check tide times here to save backtracking. Turn right here, past a golf course and houses to Hilbre Point.

Turn left on the beach and left again on a path between reedbeds and

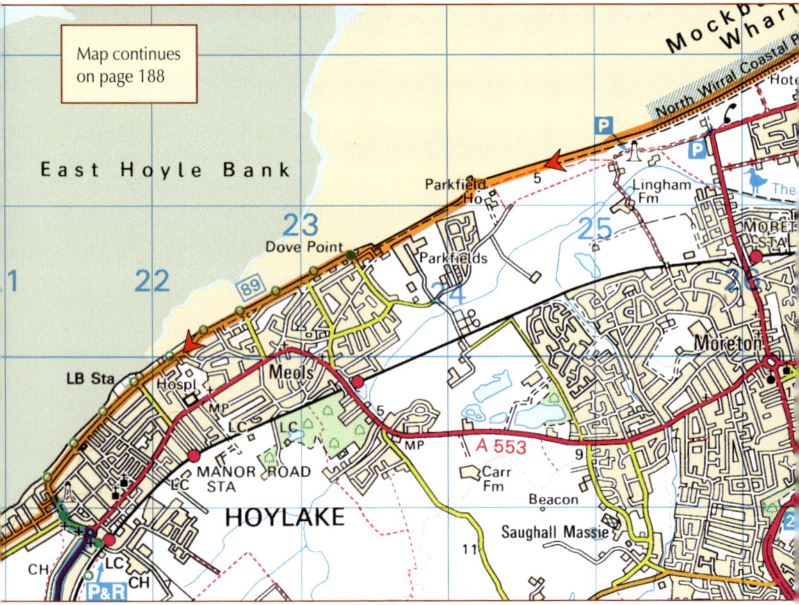

Stage 27 – New Brighton to Parkgate

dune in Cheshire Wildlife Trust's Red Rocks reserve, then on beach, to **West Kirby**. Natterjack toads may be present – please keep dogs out of ponds.

It is possible to walk to **Hilbre Island**, named after a medieval chapel dedicated to St Hildeburgh, at low tide, but see noticeboards at West Kirby for the latest safe route and timing advice.

West Kirby to Wirral Country Park (4.9km, 1hr 15min)
Leave the beach then turn right past cafés and through a car park onto Marine Lake's sea wall. Use the road if flooded or stormy. At the end, head inland past a sailing club and take the second right onto Macona Drive. Keep ahead through Cubbins Green then slightly left to meet the Wirral Way. Follow this now, past a golf course. After a caravan site and road underpass, turn right past the **Wirral Country Park** visitor centre (with toilets and café).

Wirral Country Park to Gayton Cottage (5.7km, 1hr 35min)
Turn left on the clifftop path for 1.5km, passing through the wooded Tinker's Dell partway, and the National Trust's Heswall Fields. Turn right on a short track to the

STAGE 27 – NEW BRIGHTON TO PARKGATE

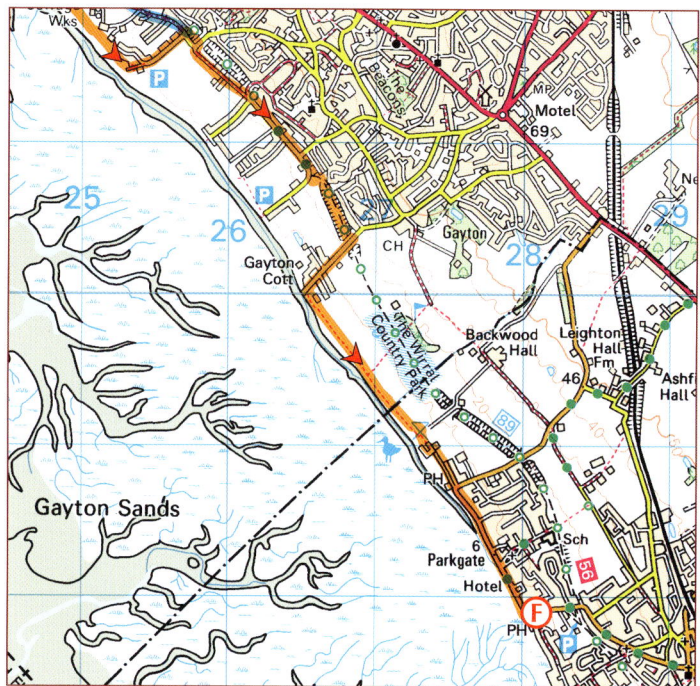

shore. Head left for 250m, then continue on shore (or high tide route as appropriate) past the sewage works. On the main route, turn left up Banks Road, where the high tide route returns. Turn right on road and right again on a tarmacked public byway. Or join the Wirral Way at Banks Road for a traffic free alternative. At the byway's end, continue on road, then 600m of the Wirral Way. At the Cottage Lane waymark turn left, then right on road, to the marsh by **Gayton Cottage**.

Gayton Cottage to Parkgate (2.8km, 45min)
Ascend steps to the sometimes narrow sea wall. Follow this to the Parkgate Old Baths car park and bathhouse remains. Continue past the Boat House pub and along Parkgate's attractive prom to the Old Quay pub on the main road corner.

Buses are available past the Old Quay pub, and at various locations on the front.

STAGE 28
Parkgate to Welsh border/Chester

Start	Old Quay pub, Parkgate, SJ 280 778
Finish	England/Wales border, SJ 305 732; Hawarden Bridge (for Shotton) railway station SJ 310 694; or Chester railway station, SJ 412 669
Time	1hr 25min / 2hr 45min / 6hr 15min
Distance	5.8km (3½ miles) to border; 11.1km (7 miles) to Hawarden Bridge station & Shotton; 23.9km (15 miles) to Chester
Ascent	10m / 35m / 55m
Terrain	Cycle path, floodbank, canal towpath
Refreshments	Old Quay and others in Parkgate; Harp Inn, Little Neston; Nets Café, near Burton Marsh; various in Shotton; various in Chester including the Town Crier Pub by the station
Toilets	School Lane, Parkgate; Chester station and city centre
Transport	Trains at Neston, Hawarden Bridge, Shotton and Chester. Bus 22 links Parkgate and Chester; 10, 10A & 11 link Shotton and Chester; 204 links WCP link route on Dee Industrial Estate (Tenth Avenue stop) with Chester
Accessibility	Good on cycle path from Little Neston to Chester
Parking	Free at Parkgate's Old Baths car park; Denhall Lane/ Station Road lane ends, Burton Marsh; Shotton station; paid at Chester station
Accommodation	Various options at Parkgate, Neston and Chester; sparse at Shotton
ECP status in 2025	Open

Welcome to the home straight as you dip into Cheshire for the last 5.6km of England, and the ECP! Somewhat inconveniently, the border sits in the middle of a marshside cycle path just north of an industrial estate, so once you're there, you'll need to retrace your steps, continue to Hawarden Bridge

STAGE 28 – PARKGATE TO WELSH BORDER/CHESTER

or Shotton stations, depending on which line you need, or even better, finish at Chester. As it's a far more attractive reward for a whole month of walking than an industrial estate, this guide describes a route to Chester station using the Wales Coast Path and associated link routes. Alternatively, because the odd border locations mean the ECP and WCP don't directly meet, a waymarked route links the two between the Welsh border and Hawarden Bridge – just in case you're planning to keep going!

PARKGATE, NESTON AND BURTON

The villages of Neston and Little Neston date back to Viking and Anglo-Saxon times. Over the years they've experienced life as a busy port and trading centre along with neighbouring Parkgate, and were the home of the Neston collieries until 1927.

Parkgate began life as a 13th-century deer park, then 17th-century fishing village, and later a port and holiday destination. It's difficult to imagine Parkgate as a shipping centre now, as centuries of silting have left the shore a well-vegetated saltmarsh with only the highest of tides coming close.

Nearby Burton Marsh is not only the link between England and Wales, but also between the RSPB's Dee Estuary and Burton Mere sites, and an MOD firing range – so keep dogs safely on the path.

Parkgate's historic black and white buildings and saltmarsh

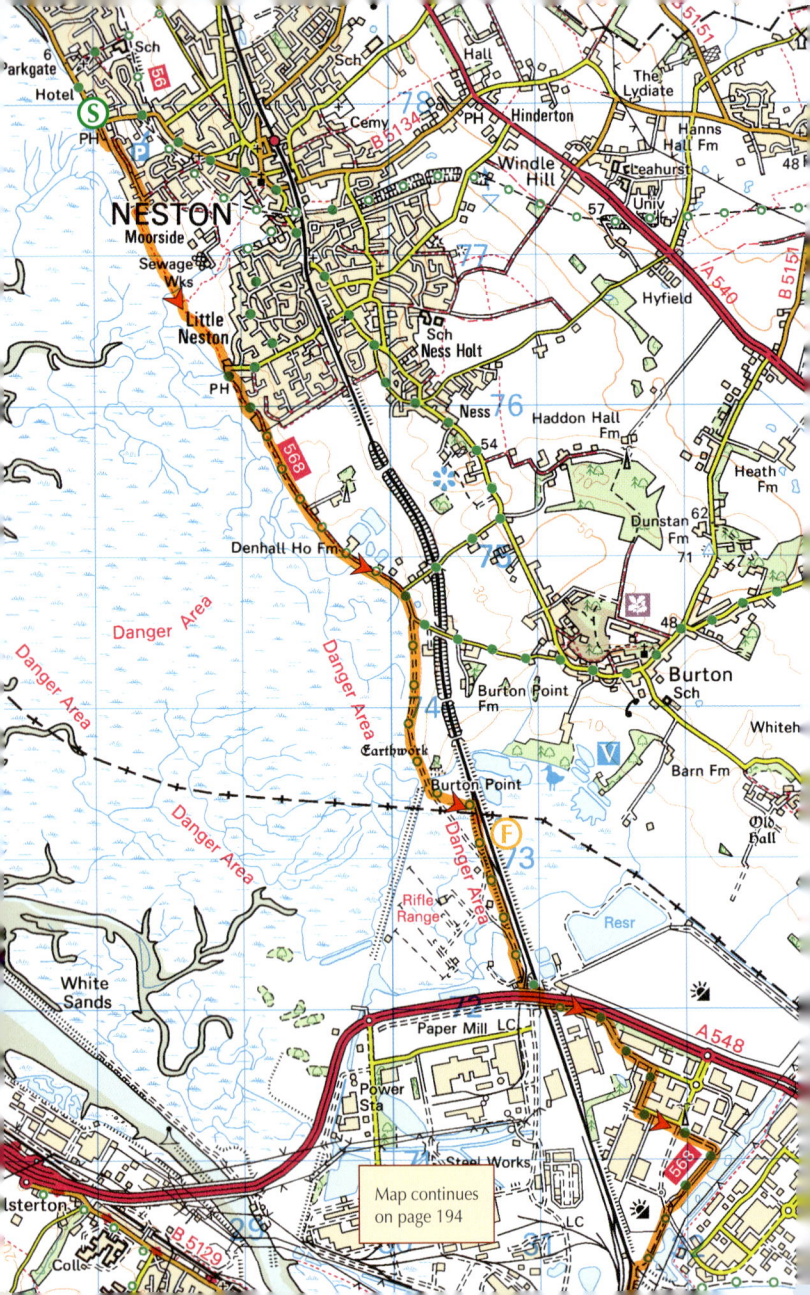

Stage 28 – Parkgate to Welsh border/Chester

Approaching Little Neston and Denhall Quay

Parkgate to Welsh border (5.8km, 1hr 30min)

At the prom's end, keep ahead then left on a walled footpath. Turn right on a residential road then short cycle link to the onward Manorial Road South. At the end, turn right to access a marshside path on gravel, fields and road, eventually passing the Harp Inn and remains of Denhall Quay. Information points en route focus on Neston and Denhall Quay's 18th- and 19th-century coal mining history.

Follow the road past houses then more marsh as it becomes a cycle path. After 1.4km continue on road briefly, then right onto the RSPB's Burton Point cycle path, with somewhat incongruous MOD warnings. After extreme tides, the path may be closed for debris clearance. When you reach the 'Croeso i Gymru' (Welcome to Wales) boulder, congratulations – you've completed the King Charles III England Coast Path – North West.

Now you just have to find your way home – or the Wales Coast Path for another 1400km!

Welsh border to Hawarden Bridge station (for Neston/Wirral rail connections and Wales Coast Path) (5.3km, 1hr 20min)

Continue on the cycle way, turning left to pass under the railway then road. Keep left for just under 1km, then right down a one-way street (against the traffic). Follow it round to the left, then go straight ahead on a vehicle-free cycleway. At a junction, continue ahead, soon joining the railway, then right at a junction in

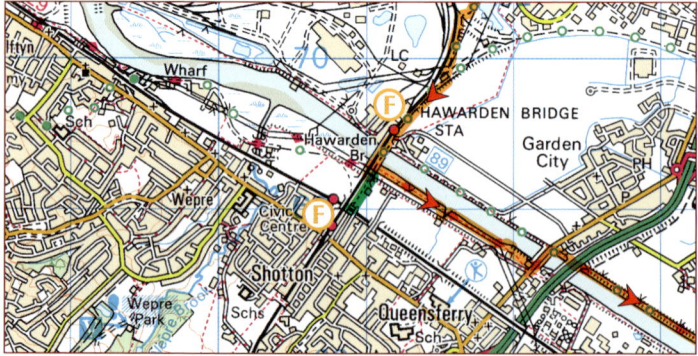

trees, to Hawarden Bridge railway station. Cross the rail and foot bridge to meet the Wales Coast Path (WCP) on the south bank of the Dee.

Hawarden Bridge station to Shotton station (for Chester/North Wales line)
(0.6km, 10min)
Cross Hawarden Bridge and continue on the cycle path (just to your left) to Shotton station, which is on two levels. The town, buses and further facilities lie just ahead.

On the brand new marshside path and lookout point near Neston

Stage 28 – Parkgate to Welsh border/Chester

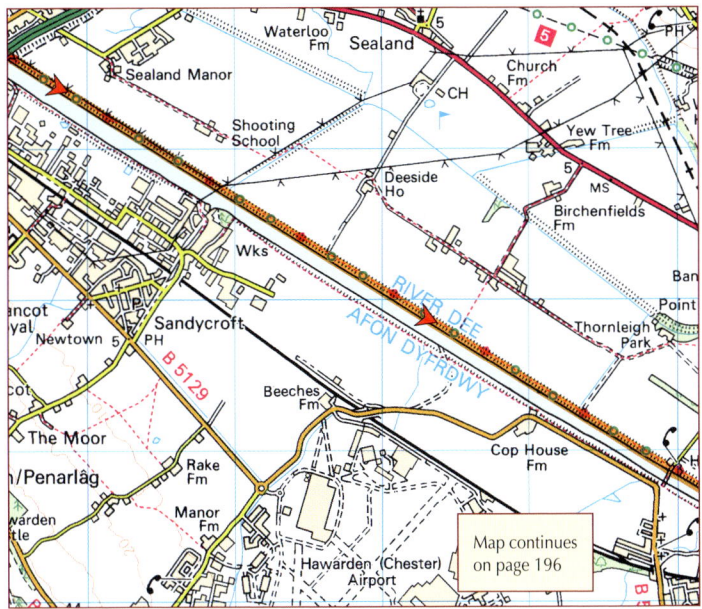

Hawarden Bridge station to Chester station (12.7km 3hr 15min)

You can turn left on a direct route just before **Hawarden Bridge**; but to lessen the tarmac, cross it then turn left on the Wales Coast Path (WCP). After 1.3km the WCP crosses back over the impressive Welsh Road bridge then turns right on a tarmac cycle path for 7.25km along the Dee. Partway along you'll pass the end of a footbridge at the historical Higher Ferry crossing point. Multiple installations mark the end (or start) of the WCP as you re-cross the border. In another 1.5km the riverside path ends.

For the recommended WCP to Chester link, keep right and right again past a skate and play park as you enter the town. At the end, go half-left across the road and up Catherine Street. Pass through a doorway in the wall ahead and turn right, crossing a lock, through the historical canal basin. Go under a road then the railway on the towpath. Pass a series of locks. Access the city walls or city centre by turning right after the locks. Stay on the towpath to the Old Harker's Arms then ascend steps and turn right on the road to the station – and a welcome pub to celebrate journey's end!

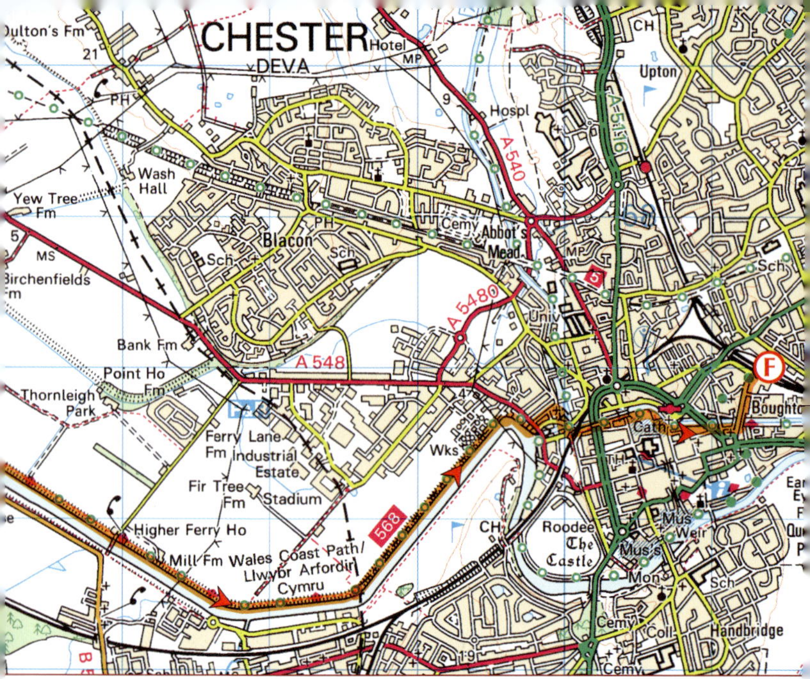

Chester's stunning architecture, including its cathedral, makes it a much more rewarding end to your journey

Don't forget your selfie with Eric Morecambe! (Stage 17)

APPENDIX A
Accommodation table

Stage	Location	Name	Type
1	Gretna	The Gretna Chase Hotel	⬡
		Braids Caravan Park	✻
1	Metal Bridge	Metal Bridge Inn	⬡ ⬡ ✻
	Todhills (off-trail)	Travelodge Carlisle Todhills	
	Rockcliffe/Cargo	King Garth	⬡
2	Knockupworth	Vallum House	⬡
		West View, Grinsdale Bridge	⬡
2	Carlisle	Plenty on booking sites, plus:	⬡ ⬡ ⬡
		Carlisle City Hostel	⬆
		Travelodge Carlisle Central	⬡
2	Boustead Hill	Highfield Farm	⬡ ⬡
		Hillside Farm	⬡ ⬆
2	Easton	Midtown Farm B&B	⬡
2	Glasson	Glendale Holiday Park	⬡
2	Port Carlisle	Hope & Anchor	⬡
3	Bowness-on-Solway	The King's Arms	⬡
		Wallsend Guest House & Glamping Pods	⬡ ⬡ ⬡
		Bowness on Solway Camping & Glamping	⬡ ⬡ ✻

Appendix A – Accommodation table

⬢ hotel ⬢ B&B/guesthouse ⬢ self-catering/glamping ⬆ hostel/bunkhouse
⬢ camping ✱ campervan/touring caravan

Tel	Web/email	Comments
01461 337517	gretnachase.co.uk enquiries@gretnachase.co.uk	Next to start of trail on Sark Bridge
07538 750803	the-braids.uk info@the-braids.uk	
01228 672492	facebook.com/metalbridgeinn metalbridgeinn508@hotmail.com	Inn, pods and campervans
08719 846127	travelodge.co.uk	
07762 286050	kinggarth.co.uk janehodgson@yahoo.co.uk	Rustic off-grid 2-bed on the riverside between the two villages
01228 521860	vallum-house-hotel.co.uk info@vallum-house-hotel.co.uk	
	booking.com	Listed as '1 bed in Carlisle'
	city-hostel.cumbriahotelsweb.com	
08719 846374	travelodge.co.uk	
01228 576060	highfield-holidays.co.uk inf@highfield-holidays.co.uk	B&B, campsite, breakfast available for both
07498 921746	hadrianswalkbnb.co.uk sandrahillsidefarm@gmail.com	Own sleeping bag and towels required for bunkbarn, breakfast available.
01228 576550 / 07967 406937	midtown-farm.co.uk janice@midtown-farm.co.uk	
	booking.com	Individually owned holiday homes & caravans rented via booking sites.
01697 351460	booking.com	
01697 351426	kingsarmsbowness.co.uk info@kingarmsbowness.co.uk	
01697 351055	thewallsend.co.uk info@thewallsend.co.uk	
	www.pitchup.com	

WALKING THE KING CHARLES III ENGLAND COAST PATH: NORTH WEST

Stage	Location	Name	Type
3	Angerton	Inn at the Bush	⬢ ⬢ ✱
3	*Kirkbride*	*White Heather Hotel*	⬢
3	Newton Arlosh	Joiners Arms	⬢
4	**Abbeytown**	No accommodation – use bus to Silloth or stay at Newton Arlosh	
4	Wheyrigg	Wheyrigg Hall Hotel	⬢ ⬢ ✱
4	Skinburness	Marsh Villa, Greenmantle and others	⬢
5	**Silloth**	Solway Holiday Park	⬢ ⬢ ✱
		Queens Hotel	⬢
		Golf Hotel	⬢
5	*Blitterlees*	*Moordale Park Caravan Park*	⬢ ⬢
5	Beckfoot	Rowanbank Caravan Park	⬢ ⬢ ✱
		Bank Mill Visitor Centre	⬢ ✱
5	Mawbray	The Lowther Arms	⬢ ⬢ ✱
		Old Kiln Farm	⬢ ⬢ ✱
5	Allonby	Spring Lea Holiday Centre	⬢ ⬢ ✱
6	**Maryport**	Golden Lion Hotel	⬢
		Harbourside Caravan Park	⬢ ✱

APPENDIX A – ACCOMMODATION TABLE

Tel	Web/email	Comments
01697 369718	roomsatthebush.co.uk manager@roomsatthebush.co.uk Tents & campervans via pitchup.com	
01697 351373	thewhiteheatherhotel.co.uk info@thewhiteheatherhotel.co.uk	*On the Kirkbridge airfield hangar*
01697 352669	facebook.com	Search 'Joiners Arms – Newton Arlosh'
01697 361242	wheyrigghall.co.uk wheyrigg-hall@tiscali.co.uk	*Includes small C&C Club Certificated Site, members only*
	airbnb.co.uk	
01697 331236	cove.co.uk/solway	
01697 331373	bedandbreakfast-silloth.co.uk moregainus@gmail.com	
01697 331438	golfhotelsilloth.co.uk info@golfhotelsilloth.co.uk	
01697 331375	springlea.co.uk mail@springlea.co.uk	
01697 331653	pitchup.com	
07753 913007	campingandcaravanningclub.co.uk	C&C Club Certificated Site, members only
01900 881044	thelowtherarms.co.uk	Campsite booking via pitchup.com; meals available in the pub but book ahead.
01900 881229 / 07747 739442	oldkilnfarmcottages.co.uk info@oldkilnfarmcottages.co.uk	Very small C&M Club Certificated Location, members only; plus glamping pods and holiday cottages
01900 881331	springlea.co.uk mail@springlea.co.uk	Sister site to Moordale Park in Blitterlees
01900 819715	thegoldenlionhotel.org.uk enquiries@thegoldenlionhotel.org.uk	
01900 814431	maryportmarina.com enquiries@maryportmarina.com	

Walking the King Charles III England Coast Path: North West

Stage	Location	Name	Type
6	Workington	Travelodge	🛑
6	Workington	Osborne House B&B	🔵
6	Workington	Washington Central Hotel and The Sleepwell Inn	🛑
6	Lowca (A595)	*Premier Inn Whitehaven*	🛑
6	Parton	*Moresby Hall*	🛑
7	**Whitehaven**	Georgian House Hotel	🛑
7	**Whitehaven**	Lismore Guest House	🔵
7	St Bees	Seacote Hotel & Holiday Park	🛑🔵🟢✱
7	St Bees	*Fairladies Barn Guest House*	🔵
7	St Bees	*Stone House Farm*	🔵
7	*Nethertown*	*Ellergill Raise Campsite (off-trail)*	🟢✱
7	Braystones	Tarnside Park	🔵🟢✱
7	*Beckermet (off-trail)*	*The White Mare*	🛑
8	**Seascale**	Bailey Ground Hotel & Lodge and Keld Green House B&B	🛑🔵🟢
8	**Seascale**	Calder House Hotel	🛑
8	**Seascale**	Westcliff B&B	🔵
8	*Stubble Green, Drigg (off-trail)*	*Shepherds Views Holidays (off-trail)*	🔵🟢✱
8	*Holmrook (off-trail)*	*Lutwidge Arms Hotel*	🛑
8	Saltcotes	Cumblands Farm Caravan and Campsite	🟢✱
7, 8, 9	*Youth Hostel Association options*	*Wasdale and Eskdale YHAs*	▲

Appendix A – Accommodation table

Tel	Web/email	Comments
08719 846 561	travelodge.co.uk	
	booking.com	
01900 65772	washingtoncentralhotel.co.uk info@washingtoncentralhotel.co.uk	
0333 321 9144	premierinn.com	
01946 696317	moresbyhallhotel.co.uk	
01946 696611	georgianhousewhitehaven.co.uk bookings@ghhwhitehaven.co.uk	
	booking.com	
01946 822777	seacote.com	Hotel, static caravans/lodges, tents and tourers
01946 822718	fairladiesbarn.co.uk info@fairladiesbarn.co.uk	
01946 822224	stonehousefarm.net csmith.stonehouse@btinternet.com	
07803 419930	ukcampsite.co.uk	
01946 841308	seacote.com	Static caravans/lodges, tents and tourers; onsite bar
	booking.com	
01946 729786	baileygroundhotel.co.uk baileygroundlodge.co.uk keldgreenhouse.co.uk info@baileygroundhotel.co.uk	Lodge residents can use hotel facilities
01946 728538	calderhouse.co.uk stay@calderhouse.co.uk	
01946 728298	booking.com	
01946 729907	shepherdsviewsholidays.co.uk contact@shepherdsviews.co.uk	
01946 724230	lutwidgearms.co.uk mail@lutwidgearms.co.uk	
01946 724616 / 07580 796559	selfcateringravenglass.co.uk cumblandsfarm@outlook.com	
	yha.org.uk	*YHAs are some distance inland – own transport may be required.*

WALKING THE KING CHARLES III ENGLAND COAST PATH: NORTH WEST

Stage	Location	Name	Type
9	Ravenglass	Ravenglass Camping & Caravanning Club Site	🟢🟢✲
9	Ravenglass	The Inn at Ravenglass The Pennington Hotel Rosegarth Guest House Muncaster Cottages	🔴🔵🟢
9	Muncaster Castle (off-trail)	The Coachman's Quarters	🟢
9	Waberthwaite (off-trail)	The Brown Cow Inn	🔴
9	Newbiggin (off-trail)	Newbiggin Farm Campsite	🟢✲
9	Tarn Bay	Captains House Campervans	✲
9	Selker	Camp Selker	🟢
9	Gutterby/Whitbeck (off-trail)	The Wayside & Whisky Barn	🟢🟢
10	**Silecroft**	*No accommodation available at Silecroft*	
10	Haverigg	Heron House	🔵
10	Haverigg	Harbour Lights campsite	🟢🟢✲
10	Haverigg	Butterflowers Holiday Park	✲
10	Millom	Estuary View Escapes	✲
10	Millom	Horama House	🔵
10	Millom	The Bear on the Square	🔴
10	The Hill (off-trail)	Deer Close	🟢
10	Broughton-in-Furness (off-trail)	Old Kings Head	🔴
11	**Foxfield**	Prince of Wales	🔴
11	Askam-in-Furness	Marsh Farm Caravan Site	🟢✲
11	Barrow-in-Furness (north, off-trail)	Travelodge Barrow-in-Furness	🔵
11	Barrow-in-Furness (north, off-trail)	Premier Inn	🔴

Appendix A – Accommodation table

Tel	Web/email	Comments
01229 717250	campingandcaravanningclub.co.uk	Non-members welcome
01229 717222	penningtonhotels.com	
01229 717222	penningtonhotels.com	Options include 6-person bunk room and bell tents. Self-catering; café available in castle grounds.
01229 717243	thebrowncow-inn.co.uk brown-cow-inn-waberthwaite@outlook.com	
07703 847074	newbigginfarm.co.uk newbiggin-farm@outlook.com	
07535 476740	captains-house.co.uk	5 campervan pitches
	pitchup.com	
01229 718883	thewayside.uk stay@thewayside.uk	The Whisky Barn is, as the name suggests, a specialist in-house bar!
	booking.com	
01229 777300	harbourlightscampsite.co.uk info@harbourlightscampsite.co.uk	
01229 772880	leisureparksltd.co.uk	
07763 490102 / 07713 530589	estuaryviewescapes.co.uk info@estuaryviewescapes.co.uk	
	booking.com	
	booking.com	
	booking.com	1-bed shepherds' hut with hot tub
	booking.com	
	facebook.com	Search 'Prince of Wales Foxfield'. Under refurbishment as of 2025.
01229 462321	ukcampsite.co.uk	
0871 984 6281	travelodge.co.uk	On main road near end of slag bank route
0333 321 9311	premierinn.com	By the Dock Museum

Walking the King Charles III England Coast Path: North West

Stage	Location	Name	Type
12	**North Scale**	Victoria House B&B	🔵
12	*North Walney*	*West Point House* *West Point Woods*	🟢 ⛺
12	South Walney	South End Caravan Park	✱
13	**Vickerstown (central)**	King Alfred Hotel	🔴
13	Barrow-in-Furness (central)	Escape Hotel	🔴
		Holiday Inn Express	🔵
13	Rampside	Clarkes Hotel	🔴
13	*Baycliff (off-trail)*	*The Farmers, Baycliff*	🟢
14	**Bardsea**	*The Ship Inn*	🔴
		Low Fell B&B	🔵
14	*Ulverston (off-trail)*	*The Sun Inn*	🔴
		Town House	🔵
14	Canal Foot	Saltcotes Farm	🔵
		Priory View Certificated Site	🟢 ✱
		The Bay Horse	🔴
15	**Cark**	The Engine Inn	🔴
15	Flookburgh (on high tide route)	Hope & Anchor	🔴

Appendix A – Accommodation table

Tel	Web/email	Comments
	booking.com	
01229 472356	westpointhousewalney.com westpointwoodswalney.com info@westpointhousewalney.com	*Individual rooms with hostel-type self-catering, plus glamping pods; between North Scale and Earnse Point*
01229 472823	southendcaravanpark.co.uk enquiries@secp.co.uk	
01229 471775	kingalfredhotel.co.uk info@kingalfredhotel.co.uk	
01229 837678	www.escapehotelscumbria.co.uk/en-GB reception@escapehotelscumbria.co.uk	
01229 444600	ihg.com hello@hiexbarrowinfurness.co.uk	
01229 830817	clarkeshotel.co.uk clarkesrampsideltd@outlook.com	
01229 869928	the-farmers-baycliff.co.uk info@the-farmers-baycliff.co.uk	*3-bed self-catering apartment above the pub*
01229 869329	theshipinnbardsea.co.uk katieclayton47@gmail.com	
01229 869304	booking.com	
01229 481869	thesuninnulverston.co.uk info@thesuninnsulverston.co.uk	
01229 580172 / 07776 057763	townhouseulverston.co.uk enquiries@townhouseulverston.co.uk	
	booking.com	
01229 586805	campingandcaravanningclub.co.uk	C&C Club Certificated Site, members only
01229 583972	thebayhorsehotel.co.uk reservations@thebayhorsehotel.co.uk	
01539 558341	theengineinncartmel.co.uk engineinnmanager@gmail.com	
01539 559202	robinsonsbrewery.com bookings@hopeandanchorlakes.co.uk	

Walking the King Charles III England Coast Path: North West

Stage	Location	Name	Type
15	Lakeland Leisure Park	Haven Lakeland Leisure Park	🟢 🟢 ✻
15	Allithwaite (off-trail)	The Pheasant Inn	🔴
15	**Grange-over-Sands**	Corner Beech House	🔵
15	**Grange-over-Sands**	The Commodore Inn	🔴
15	**Grange-over-Sands**	High Fellgate Farm Caravan Park	🟢 ✻
15	Meathop (off-trail)	Woodlands Hotel & Pine Lodges	🔴 🟢
15	Meathop (off-trail)	Meathop Fell Caravan & Motorhome Club Site & Cottages	🟢 ✻
15	Sandside & Storth (off-trail)	Hazelslack Caravan Site	✻
16	**Arnside**	Parkside Guest House	🔴
16	**Arnside**	Ye Olde Fighting Cocks	🔴
16	Far Arnside	Hollins Farm Holiday Park	🟢 🟢 ✻
16	Silverdale	Silverdale Holiday Park	🔴 🟢 🟢 ✻
16	Silverdale	The Silverdale Hotel	🔴
16	Silverdale	Gibraltar Farm Campsite	🟢 ✻
16	Warton	George Washington Inn	🔴
16	Cote Stones	Cotestones Farm Certificated Location	✻
16	Carnforth (off-trail)	The Royal Station Hotel	🔴
16	Carnforth (off-trail)	The County Lodge Hotel	🔵

Appendix A – Accommodation table

Tel	Web/email	Comments
01539 558556	haven.com	Individually owned holiday homes & caravans can also be rented via booking sites.
01539 532239	thepheasantinnallithwaite.co.uk thepheasantinnreservations@outlook.com	
01539 533088	cornerbeech.co.uk info@cornerbeech.co.uk	
01539 555880	thecommodoreinn.co.uk info@thecommodoreinn.co.uk	
01539 536231	highfellgate.co.uk	
01539 534128	whpl.co.uk whpl.admin@gmail.com	
01539 532912	camc.com/meathopfellcottage	
01539 563368	ukcampsite.co.uk	
01524 761815	parksideholidays.co.uk office@parksideholidays.co.uk	
01524 761176	oldefightingcocksarnside.co.uk	
01524 701508	holgates.co.uk info@holgates.co.uk	
01524 701508	holgates.co.uk info@holgates.co.uk	
01524 701118	thesilverdalehotel.co.uk goodtimes@thesilverdalehotel.co.uk	
01524 701736	gibraltarfarm.co.uk camping@gibraltarfarm.co.uk	
01524 732865	www.georgewashingtonwarton.co.uk james@georgewashingtonwarton.co.uk	
07977 512134	caravanclub.co.uk	Very small C&M Club Certificated Location, members only
01524 733636	royalstation.co.uk office@royalstation.co.uk	
	booking.com	

WALKING THE KING CHARLES III ENGLAND COAST PATH: NORTH WEST

Stage	Location	Name	Type
16	Bolton-le-Sands	Bay View Holiday Park	🛖 🛖 ✱
		Archers at Red Bank Farm	🛖 ✱
16	Bolton-le-Sands (off-trail)	The Royal Hotel	🛖
17	**Hest Bank**	The Gateway at Hest Bank	🛖
		Morecambe Lodge Caravan Park	✱
17	Morecambe (north)	Plentiful via booking websites throughout Morecambe; plus:	🛖 🛖
		The Strathmore Hotel	🛖
		Craigwell Hotel	🛖
17	Morecambe (central)	Travelodge	🛖
		Midland Hotel	🛖
		Sunnyside Caravan and Camping Site	🛖 ✱
17	Morecambe (south)	The Clarendon Hotel	🛖
17	Heysham	The Royal Heysham	🛖
17	Middleton Sands	Ocean Edge Holiday Park	🛖
18	**Overton**	No accommodation at Overton	
18	Snatchems	The Golden Ball Hotel & Camping Pods	🛖 🛖
18	Lancaster	Plentiful via booking websites, plus:	🛖 🛖
		Wagon & Horses	🛖
		Sun Hotel & Bar	🛖
		Crows Hotel	🛖

Appendix A – Accommodation table

Tel	Web/email	Comments
01524 701508	holgates.co.uk info@holgates.co.uk	
01524 823196	archers-redbankfarm.co.uk info@archers-redbankfarm.co.uk	
01524 572326	royalhotelboltonlesands.co.uk	
01524 823762 / 07926 985767	thegatewayathestbank.co.uk	Packed lunches available
01524 824361	morecambe-lodge.co.uk andrew@morecambe-lodge.co.uk	
01524 888838	thestrathmore.co.uk stay@thestrathmore.co.uk	
01524 410095 / 07983 448738	craigwellhotel.co.uk craigwellhotel@gmail.com	
0871 984 6479	travelodge.co.uk	
01524 424000	inncollectiongroup.com info@themidlandmorecambe.com	
01524 418373 / 07881 478919	sunnysidecamping.com enquiries@sunnysidecamping.com	
01524 951798	clarendonhotelmorecambe.com clarendonhotel@eagleideas.co.uk	
01524 859298	theroyalheysham.co.uk relax@theroyalheysham.co.uk	
0344 381 9128	parkdeanresorts.co.uk	
01524 259352 / 07426 803668	snatchems.co.uk info.goldenballhotel@gmail.com	
01524 846094	robinsonsbrewery.com/pubs/ wagon-horses-lancaster	
01524 66006	thesunhotelandbar.co.ukk	*Near station*
01524 382888	sleepinngroup.co.uk info@sleepinngroup.co.uk	

WALKING THE KING CHARLES III ENGLAND COAST PATH: NORTH WEST

Stage	Location	Name	Type
19	**Conder Green**	Berrys Farm Campsite	🟢✱
		The Stork Hotel	🔴
19	Cockerham Sands	Cockerham Sands Caravan Park	🟢
19	Pilling (winter route)	Sandvilla Stays	🟢✱
19	*Preesall*	*Boothfield House Caravan Park*	✱
		Muffys Platt Farm Certificated Site	🟢✱
		Bluebell Cottage Certificated Site	🟢✱
19	**Knott End**	Knott End on Sea Self Catering	🟢
20	Fleetwood	Plentiful via booking websites throughout Stage 20; plus:	
		The North Euston Hotel	🔴
		The New Sandpiper Holiday Apartments	🟢
20	Cleveleys	The Briardene Hotel	🔴
20	Bispham	The Norbreck Castle Hotel	🔴
		Queens Plaza Hotel	🔵
20	Blackpool (north)	The Savoy Hotel	🔴
		Doric Hotel	🔴
20	Blackpool (central)	Grand Hotel Blackpool and Metropole Hotel	🔴
		Premier Inn North Pier	🔴
		The Claremont	🔴

Appendix A – Accommodation table

Tel	Web/email	Comments
07734 581291	campingandcaravanningclub.co.uk	C&C Club Certificated Site, members only
	booking.com	
01524 917311	pure-leisure.co.uk	
07791 165280	sandvillastays.co.uk info@sandvillastays.co.uk	On a smallholding with alpacas
07721 587108 / 07547 202801	slynecaravanpark.co.uk/boothfield info@slynecaravanpark.co.uk	
01253 810373	campingandcaravanningclub.co.uk	*C&C Club Certificated Site, members only*
01253 811564	campingandcaravanningclub.co.uk	*C&C Club Certificated Site, members only*
01253 810159	selfcateringknottend.co.uk knottsquash@aol.com	Above the Squash pub
01253 876525	northeustonhotel.com reception@northeustonhotel.com	
07752 721344	new-sandpiper.co.uk enquiries@new-sandpiper.co.uk	
01253 338300	thebriardenehotel.co.uk briardenehotel@yahoo.co.uk	
01253 352341	britanniahotels.com	With swimming pool
01253 429010	queensplazahotel.co.uk enquiries@queensplazahotel.co.uk	
0871 222 0034	britanniahotels.com	
01253 272553	watersidehotels.co.uk customer.services@watersidehotels.co.uk	With swimming pool
0871 222 7768	britanniahotels.com	
0333 323 1574	premierinn.com	
0844 811 5585	claremonthotelblackpool.co.uk claremont@choicehotels.co.uk	

WALKING THE KING CHARLES III ENGLAND COAST PATH: NORTH WEST

Stage	Location	Name	Type
20	Blackpool (south)	South Beach Hotel	⬠ (red)
20	Blackpool (south)	Travelodge Blackpool South Promenade	⬠ (red)
20	Blackpool (south)	Hampton Road Caravan Park	✲
20	Starr Gate	Blackpool Airport Hotel	⬠ (red)
20	St Anne's	Travelodge Lytham St Annes	⬠ (blue)
20	St Anne's	St Ives Hotel	⬠ (red)
20	St Anne's	Inn on the Prom	⬠ (red)
21	Lytham	The County Hotel	⬠ (red)
21	Lytham	The Queens Lytham	⬠ (red)
21	Lytham	Mode Lytham	⬠ (blue)
21	Freckleton	Donkey Creek Farm Caravan Park	✲
21	Lea Gate/Savick Bridge (A583)	Lea Gate Hotel	⬠ (red)
22	Preston (Penwortham Bridge area)	The Spring Bank Aparthotel	⬠ (green)
22	Preston (Penwortham Bridge area)	Riverside by Teil	⬠ (blue)
22	Preston (central; off-trail)	Legacy Preston International Hotel	⬠ (red)
22	Preston (central; off-trail)	Premier Inn Preston Central	⬠ (red)
22	Bretherton (off-trail)	Longfold Farm Campsite	⬠ ⬠ ✲ (green)
23	Tarleton	Bank Bridge House	⬠ (green)
23	Becconsall & Hesketh Bank (off-trail)	Old Manor Farm Certificated Site (off-trail)	⬠ ✲ (green)
23	Becconsall & Hesketh Bank (off-trail)	Landsdowne Camping Certificated Site	⬠ ✲ (green)
24	Crossens	No accommodation but various buses towards Preston and Southport	

Appendix A – Accommodation table

Tel	Web/email	Comments
01253 342250 / 07568 739777	southbeachhotel.co.uk info@southbeachhotel.co.uk	
0871 984 6191	travelodge.co.uk	
01253 341020	hamptonroadcaravanparkandsocialclub.co.uk hrcp22@gmail.com	
0333 777 3919	premierinn.com	
0871 984 6167	travelodge.co.uk	
01253 720011	thestiveshotel.co.uk book@thestiveshotel.co.uk	
01253 726726	innontheprom.co.uk info@innontheprom.co.uk	
01253 795128	thecountyhotellytham.co.uk	
01253 737316	queenslytham.co.uk enquiries@queenslytham.co.uk	
01253 713535	modehotel.co.uk	
01772 631323	donkeycreekfarm.co.uk	
01772 329760	greenekinginns.co.uk	
	booking.com	500m from trail
	booking.com	200m from trail
	booking.com	
0333 321 8335	premierinn.com	*Close to station*
01772 600304	popesfarms.co.uk/longfold.html popesfarms@yahoo.co.uk	
	airbnb.co.uk	Room in owner's house; on A59 on link route
07932 277025	old-manor-farm.co.uk enquiries@old-manor-farm.co.uk	
01772 814075 / 07751 249272	landsdownecamping.org.uk info@landsdownecamping.org.uk	

Walking the King Charles III England Coast Path: North West

Stage	Location	Name	Type
24	Southport	Southport Central Hotel	⬭
		Waterfront Southport Hotel	⬭
		Adventure Coast Southport motorhome site	✱
24	*Ainsdale (off-trail)*	*Willowbank Holiday Home & Touring Park*	✱
25	**Freshfield (Formby) (trail)**	Freshfields Caravan Park	✱
25	Crosby	Aberley House	⬭
		The Lake House	⬭
26	**Seaforth**	The Royal Hotel	⬭
26	Liverpool dockside (Regent Road)	The Royal Crest	⬭
		Titanic Hotel Liverpool	⬭
		Mercure Liverpool Atlantic Tower Hotel	⬭
26	Pier Head/Albert Dock	Holiday Inn Express Liverpool – Albert Dock	⬭
		YHA Liverpool Albert Dock	▲
26	*Liverpool centre (off-trail)*	*Plentiful on booking sites, plus:*	
		Travelodge's Liverpool Central – The Strand and Liverpool Central – Exchange Street branches	⬭
		Hatters Hostel	▲
		Kabannas Hostel	▲
26	Seacombe	The Liver View Hotel	⬭
		Luxury Rooms Liverpool Aparthotel	⬭
26	Egremont	King Street B&B	⬭
		Sea-Quinn Views	⬭

Appendix A – Accommodation table

Tel	Web/email	Comments
0333 321 9016	premierinn.com	
01704 516220	waterfrontsouthporthotel.co.uk	*On Marine Lake, closer to trail*
01704 531957	adventurecoastsouthport.co.uk hello@adventurecoastsouthport.co.uk	
01704 571566	willowbankcp.co.uk	
	caravanclub.co.uk	C&M Club members only
07393 502906	aberleyhouse.com farrerjb@gmail.com	
0151 351 9076	thelakehousewaterloo.co.uk	
0151 928 2332	liverpool-royalhotel.co.uk	
07859 487782	royalcrestliverpool.com contact@royalcrestliverpool.com	
0151 559 1444	titanichotelliverpool.com info@titanichotelliverpool.com	
	all.accor.com	
0800 404040	ihg.com	
	yha.org.uk	
0871 984 6486	travelodge.co.uk	
	ph-hostels.com	
	kabannas.com	
0151 639 5723	liverview.com liverview@live.co.uk	
	booking.com	
0151 640 0153	kingstreetbnb.com hello@kingstreetbnb.com	
07572 388625	seaquinnviews.mydirectstay.com seaquinnviews@gmail.com	

Walking the King Charles III England Coast Path: North West

Stage	Location	Name	Type
27	**New Brighton**	New Brighton Hotel	🔴
		Travelodge Wallasey New Brighton	🔵
27	Leasowe	Leasowe Castle	🔴
27	Meols	Salthaze B&B	🔵
27	*Hoylake*	*Green Lodge Hotel*	🔴
27	West Kirby	Brookfield Cottage	🔵
		42 Caldy Road	🔵🟢
		22 Mostyn Avenue Victorian Guest House	🔵
27	Thurstaston (Country Park)	Wirral Country Park Caravan and Motorhome Club Site	✱
		Thurstaston Field Popup Campsite	🟢✱
27	*Heswall (off-trail)*	*The Jug and Bottle*	🔴
28	**Parkgate**	The Ship Hotel	🔴
28	*Burton (off-trail)*	*Trustwood B&B*	🔵
28a	*Queensferry (off-trail)*	*Greenacres Farm Park (off-trail)*	🟢✱
28b	*Higher Ferry (off-trail)*	*Fir Trees Holiday Park*	🟢
		Thornleigh Park Farm	🟢✱
28	**Chester**	Mill Hotel and Spa	🔴
		The Queen at Chester	🔴
		Travelodge's Chester Central and Chester Central – Bridge Street branches	🔴

Appendix A – Accommodation table

Tel	Web/email	Comments
0151 638 3568	newbrighton-hotel.co.uk info@newbrighton-hotel.co.uk	
08719 846476	travelodge.co.uk	
0151 606 9191	leasowecastle.com reception@leasowecastle.com	
07710 598560	airbnb.co.uk	
0151 632 2321	greenlodgehotelpub.co.uk greenlodgehotel.wirral@marstons.co.uk	
	booking.com	
0151 625 8740 / 07973 418551	42caldyroad.co.uk info@42caldyroad.co.uk	
	booking.com	
01342 327490	caravanclub.co.uk	Non-members welcome
07866 368355	ukcampsite.co.uk	Limited seasonal opening only
	booking.com	
0151 336 3931	the-shiphotel.co.uk info@the-shiphotel.co.uk	
0151 336 7118	trustwoodbnb.uk p.j.friend@icloud.com	
01244 531147	greenacresanimalpark.co.uk info@greenacresanimalpark.co.uk	*On an exotic animal park*
01244 398365	firtreescaravanpark.com info@firtreescaravanpark.com	
01244 371718	caravanclub.co.uk	*Very small C&M Club Certified Location, members only*
01244 350035	millhotel.com reservations@millhotel.com	Close to trail
0330 028 3402	thequeenatchesterhotel.co.uk info@thequeenatchesterhotel.co.uk	Next to station
0871 984 6363	travelodge.co.uk	*Both very close together in city centre – evening meals available at Bridge Street*

APPENDIX B
Useful contacts

Official websites

King Charles III England Coast Path
National Trail
www.nationaltrail.co.uk

Coastal Access and Open Access
restrictions and exclusions
www.openaccess.naturalengland.org.uk

Progress on all stretches
www.gov.uk/englandcoastpath

Tourism and local interest resources

Solway Coast National Landscape
www.solwaycoast-nl.org.uk

Cumbria Tourism
www.visitlakedistrict.com

Lake District National Park
www.lakedistrict.gov.uk

Morecambe Bay Partnership
www.morecambebay.org.uk

Arnside & Silverdale National
Landscape
www.arnsidesilverdaleaonb.org.uk

Visit Lancashire
www.visitlancashire.com

Visit Blackpool
www.visitblackpool.com

Visit Sefton
www.visitseftonandwestlancs.co.uk

Visit Liverpool (City Region)
www.visitliverpool.com

Visit Wirral
www.visitwirral.com

Visit Cheshire
www.visitcheshire.com

Trail management

Cumbria to Lancashire
To report issues, contact the North West
Trail Partnership via:

www.cumberland.gov.uk
countrysideaccess@cumberland.gov.uk

Sefton to Cheshire:
To report issues, contact individual
councils as follows:

Sefton Council
www.sefton.gov.uk

Liverpool City Council
www.liverpool.gov.uk

Wirral Council
www.wirral.gov.uk

Cheshire West & Chester Council
www.cheshirewestandchester.gov.uk

Appendix B – Useful contacts

Related trails

Hadrian's Wall Path and Coast to Coast Path National Trails
www.nationaltrail.co.uk

Wales Coast Path/Llwybr Arfordir Cymru
www.walescoastpath.gov.uk

Transport

Cumberland Council
www.cumberland.gov.uk

Westmorland and Furness Council
www.westmorlandandfurness.gov.uk

Lancashire County Council
www.lancashire.gov.uk

Merseytravel (Sefton, Liverpool, Wirral)
www.merseytravel.gov.uk

Cheshire and Chester
www.cheshirewestandchester.gov.uk

Traveline (national)
www.traveline.info

National Rail
www.nationalrail.co.uk

National Express coaches
www.nationalexpress.com

Megabus
www.megabus.co.uk

BusTimes
www.bustimes.org

APPENDIX C
Day walk options

You can also walk the route in short sections or day trips, or choose a selection of highlights to explore or create circular routes around. The table below includes suggestions of various lengths, covering all areas, all open and walkable now – so no need to wait for ECP completion.

Area	Linear/circular	Walk	Distance	Route stage
Solway Firth/ Hadrian's Wall	Circular – by car from Skinburness or longer walk from bus at Silloth	Grune Point. Park at old pub site off Skinburness Road (NY127559) and use ECP round peninsula. Check tides.	4km	4
West Cumbria	Linear using train	Whitehaven to Seascale via St Bees, where it can be split or shortened.	26km (11 & 15km if split)	7
Duddon Estuary	Circular from Millom station	Millom loop. Use ECP around old ironworks and Hodbarrow lagoon, returning via byway & Mainsgate road.	9km	10
Morecambe Bay – Westmorland	Circular by car or bus from Bardsea beach	Birkrigg Common and stone circle. Use ECP from Bardsea to Conishead Priory then past its lake to Birkrigg Common via Gascow Farm, and back via Sea Wood.	10km	13–14
Arnside & Silverdale National Landscape	Circular from Arnside station	Arnside & Arnside Knott. From the station, take ECP (or existing footpaths) to Far Arnside then back over Arnside Knott.	9km	16

Appendix C – Day walk options

Area	Linear/circular	Walk	Distance	Route stage
Morecambe Bay – Lancashire	Circular	Sunderland Point. Park at Potts Corner and walk south for a circuit of the Point via Sambo's Grave, the shore, and mouth of the Lune. Check tides.	5km	17
Fylde	Linear using tram	Blackpool to Lytham. Walk from Blackpool Central via St Anne's for a bit of everything the coast has to offer. Easy to split.	14km	20
Ribble Estuary	Circular from RSPB car park or longer walk from bus at Hesketh Bank.	Hesketh Out Marsh. Combine floodbank ECP with grid of public footpaths through arable fields for walks of varying lengths.	5–10km	23
Merseyside	Linear using train/bus	Formby to Crosby. Walk from Freshfield station; use ECP through dunes to Anthony Gormley beach statues then Waterloo station. Can be split at Hightown.	18km (9.5km & 8.5km if split)	25
Wirral	Linear using train/bus	New Brighton to West Kirby on ECP – prom, dune and beach including optional 2.5km circuit of Marine Lake. Check tides.	18.5km (or 16km)	27

APPENDIX D
Further reading

Coppack, John *The Comedy Way – A semi-circular walk around Morecambe Bay via Silverdale* (Follifoot Publishing Limited, 2021)

Dillon, Paddy *Walking the Wales Coast Path* (Cicerone, 2025)

Groom, Brian *Northerners – A History* (Harper Collins, 2023)

Jordan, David *15 Short Walks in Arnside and Silverdale* (Cicerone, 2023)

Richards, Mark *Walking Hadrian's Wall Path National Trail* (Cicerone, 2015)

Scanlan, John *West Cumbria – On the Edge* (In Certain Places, University of Central Lancashire, 2019)

Sene, Kevin *The Cumbria and Lake District Coast* (Matador, 2021)

Stenhouse, David *The North West* (Batsford, 1977)

NOTES

WALKING THE KING CHARLES III ENGLAND COAST PATH: NORTH WEST

This guide is accompanied by a two-volume set of map booklets covering the route in Cumbria, and Merseyside and Lancashire. These convenient and compact booklets of Ordnance Survey 1:25,000 maps show the route, providing all of the mapping you need to walk the trail in either direction.

The beach and cliffs at St Bees, where the Coast to Coast National Trail starts (Stage 7)

DOWNLOAD THE GPX FILES

All the routes in this guide are available for download from:

www.cicerone.co.uk/1027/GPX

as standard format GPX files. You should be able to load them into most online GPX systems and mobile devices, whether GPS or smartphone. You may need to convert the file into your preferred format using a conversion programme such as gpsvisualizer.com or one of the many other such websites and programmes.

When you follow this link, you will be asked for your email address and where you purchased the guidebook, and have the option to subscribe to the Cicerone e-newsletter.

www.cicerone.co.uk

LISTING OF CICERONE GUIDES

BRITISH ISLES CHALLENGES, COLLECTIONS AND ACTIVITIES

Great Walks on the England Coast Path
Map and Compass
The Big Rounds
The Book of the Bivvy
The Book of the Bothy
The Mountains of England and Wales:
  Vol 1 Wales
  Vol 2 England
The National Trails
Walking the End to End Trail
Cycling Land's End to John o' Groats

SHORT WALKS SERIES

15 Short Walks Hadrian's Wall
15 Short Walks in the Lake District: Keswick, Borrowdale and Buttermere
15 Short Walks in the Lake District: Windermere Ambleside and Grasmere
15 Short Walks Lake District: Coniston and Langdale
15 Short Walks in Arnside and Silverdale
15 Short Walks in the Ribble Valley
15 Short Walks in Nidderdale
15 Short Walks in Northumberland: Wooler, Rothbury, Alnwick and the coast
15 Short Walks in the Yorkshire Dales: Grassington, Skipton, Malham and Ilkley
15 Short Walks in the Peak District: Bakewell and the White Peak
15 Short Walks on the Malvern Hills
15 Short Walks in Cornwall: Falmouth and the Lizard
15 Short Walks in Cornwall: Land's End and Penzance
15 Short Walks in the South Downs: Brighton, Eastbourne and Arundel
15 Short Walks in the Surrey Hills
15 Short Walks on Dartmoor North: Okehampton and Chagford
15 Short Walks on Dartmoor South: Ivybridge and Princetown
15 Short Walks on Exmoor
15 Short Walks Winchester
15 Short Walks in Bannau Brycheiniog: Brecon Beacons
15 Short Walks in Pembrokeshire: Tenby and the south
15 Short Walks in Dumfries and Galloway
15 Short Walks in the Trossachs: Callander and Aberfoyle
15 Short Walks on the Isle of Mull
15 Short Walks on the Orkney Islands
15 Short Walks on the Shetland Islands

SCOTLAND

Ben Nevis and Glen Coe
Cycling in the Hebrides
Cycling the North Coast 500
Great Mountain Days in Scotland
Mountain Biking in Southern and Central Scotland
Mountain Biking in West and North West Scotland
Not the West Highland Way: A Mountain High Way
Scotland
Scotland's Best Small Mountains
Scotland's Mountain Ridges
Scottish Wild Country Backpacking
Skye's Cuillin Ridge Traverse
The Borders Abbeys Way
The Great Glen Way
The Great Glen Way Map Booklet
The Hebridean Way
The Hebrides
The Isle of Mull
The Isle of Skye
The Skye Trail
The Southern Upland Way
The West Highland Way
The West Highland Way Map Booklet
Walking Ben Lawers, Rannoch and Atholl
Walking in the Cairngorms
Walking in the Pentland Hills
Walking in the Scottish Borders
Walking in the Southern Uplands
Walking in Torridon, Fisherfield, Fannichs and An Teallach
Walking Loch Lomond and the Trossachs
Walking on Arran
Walking on Harris and Lewis
Walking on Jura, Islay and Colonsay
Walking on Mull, Coll and Tiree
Walking on Rum and the Small Isles
Walking on the Orkney and Shetland Isles
Walking on Uist and Barra
Walking the Cape Wrath Trail
Walking the Corbetts
  Vol 1 South of the Great Glen
  Vol 2 North of the Great Glen
Walking the Fife Pilgrim Way
Walking the Galloway Hills
Walking the John o' Groats Trail
Walking the Munros
  Vol 1 Southern, Central and Western Highlands
  Vol 2 Northern Highlands and the Cairngorms
Winter Climbs in the Cairngorms
Winter Climbs: Ben Nevis and Glen Coe

NORTHERN ENGLAND ROUTES

Cycling the Reivers Route
Cycling the Way of the Roses
Hadrian's Cycleway
Hadrian's Wall Path
Hadrian's Wall Path Map Booklet
The Coast to Coast Cycle Route
The Coast to Coast Map Booklet
The Coast to Coast Walk
Walking the Dales Way
The Dales Way Map Booklet
Walking the Pennine Way
Pennine Way Map Booklet

LAKE DISTRICT

Bikepacking in the Lake District
Cycling in the Lake District
Great Mountain Days in the Lake District
Joss Naylor's Lakes, Meres and Waters of the Lake District
Lake District Winter Climbs
Lake District:
  High Level and Fell Walks
  Low Level and Lake Walks
Mountain Biking in the Lake District
Outdoor Adventures with Children — Lake District
Scrambles in the Lake District —
  North
  South
Trail and Fell Running in the Lake District
Walking The Cumbria Way
Walking the Lake District Fells —
  Borrowdale
  Buttermere
  Coniston
  Keswick
  Langdale
  Mardale and the Far East
  Patterdale
  Wasdale
Walking the Tour of the Lake District

NORTH-WEST ENGLAND AND THE ISLE OF MAN

Cycling the Pennine Bridleway
Isle of Man Coastal Path
The Lancashire Cycleway
The Lune Valley and Howgills
Walking in Cumbria's Eden Valley
Walking in Lancashire
Walking in the Forest of Bowland and Pendle
Walking on the Isle of Man
Walking on the West Pennine Moors
Walking the Ribble Way
Walks in Silverdale and Arnside

NORTH-EAST ENGLAND, YORKSHIRE DALES AND PENNINES

Cycling in the Yorkshire Dales
Great Mountain Days in the Pennines
Mountain Biking in the Yorkshire Dales
The Cleveland Way and the Yorkshire Wolds Way
The Cleveland Way Map Booklet
The North York Moors
Trail and Fell Running in the Yorkshire Dales
Walking in County Durham
Walking in Northumberland
Walking in the North Pennines
Walking in the Yorkshire Dales:
  North and East
  South and West
Walking St Cuthbert's Way
Walking St Oswald's Way and Northumberland Coast Path

DERBYSHIRE, PEAK DISTRICT AND MIDLANDS

Cycling in the Peak District
Dark Peak Walks
Scrambles in the Dark Peak
Walking in Derbyshire
Walking in the Peak District -
  White Peak East
  White Peak West

WALES AND WELSH BORDERS

Cycle Touring in Wales
Cycling Lon Las Cymru
Great Mountain Days in Snowdonia
Hillwalking in Shropshire
Mountain Walking in Snowdonia
Offa's Dyke Path
Offa's Dyke Map Booklet
Scrambles in Snowdonia
Snowdonia: 30 Low-level and Easy Walks — North, South
The Cambrian Way
The Pembrokeshire Coast Path
The Pembrokeshire Coast Path Map Booklet
The Snowdonia Way
The Wye Valley Walk
Walking Glyndwr's Way
Walking in Carmarthenshire
Walking in Pembrokeshire
Walking in the Brecon Beacons
Walking in the Wye Valley
Walking on Gower
Walking the Severn Way
Walking the Shropshire Way
Walking the Wales Coast Path

SOUTHERN ENGLAND

20 Classic Sportive Rides
  in South East England
  in South West England
Cycling in the Cotswolds
Mountain Biking on the North Downs
Mountain Biking on the South Downs
The North Downs Way

The North Downs Way Map Booklet
The South Downs Way
The South Downs Way Map Booklet
The Cotswold Way
The Cotswold Way Map Booklet
The Ridgeway National Trail
The Ridgeway Map Booklet
The Thames Path
The Thames Path Map Booklet
The Two Moors Way
Two Moors Way Map Booklet
Walking the South West Coast Path
South West Coast Path Map Booklet
  Vol 1: Minehead to St Ives
  Vol 2: St Ives to Plymouth
  Vol 2: St Ives to Plymouth
  Vol 3: Plymouth to Poole
Suffolk Coast and Heath Walks
The Kennet and Avon Canal
The Lea Valley Walk
The Peddars Way and Norfolk Coast Path
The Pilgrims' Way
Walking Hampshire's Test Way
Walking in Essex
Walking in Kent
Walking in London
Walking in Norfolk
Walking in the Chilterns
Walking in the Cotswolds
Walking in the Isles of Scilly
Walking in the New Forest
Walking in the North Wessex Downs
Walking on Dartmoor
Walking on Guernsey
Walking on Jersey
Walking on the Isle of Wight
Walking the Dartmoor Way
Walking the Jurassic Coast
Walking the Sarsen Way
Walks in the South Downs National Park

ALPS CROSS-BORDER ROUTES

100 Hut Walks in the Alps
Alpine Ski Mountaineering Vol 1 — Western Alps
The Karnischer Hohenweg
The Tour of the Bernina
Trail Running — Chamonix and the Mont Blanc region
Trekking Chamonix to Zermatt
Trekking in the Alps
Trekking in the Silvretta and Ratikon Alps
Trekking Munich to Venice
Trekking the Tour du Mont Blanc
Tour du Mont Blanc Map Booklet
Walking in the Alps

FRANCE, BELGIUM, AND LUXEMBOURG

Camino de Santiago — Via Podiensis
Chamonix Mountain Adventures
Cycling London to Paris
Cycling the Canal de la Garonne
Cycling the Canal du Midi

Mont Blanc Walks
Mountain Adventures in the Maurienne
Short Treks on Corsica
The GR5 Trail
The GR5 Trail —
  Vosges and Jura
  Benelux and Lorraine
The Moselle Cycle Route
Trekking in the Vanoise
Trekking the Cathar Way
Trekking the GR10
Trekking the GR20 Corsica
Trekking the Robert Louis Stevenson Trail
Via Ferratas of the French Alps
Walking in Provence — East
Walking in Provence — West
Walking in the Auvergne
Walking in the Brianconnais
Walking in the Dordogne
Walking in the Haute Savoie: North
Walking in the Haute Savoie: South
Walking on Corsica
Walking the Brittany Coast Path
Walking in the Ardennes

PYRENEES AND FRANCE/SPAIN CROSS-BORDER ROUTES

Shorter Treks in the Pyrenees
The Pyrenean Haute Route
The Pyrenees
Trekking the Cami dels Bons Homes
Trekking the GR11 Trail
Walks and Climbs in the Pyrenees

SPAIN AND PORTUGAL

Camino de Santiago: Camino Frances
Coastal Walks in Andalucia
Costa Blanca Mountain Adventures
Cycling the Camino de Santiago
Mountain Walking in Mallorca
Mountain Walking in Southern Catalunya
Spain's Sendero Historico: The GR1
The Andalucian Coast to Coast Walk
The Camino del Norte and Camino Primitivo
The Camino Ingles and Ruta do Mar
The Mountains Around Nerja
The Mountains of Ronda and Grazalema
The Sierras of Extremadura
Trekking in Mallorca
Trekking in the Canary Islands
Trekking the GR7 in Andalucia
Walking and Trekking in the Sierra Nevada
Walking in Andalucia
Walking in Catalunya —
  Barcelona
  Girona Pyrenees
Walking in the Picos de Europa
Walking La Via de la Plata and Camino Sanabres
Walking on Gran Canaria
Walking on La Gomera and El Hierro

Walking on La Palma
Walking on Lanzarote and Fuerteventura
Walking on Tenerife
Walking on the Costa Blanca
Walking the Camino dos Faros
Portugal's Rota Vicentina
The Camino Portugues
Walking in Portugal
Walking in the Algarve
Walking on Madeira
Walking on the Azores

SWITZERLAND
Switzerland's Jura Crest Trail
The Swiss Alps
Tour of the Jungfrau Region
Trekking the Swiss Via Alpina
Walking in Arolla and Zinal
Walking in the Bernese Oberland — Jungfrau region
Walking in the Engadine — Switzerland
Walking in Ticino
Walking in Zermatt and Saas-Fee

GERMANY
Hiking and Cycling in the Black Forest
The Danube Cycleway Vol 1
The Rhine Cycle Route
The Westweg
Walking in the Bavarian Alps

POLAND, SLOVAKIA, ROMANIA, HUNGARY AND BULGARIA
The Danube Cycleway Vol 2
The High Tatras
The Mountains of Romania

SCANDINAVIA, ICELAND AND GREENLAND
Hiking in Norway —
  North
  South
Trekking the Kungsleden
Trekking in Greenland — The Arctic Circle Trail
Walking and Trekking in Iceland

SLOVENIA, CROATIA, SERBIA, MONTENEGRO AND ALBANIA
Hiking Slovenia's Juliana Trail
Mountain Biking in Slovenia
The Islands of Croatia
The Julian Alps of Slovenia
The Mountains of Montenegro
The Peaks of the Balkans Trail
The Peaks of the Balkans Trail
The Slovene Mountain Trail
Walking in Slovenia: The Karavanke
Walks and Treks in Croatia

ITALY
Alta Via
  1 — Trekking in the Dolomites
  2 — Trekking in the Dolomites
Day Walks in the Dolomites
Italy's Grande Traversata delle Alpi
Italy's Sibillini National Park
Ski Touring and Snowshoeing in the Dolomites
The Way of St Francis: Via di Francesco
Trekking Gran Paradiso: Alta Via 2
Trekking in the Apennines
Trekking the Giants' Trail: Alta Via 1 through the Italian Pennine Alps
Via Ferratas of the Italian Dolomites:
  Vol 1
  Vol 2
Walking in Abruzzo
Walking in Italy's Cinque Terre
Walking in Italy's Stelvio National Park
Walking in Sicily
Walking in the Aosta Valley
Walking in the Dolomites
Walking in Tuscany
Walking in Umbria
Walking Lake Como and Maggiore
Walking Lake Garda and Iseo
Walking on the Amalfi Coast
Walking the Via Francigena Pilgrim Route
  Part 1
  Part 2
  Part 3
  Part 4
Walks and Treks in the Maritime Alps

IRELAND
The Wild Atlantic Way and Western Ireland
Walking the Kerry Way
Walking the Wicklow Way

EUROPEAN CYCLING
Cycling the Route des Grandes Alpes
Cycling the Ruta Via de la Plata
The Elbe Cycle Route
The River Loire Cycle Route
The River Rhone Cycle Route

INTERNATIONAL CHALLENGES, COLLECTIONS AND ACTIVITIES
Europe's High Points
Pocket First Aid and Wilderness Medicine

AUSTRIA
Innsbruck Mountain Adventures
Trekking Austria's Adlerweg
Trekking in Austria's Hohe Tauern
Trekking in Austria's Stubai Alps
Trekking in Austria's Zillertal Alps
Walking in Austria
Walking in the Salzkammergut: the Austrian Lake District

MEDITERRANEAN
The High Mountains of Crete
Trekking in Greece
Walking and Trekking in Zagori
Walking and Trekking on Corfu
Walking on the Greek Islands — the Cyclades
Walking in Cyprus
Walking on Malta

HIMALAYA
8000 metres
Everest: A Trekker's Guide
Trekking in the Karakoram

NORTH AMERICA
Hiking and Cycling the California Missions Trail
Hiking the Pacific Crest Trail
The John Muir Trail

SOUTH AMERICA
Aconcagua and the Southern Andes
Hiking and Biking Peru's Inca Trails
Trekking in Torres del Paine

AFRICA
Climbing Toubkal
Kilimanjaro
Walking in the Drakensberg
Walks and Scrambles in the Moroccan Anti-Atlas

NEW ZEALAND AND AUSTRALIA
Hiking the Overland Track

CHINA, JAPAN AND ASIA
Annapurna
Hiking and Trekking in the Japan Alps and Mount Fuji
Hiking in Hong Kong
Japan's Kumano Kodo Pilgrimage
Japan's Kumano Kodo Pilgrimage
Trekking in Bhutan
Trekking in Ladakh
Trekking in Tajikistan
Trekking in the Himalaya

TECHNIQUES
Fastpacking
The Mountain Hut Book

MINI GUIDES
Alpine Flowers
Navigation

MOUNTAIN LITERATURE
A Walk in the Clouds
Abode of the Gods
Fifty Years of Adventure
The Pennine Way — the Path, the People, the Journey
Unjustifiable Risk?

For full information on all our guides, books and eBooks, visit our website:
www.cicerone.co.uk

CICERONE

Trust Cicerone to guide your next adventure, wherever it may be around the world...

Discover guides for hiking, mountain walking, backpacking, trekking, trail running, cycling and mountain biking, ski touring, climbing and scrambling in Britain, Europe and worldwide.

Connect with Cicerone online and find inspiration.

- buy books and ebooks
- articles, advice and trip reports
- GPX files and updates
- regular newsletter

cicerone.co.uk